DEALING WITH WORKPLACE BULLYING

Society's corporate Disgrace!

REVISED EDITION

ROBERTA CAVA

Dealing with Workplace Bullying

- Society's Corporate Disgrace!

Revised Edition

Roberta Cava

Published by Cava Consulting

14 Whitehall Road, Golden Crest Manor

Highland Park, 4211, Queensland, Australia

info@dealingwithdifficultpeople.info

Discover other titles by Roberta Cava at:
  www.dealingwithdifficultpeople.info/books/index.htm

National Library of Australia

Cataloguing-in-publication data:

ISBN 978-0-9925659-7-8

BOOKS BY ROBERTA CAVA

Dealing with Difficult People

(22 publishers – in 16 languages)

Dealing with Difficult Situations – at Work and at Home

Dealing with Difficult Spouses and Children

Dealing with Difficult Relatives and In-Laws

Dealing with Domestic Violence and Child Abuse

Dealing with School Bullying

Dealing with Workplace Bullying - Revised

What am I going to do with the rest of my life?

Before tying the knot – Questions couples Must ask each other

Before they marry!

How Women can advance in business

Survival Skills for Supervisors and Managers

Human Resources at its Best!

Human Resources Policies and Procedures

Employee Handbooks

Easy Come – Hard to go – The Art of Hiring,

Disciplining and Firing Employees

Time and Stress – Today's silent killers

Take Command of your Future – Make things Happen

Belly Laughs for All! – Volumes 1 to 4

Wisdom of the World– The happy, sad and wise things in life

ACKNOWLEDGEMENTS

Without the valuable contributions of Tim Field (in the UK) through his website *"Bully OnLine"* and the CEO and executive of Members Equity in Melbourne - this book would not have been written. Many thanks to other company representatives and victims who took the time to tell me their horror stories about the bullying they've either observed or been part of.

Special thanks to Doreen Orion, MD; UP Magazine; Clinical Psychiatry News; CGU Workers Insurance; Victorian WorkCover Authority; WorkCover NSW; NSW Labour Council - Unionsafe; WorkCover Corporation SA; CCH's Australian OH&S Magazine; VicHealth; National Research Centre for Occupational Health & Safety Regulations; ACTU Queensland; Occupational Health & Safety, Canberra; Occupational Health, Safety and Welfare S.A.; ACTU Australia; Victoria Trades Hall Council; WorkSafe Victoria; SAEBOW (Southern Australia Employees Bullied Out of Work); Sandra Dann, Working Women's Centre SA Inc.; S.A. Employer Ombudsman; Paul McCartney, Griffith University; Division of Workplace Health & Safety, Department of Industrial Relations, Queensland; United Church of Canada; Women's Executive Network - Canada; TMP Worldwide; Anti-Discrimination Commission Tasmania; Workplace Standards Tasmania; Oonagh Barron of Job Watch; BNJ Publishing; International Labour Organisation - Geneva; Independent Education Union; Australian Manufacturing Workers Union (AMUW); N.T. Department of Industries and Business; and ANF (Australian Nursing Federation) for giving me permission to use their information.

Memorial to Tim Field:

Tim Field died on January 15, 2006 at the age of 53 from cancer. He was a world authority on bullying and psychiatric injury and author of the best-selling book, *Bully in Sight* (1997). His vision was to attain a bully-free world and he campaigned in schools, further and higher education and the workplace to achieve this.

He lectured all over the world and worked personally on more than 5,000 bullying cases, highlighting the lack of understanding for victims.

He revealed patterns showing how trade unions often failed to deal effectively with the problem among their members.

Field believed that bullying was the single most important social issue today. His work inspired and influenced international anti-bullying organisations, while his personal energy, commitment and knowledge restored sanity and saved lives. The world misses this dedicated anti-bullying campaigner.

Dealing with Workplace Bullying
Australia's Corporate Disgrace
Revised Edition
Table of Contents

INTRODUCTION

Bullying in the workplace has proven to be one of the most costly disciplinary matters a company can deal with. If not dealt with swiftly and aggressively, it can result in loss of productivity and de-motivation of any staff that have either observed or been subjected to the bullying. It can cause high absenteeism, loss of job satisfaction and often involves the loss of good employees who will not tolerate such seemingly condoned behaviour in their companies.

In Australia, estimates of harassment in the workplace range from 400,000 to two million workers affected each year! This affects up to five million workers at some point during their working lives (Beyond Bullying Association 2001). With a total Australian population of 22 million people and over 11.5 million people in the workplace - this is not a problem - it's an epidemic!

Bullying costs the Australian economy up to $13 Billion a year in absenteeism, compensation, management time and lost productivity. 1,100 Victorian claims for compensation as a result of workplace violence, harassment and bullying cost $26 Billion. Half of workplaces employ bullies and up to half of all workers will be bullied at least once during their careers.

Bullying and intimidation has a large impact on the culture of all businesses and must not be ignored by senior executives. Anti-bullying policies need to be built into the way all businesses function with both its staff members and its customers. Many supervisory and management staff desperately need anti-bullying courses to learn how to deal with and stop bullying. Only then, will many be forced to consider whether their own behaviour could be considered as harassment or bullying.

Senior people need to examine their company's vision. Many company visions state that they care about the people that work for them and provide an environment free of harassment of any kind - but fail to enforce that vision. It doesn't matter how good technology is in a company - it's the people that make things happen. Unhappy, harassed employees simply can't accomplish this.

When I started writing this book I intended to concentrate only on workplace bullying, but soon recognised that most bullies begin their harassment of others very early in their lives - often in the home. There's a lot of anecdotal evidence to suggest that people who are bullies as adults witnessed bullying in their home. Most were bullies at school and learned they could get away with it.

Children watch how their parents and siblings settle disputes. If conflicts are settled by negotiation and discussion, children learn to use their heads instead of their fists or bullying behaviour to deal with difficult situations. However, if the parents (their role models) deal with disputes by having shouting matches or using aggressive behaviour - these children will likely clone this behaviour with their friends and siblings.

Do all children from such homes become bullies - of course not, but the apple seldom falls far from the tree. Under most circumstances, the bullying child will have bullying parents.

And then there's the school system. Slowly, but surely government bodies have taken the control away from teachers and administrators. These teachers are forced to teach at the level of the lowest common denominator in their classes and spend much of their valuable time trying to re-channel the energies of their hyperactive or bullying students. There are too many students per teacher, so teachers spend less time with each child. School curriculum puts heavy emphasis on knowledge and little on how to work co-operatively with others. Sometimes teachers and schools find it easier to "look the other way" when faced with a bullying episode.

If bullies get away with their actions at home and at school - their next targets are in the workplace. This book tackles the treatment of workplace bullying, harassment and violence. It includes definitions of what is harassment and bullying; how and why it happens; see bullying from both the victim and bully's sides; and identifies the appalling lack of governmental action that's required to improve the handling of such cases.

Some of the information is duplicated in this book, but I did not want to alter the information that I have quoted from different state agencies.

It became apparent that, although there were **Codes of Conduct** and **Guidance Notes** relating to workplace bullying – it is obvious that neither of these have any teeth when it comes to taking a company to court about a bullying or harassment issue. Most countries cover workplace bullying in their **Occupational Health and Safety** laws. I did a spell-check of the Australian Federal and States' ***Occupational Health and Safety*** laws and not once did they mention bullying, harassment or violence!

And what do the business owners say? We need protection from being charged with unfair dismissal when we try to get rid of bludgers and bad employees. Well - that falls under the Industrial Relations/Labour/ Employment laws that should clearly point out what employers need to do to document, discipline and fire employees. There needs to be special laws protecting employees against bullying, harassment and violence in the workplace.

Update: March, 2006

If we thought workplace bullying and harassment were bad before – just wait till John Howard's Industrial Relations Act kicks in. It can't help but reduce Australia's level of employee productivity and we'll likely find the value of the Australian dollar will plummet. How can it not – when employees are faced on a daily basis with *sanctioned* bullying and have NO security that they will have a job the next day.

Update: September, 2013

Now it's up to the new LNP government to correct this problem.

Note:

This book was originally written in 2005, but the contacts throughout this book can provide updates on the current status of their workplace bullying strategies.

Update: July 1, 2014 – Fair Work Commission update

Chapter 1

WHAT IS BULLYING?

Bullying is a pattern of constant, daily faultfinding, criticism, segregation, exclusion and undermining that occurs for weeks or months. Each incident can be trivial and on its own does not represent an offence or grounds for disciplinary action. The average bullying episode is brief, approximately 37 seconds long, but emotional scars from bullying can last a lifetime. Recovery from a bullying experience can take between two to five years and some people never fully recover. Bullying differs from harassment and assault because the latter can result from a single incident or a small number of incidents, whereas bullying tends to be an accumulation of many small incidents over a long period of time.

The most despicable bullies on this earth are terrorists, murderers, rapists, paedophiles and pimps. These dregs of the earth all have one insatiable and obsessive need - to control others. They know of no other way to live life except to overpower others. However, they're cowards and have yellow streaks down their backbones. Anyone who feels confident about him- or herself does not need to use power to influence or control others.

This control is gained through terror, intimidation, harassment or just plain aggressiveness. The extrovert bullies tend to be shouters and screamers - are highly visible and bully from the top. A discussion becomes a debate and often ends up in a shouting match. They manipulate others into believing that they caused the bullying behaviour. Introverted bullies (the most dangerous types) tend to sit in the background and recruit others to do the bullying for them.

Bullies are cunning, conniving, scheming, calculating, sadistic, violent, cruel, nasty, ruthless, treacherous, pre-meditated, exploitive, parasitic, obnoxious, opportunist, ominous, menacing, sinister, ferocious, forceful, annoying and aggressive. They are experts in the use of sarcasm but lack communication, interpersonal and social skills. Some rely excessively or exclusively on texts, emails or third parties and other strategies for avoiding face-to-face contact.

Rational human beings strive to coexist with others. Bullies don't understand this concept. Their need to control can reach obsessive heights and they can even have panic attacks if they feel they're not in control of every situation. These are sick people.

Bullies like pimps, relish having control over other human beings. However, they are insecure cowards whose only source of confidence is to be in control of situations and of others. This control is gained through terror, intimidation, harassment or just plain aggressiveness.

Bullies lack emotional intelligence. Emotional intelligence helps people understand and control their own emotions. It also helps them recognise and respond correctly to others' emotions. Those with emotional intelligence recognise emotions in others and know how to control their reactions to those emotions. They also know their own emotions and how to control them when they are getting upset or angry. Bullies are either born without emotional intelligence or they suppress it by copying their defective role models. Often extensive counselling is the only way to change their destructive behaviour.

Abuse is defined in the dictionary as "an evil or corrupt practice; deceit, betrayal, molestation, violation" and comes in many forms. The common denominator of all abuse is the collection of behaviours related to bullying.

- Abusers *choose* to abuse,
- Molesters *choose* to molest,
- Rapists *choose* to rape,
- Harassers *choose* to harass,
- Paedophiles *choose* to abuse children and
- Bullies *choose* to bully.

Symptoms of Bullying

- Being belittled, demeaned or patronised especially in front of others. This chips away at the person's status, self-confidence, worth and potential;
- Being disgraced, shouted at and threatened, often in front of others;
- Making snide comments to see if the person will fight back;
- Finding fault and criticising everything the victim says and does or twisting, distorting and misrepresenting the victim. The criticism is of a trivial nature and often contains a grain of truth. This can dupe the victim into believing the criticism is valid.
- An unvarying refusal to recognise the victim's contributions;
- Treating them differently by showing favouritism to others and bias towards the victim.

14

Forms of bullying

- Terrorism and murder;
- Child abuse; child sexual abuse and child neglect;
- Pimping (selling of prostitution);
- Wife battering (domestic violence);
- School bullies;
- Armed forces bullying;
- Elderly abuse;
- Sports sexual abuse;
- Prison bullying;
- Road rage
- Queue rage;
- Stalking;
- Email abuse;
- On-line dating abuses;
- Neighbour abuse;
- Phone abuse;
- Cyber bullying;
- Workplace bullying;
- Sexual harassment: at work, at home, at school, in public (such as restaurants;
- Discrimination: age, sex, disabled, culture or nationality, religion;
- Mobbing (group bullying).

Where are people bullied?

- At home; (by parents, siblings or partners through bullying, assault, domestic violence, wife/child abuse, verbal abuse, neglect, emotional abuse);
- At school; (by other students, teachers or school staff);
- Under the care of others; (at child- or aged-care facilities – retirement villages - in hospitals, care homes, group homes, convalescent or rehabilitation facilities);
- At work; (by managers, clients, co-workers and subordinates through bullying/harassment, mobbing, falsifying time sheets, pilfering, embezzlement, fraud, malpractice, conspiracy, breaches of health and safety regulations, sexual harassment and/or discrimination);

- In prison; (by guards or other prisoners - by bullying, harassment, discrimination, assault);
- In the armed forces; (bullying, harassment, discrimination, assault);
- By those in authority; (harassment, abuse of power);
- By neighbours, landlords and even friends; (bullying, stalking, harassment);
- By strangers in restaurants and in line-ups; (that can involve harassment, stalking, assault, sexual assault, rape, grievous bodily harm and even murder).
- On the road; (road rage).

Why do bullies bully?

Some bully because their role models (often their parents or older siblings) bully. It's natural for children to mimic the behaviour of these role models. Others seem to be born with a lack of empathy towards others or a feeling that they are superior to others. It's almost impossible for these individuals to understand what their bullying behaviour does to their victims. Only professional counselling (lasting sometimes for years) can reverse these flawed individuals.

Kinds of abuse

Bullying occurs in virtually all situations of life in which people interact with others. Thus we have bullying at home, at school, by caregivers in various situations, at work, in prison, in the armed forces, as neighbours interact and in public places through stalking, assault and road rage.

In terms of abuse and criminal acts in general, there are glaring differences between the genders. Young men are more likely to commit murder, arson, assault, fraud and sexual and drug-related offenses. For such acts, male offenders typically outnumber female offenders 4 to 1. As many of the factors causing bullying and abuse also lead to these behaviours, we need to give proper guidance to our boys and young men.

Although this book is about workplace bullying, it is important to know the different kinds of abuse, because bullies are often abusive in many areas of their lives. There are many kinds of abuse:

Discrimination: This is done on grounds of age, sex, disability, culture, nationality and religion.

Violence: this includes wife and child battering, violent crime such as murder and road rage. Intimidation and threats on the telephone, on-line or from neighbours are also a form of violence.

Bullying: This form of abuse occurs in schools, in prison, in the military and at the workplace. Elderly people and children may also be bullied on account of their age.

Sexual abuse: Sexual harassment occurs at work, home, school and in places such as restaurants. This form of abuse also includes child sexual harassment, rape in all its forms and online dating abuse.

Other forms of abuse: These include child neglect, stalking, pornography, road rage, queue rage and arson.

Who are the targets of bullying?

It is often assumed that victims of bullying are weak and inadequate. Targets of bullying are assumed to be loners, but most are independent, self-reliant and have no need for gangs or cliques. They have neither a need to impress nor are they interested in office politics. Bullies select individuals who prefer to use dialogue to resolve conflict and who will go to great lengths to avoid conflict. They constantly try to use negotiation rather than resorting to grievance and legal action. Targets are chosen because they are competent and popular. Bullies are jealous of the easy and stable relationships targets have with others.

Many targets are so traumatised by the bullying that they need professional help or take stress leave until the incidence of bullying is investigated. Bullies love this because they can claim that their target is "mentally ill" or "mentally unstable" or has a "mental health problem." It's much more likely that this allegation is a projection of the bully's own mental health problems which have not been treated.

Kinds of Bullies

- Adult bullies in the workplace;
- Abusive and violent partners;
- Abusive and violent parents;
- Abusive and violent children (abuse their parents and others);
- Abusers of those in care;
- Bullying neighbours, landlords, authorities;
- Con artists and swindlers;
- Cult leaders;

- Child bullies who can grow up to be adult bullies;
- Racial and sexual harassers;
- Sexual abusers and paedophiles;
- Rapists (also date rape) and those who commit acts of sexual violence;
- Cyber bullies;
- Advocates of hard pornography;
- Stalkers;
- Arsonists;
- Violent offenders including organised serial killers.

They are also found in a variety of situations:

Physical Bullies: They act out their anger in physical ways. They resort to hitting or kicking their victims or damaging the victim's property. Of all the types of bullies, this one is easiest to identify because his or her behaviour is so obvious. This is the type of bully our imagination conjures up when we picture a bully. As they get older, physical bullies can become more aggressive in their attacks. As adults this aggressive attitude is so deeply ingrained in the bully's personality that serious long-term counselling is required to change the behaviour.

Verbal Bullies: It is quite difficult for a victim to ignore this type of bully. They use words to hurt and humiliate, resorting to name-calling, insulting, teasing and making racist, chauvinistic or paternalistic comments. While this type of bullying does not result in physical scars, its effects can be devastating. It is often the easiest form of attack for a bully. It is quick and painless for the bully, but often remarkably harmful for the victim.

Pornography: has been a traditional outlet for sexual frustration and probably always will be. Its acceptability is determined by current social values. Most people do not object to "soft" pornography and may even secretly indulge occasionally in order to see what they are missing. The harder the pornographic content, the more abusive it tends to be. The individual's need and hence dependency on pornography, is directly proportional to that individual's feelings of sexual inadequacy.

Female Bullies: Society makes the assumption that in a violent situation, there is a male aggressor and a female victim, but females can be as vicious as males. Female bullies are spiteful, devious, manipulative and vengeful. These individuals use gossip and backstabbing to undermine, discredit or devaluate other's contributions. They have poorly-defined moral and ethical boundaries and put others down to make themselves feel important. They are experts in the use of sarcasm but lack communication, interpersonal and social skills.

Group Bullies: These are predominantly female bullies who exclude their victims from feeling part of a group. They exploit the feeling of insecurity in their victims by ambushing their victims and convincing peers to exclude or reject the victim. They often use the same tricks that the verbal bullies use with their victims to isolate them. Spreading nasty rumours about the victim is part of the pattern. It can be an extremely harmful form of bullying especially in children when they are making their first social connections, because it excludes the victim from his or her peer group.

Bullies who were victims: Some bullies have been bullied or abused themselves. There is evidence that many murderers, especially those involving serial killings, have received brain damage from parental beatings. Those beatings can leave them with the inability to control their violent tendencies.

The first time bullies get a taste of their own medicine, they run whining to authorities for protection. They bully to feel competent, to get some relief from their own feelings of powerlessness. They are stuck between the state of a victim and a bully and are usually the most difficult to identify because they, at first glance, appear to be targets of other bullies and fiercely attack their bullies. They are usually impulsive and react quickly to intentional or unintentional physical encounters, claiming self-defence for their actions. Rather than lashing out at his or her bully, this victim needs to learn how to avoid other bullies.

Many abusers, molesters, harassers and bullies who end up in court because of their actions insist they were victims too.

These bullies seem to rely on their past problems as a victim to gain supporters. Such "do-gooders" will take advantage of any form of support they can get to evade taking responsibility for their actions. When asked to account for the way they choose to behave, bullies use a variety of strategies to evade accountability such as denial, counter-attack and feigned victimhood.

They are experts at buck-passing. They have not learned how to take responsibility for their actions, lack self-discipline and will often blame someone else for why they reacted as they did.

Road Rage:

Workplace bullies are also prone to road rage. Road rage occurs when one driver expresses his or her anger towards another driver for something s/he did on the road. People are encouraged to engage in road rage by the fact that they will not see each other again. They also feel that the other motorist is just some idiot who has endangered their lives. Road rage can be expressed through screaming, beeping the horn, flashing headlights, slamming on the brakes to teach a tailgater a lesson, cutting a person off to retaliate, throwing things, hostile stares, sticking out the middle finger and profanities. Others even get out of their cars and start fighting.

Most people who demonstrate road rage are aggressive drivers, but do not consider their actions a problem to others. They think of the other drivers as being stupid, rude and discourteous. The stresses of modern urban life are no reason to take it out on other drivers.

Stalkers:

Stalkers include intimate partner stalkers, delusional stalkers and vengeful stalkers. Studies show that the overwhelming number of stalkers are men and the overwhelming number of their victims are women.

Intimate partner stalkers refuse to believe that the relationship has ended. The vast majority of these stalkers are not lonely people who are still hopelessly in love. On the contrary, they are emotionally abusive and controlling both during and after the relationship has ended. The only thing to say to the stalker is *"No"* once only and then never say anything to him again. If the stalker cannot have his victim's love, he will settle for her hatred or her fear. The worst thing in the world for stalkers is to be ignored.

Delusional stalkers frequently have had little, if any, contact with their victims. They may have major illnesses like schizophrenia, manic-depression or erotomania. In erotomania, the stalker's delusional belief is that the victim loves him and he believes that he is having a relationship even though they might never have met. Another more tenacious type might believe that he is destined to be with someone and that if he only pursues her hard enough and long enough, she will come to love him. Most are unmarried and socially immature.

The vengeful stalker is driven by vengeance, rather than love. They become angry with their victims over some slight, either real or imagined. This could be anger at a politician because of some piece of legislation they introduced or it could be disgruntled ex-employees.

Queue Rage:

Public servants are being bashed, stalked and threatened with weapons in unprecedented abuse from customers forced to wait in long queues and being forced to fill in official forms. In one case they found the name of the person on the other side of the counter, found out where she lived and followed her. This employee's health has been totally destroyed and she will never be able to work again. Others have been threatened with syringes. Government employees at all levels are vulnerable to the danger. This could be classed as workplace abuse and their employers need to know this. By not having enough employees available to "service" their clients, they are setting their staff up for abuse by the clients.

The alarming increase in queue rage has prompted special training programs for frightened counter staff. This behaviour includes people jumping the counter, threatening, jumping the queue and performing in the waiting area for the benefit of others. And the public servants are wilting. Society in general and clients being served by government staff are more aware of their rights now than ever before. This has made them become more assertive and they can become very angry when trying to get what they want.

Employees are being trained to recognise the danger signals. They see clients fuming and know something is happening. This is where an alert supervisor can anticipate trouble. Employees are given alarm bells and a system of security that they can use if the situation escalates into abusive behaviour.

Cyber Bullying:

Cyber bullying occurs when an adult or child is tormented, threatened, harassed, humiliated, embarrassed or otherwise targeted by another adult or child, using the Internet, interactive and digital technologies or mobile phones.

Cyber bullying is usually not a one time communication, unless it involves a death threat or a credible threat of serious bodily harm. In extreme cases people have killed each other or committed suicide after being involved in a cyber bullying incident.

Penalties for Cyber Bullying:

Most of the time the cyber bullying does not go so far that the law intervenes, although victims often might attempt to lodge criminal charges. Cyber bullying however, may result in a misdemeanour cyber harassment charge or if the bullying child is young enough may result in the charge of juvenile delinquency. It has to have a minor on both sides or at least have been instigated by a minor against another minor.

It typically can result in the person losing his/her ISP or IM accounts because s/he violated the terms of service rules. In some cases, if hacking or password and identity theft is involved, s/he can be charged with serious criminal charges by state and federal law enforcement agencies.

Cyber Bullying is NOT ...

Once adults cyber bully children, it is called **cyber harassment or cyber stalking.** Adult cyber-harassment or cyber stalking is not cyber bullying.

It isn't when adults are trying to lure children into offline meetings. That is called **sexual exploitation** or luring by a sexual predator. The methods used are limited only by the bully's imagination and access to technology. And the cyber bully one moment may become the victim the next. They often change roles, going from victim to bully and back again.

Sports Bullying:

A recent report released in Italy on violence in sport by UNICEF, said nearly one in ten Australians had suffered sexual abuse in a sporting context. Sexual violence against children in sport in Australia could be as high as 8 per cent compared to Canada, where 2.6 per cent of children reported experiencing unwanted sexual touching.

Trisha Layhee, one of the report's authors said the rates of sexual violence may be much higher and work was needed to assess the issue.

22

Dr. Layhee, who now heads the Hong Kong Sports Institute, said Australia was unique in the world for having a coaching culture that encouraged extreme psychological abuse.

'What we found was the complete normalisation of psychologically abusive behaviour by coaches, particularly at the elite level. I mean coaches screaming at kids,' she said.

Her survey of 370 elite and club athletes in Australia found 31 per cent of female and 21 per cent of male athletes reported sexual abuse under the age of 18. Of these, 41 per cent of females and 29 per cent of males said the abuse occurred in a sporting context.

Conclusion

Workplace bullying, harassment and violence are the subjects of much of this book. This bullying is done by supervisors, managers, colleagues, clients and even subordinates. Workplace bullying includes harassment, emotional, verbal and physical abuse and violence. All of these aspects of workplace bullying will be examined together with suggested solutions.

Our children are constantly exposed to violence - and I don't just mean watching gun battles and murder scenes on the television. Have you really paid attention to what they're watching in our sports-addicted society? If you have, you'll notice how much aggression and violence is now used in the name of 'sport.' Grown men poke other players, gouge bodies and generally act the part of the school bully. And we wonder why our children clone that behaviour!

Our society needs to look seriously at cleaning up the violence we now see in several of our sports. Sport used to be "sportsmanlike" but the violent actions we see in our football players can not be called sporting at all. The AFL and Aussie Rules administratiuon staff should look at the image they are giving to young Australian supporters. This is not sportsmanship – *it's bullying* and sets a terrible example for the impressionasble youngsters of Australia. They should be ashamed of themselves.

Chapter 2

IDENTIFYING BULLIES

Identifying bullies is an important skill. This is Human Resource specialists, union representatives, colleagues and others who witness the bullying.

Bullies completely lack empathy and instead, are arrogant, self-absorbed, egotistical and selfish. They torment, intimidate, persecute, terrorise, oppress, browbeat, harass, irritate, molest, batter, hurt and manipulate their targets. They also use coercion, threats, pressure, brutality and sadism to control their targets.

Relational characteristics of bullies:

They are autocratic and dictatorial, often using phrases like *"you shouldn't ..."* or *"you ought to ..."* Some people mistake these behaviours as showing high self-esteem, which they are not. They appear competent and professional at their job, but behind the facade they are inadequate, inept, often incompetent individuals. They survive only by plagiarising other people's work and being carried by those they bully. They find fault with or pour scorn on other people's ideas, only to later regurgitate them and claim to be the originator.

Their attempts at humour usually involve sarcasm that has either sexual or discriminatory connotations that can fall flat with some listeners. Some rely excessively or exclusively on texts, emails or third parties and other strategies for avoiding face-to-face contact.

They display inappropriate body language and eye contact, either too much or too little. Their gaze is often reported as having an evil stare. They may invade intimate body space zones and use gestures or comments that include inappropriate sexual references or innuendo. If working in a service firm, they tend to be inappropriately intimate with clients. Bullies are also prone to being too friendly too soon in their relationships.

They are rigid and unbending if other people's ideas go against their wishes. If the person's ideas have a hint of criticism about how they are completing a task or project they retaliate. They exhibit duplicity and hypocrisy saying one thing one day and denying it the next. They are unwilling to apologise for mistakes, except when witnesses are present.

Even then the apology is artificial and inappropriate but sufficiently convincing for peers and superiors.

Psychological characteristics of bullies:

They have unpredictable mood swings, blowing hot and cold, often suddenly and without warning. They are literally time bombs. Bullies learn that bullying results in relief from their anxiety, which produces that warm feeling called satisfaction. Gratification is the indulgence in the feeling of satisfaction resulting from relief from anxiety brought about by bullying. Gratification is a behaviour loop in which the adult is trapped and is the common denominator behind most forms of violence, especially sexual abuse and violence. They are unable to assess the importance of events and tasks, often making an unnecessary fuss over trivia while ignoring important or urgent matters. Some have an unhealthy obsession with cleanliness or orderliness.

Vulnerability of others is a major stimulant to the serial bully. They gain gratification from provoking people into emotional or irrational responses, but are quick to claim provocation by others when challenged. They are unable or unwilling to reciprocate any positive gesture. Instead, they see anyone attempting to be conciliatory as a sucker who should be exploited.

They may have poor social skills and do not fit into society or they cannot meet the expectations of their family, school or boss. Jealousy and envy can be the conduit for the release of the seething inner anger, hatred and resentment that bullies harbour against their targets. Bullies often do not outgrow their aggressive behaviour and it becomes a perpetual personality characteristic.

In the workplace, bullies hoard crucial information. They form or join committees to look busy and important, but never achieve anything of significance or value. They abuse disciplinary procedures by using criticism and humiliation in the guise of addressing shortcomings in others' performance. Their aim is only to control or subjugate others, rather than to obtain performance improvement. They do not trust others, which partly explains their compulsion for excessive monitoring. Their departments are dysfunctional and inefficient and their behaviour prevents staff from performing their duties.

Some people mistake these behaviours as showing high self-esteem, which they are not. They appear competent and professional at their job, but behind the façade they're inadequate, inept, often incompetent individuals.

Psychopath

Mad, bad and dangerous to know. They're glib, superficial and remorseless and they're sitting at the next desk to you.

Have a look around your office. These days a psychopath is as likely to be wearing a three-piece suit as an ice hockey mask with a chainsaw as accessory. Dubbed industrial psychopaths or more accurately, sub-criminal psychopaths, they are invariably male and thrive in organisations that are rapidly changing. In other words, the company of today.

By psychopath, we are not talking about axe-wielding, homicidal maniacs. **Paul Babiak**, an industrial-organisational psychologist based in New York has identified the industrial psychopath's behaviour within the company. In a groundbreaking article in Clinical Psychiatry News, he explains how they work.

The first stage, what he calls organisational entry, is accomplished by charming the interviewer. The next stage - assessment - involves the psychopath using his skills to gauge how useful various members of the organisation are. He begins to charm people in power and others of use to him and establishes a communication network.

During the manipulation stage, the psychopath spreads disinformation to enhance his image and disparage others. He is adept at creating conflict between those who might pool negative information about him. In these efforts, he mobilises a full arsenal of effective social tools, such as rational persuasion, ingratiation and coalition.

This is followed, eventually, by a confrontation stage, in which he abandons the pawns that are no longer useful to him and takes steps to neutralise detractors. Finally, the most successful psychopath enters an ascension phase during which he abandons his patrons, those who have helped his rise to power.

While the number of psychopaths in organisations is impossible to estimate, many entrepreneurs share some of the characteristics that psychopaths exhibit - glibness, lack of guilt and dishonesty. Babiak's study reckoned that fifteen per cent of executives misrepresent their education and that one-third of all CVs contain lies. Take the example of Richard Li, chairman and CEO of Pacific Century Cyberworks, who was recently exposed as not having a Stanford degree as claimed.

Childhood bullies:

Bullying behaviour can be identified as early as pre-school age and some children who are bullies continue this behaviour into adulthood. Most children learn to control their anger and fighting instincts as they grow older, but not the bully. These children have special characteristics such as:

- Greater than average aggressive behaviour patterns;
- The desire to dominate peers;
- The need to feel in control and to win;
- No sense of remorse for hurting another child;
- A refusal to accept responsibility for his/her behaviour.

Lethal employees:

In recent years, there's been an interest in "profiling" the lethal employee. These are employees who end up killing those they perceive as having harmed them. One of the first attempts to profile lethal employees was by *Anthony Baron* in 1993 who says that there's a 90 per cent probability of lethality if the offender has one or more of the following characteristics:

- History of violence;
- Psychosis and/or projection;
- Romantic obsession;
- Chemical dependence;
- Depression;
- Pathological blaming;
- Impaired neurological functioning;
- Elevated frustration level;
- Interest in weapons;
- Evidence of personality disorder;
- Vocalisation of violent intentions prior to act.

A second type of workplace violence resembles stalking and consists of sexual obsession. Like church and school, the workplace is traditionally considered an appropriate place to find one's life partner or spouse.

Hence, unmarried employees (and even married ones sometimes) look at their place of work to find new boyfriends or girlfriends. It's assumed that it's better to find your mate at work rather than pick him or her up in a bar or tavern. Sexual obsession is sometimes called love obsession or romantic stalking and it occurs in at least three varieties:

- The spurned ex-lover or spouse whose primary motivation is revenge;
- The delusional erotomaniac who engages in bizarre, unrealistic fantasies;
- The pathological dependent that finds it difficult to function without the attention of another.

In the second type, the offenders believe that their victims are in love with them. Much more common are cases in which the victim has clearly communicated something like *"I wouldn't go out with you if you were the last man on earth,"* and the offender simply refuses to give up.

Conclusion

Normal people do not need to bully; only weak people need to bully in order to hide their weakness and inadequacy. Learning to control our anger and fighting instincts is a part of growing up. Most of us manage the process with little difficulty, but the bully usually possesses personality traits that work as obstacles to his or her maturation.

Chapter 3

DIAGNOSIS OF BULLYING

Chapter 1 defined bullying and abuse and gave some common characteristics of a bully. This Chapter goes further to give psychological insights into the mind of an abuser as developed by **Tim Field** and **David Kinchin.** This is followed by an examination of the effects of bullying.

Abuse and antisocial personality disorder (APD)

Many abusers fit the criteria for *Antisocial Personality Disorder* (APD). Although most people think those with APD are of a low socio-economic status, tend to be of lower intelligence and are associated with certain urban settings, this is not the case. They come from all environments. These individuals have a complete disregard for and violate the rights of others. They indicate at least three of the following symptoms:

- Failure to conform to social norms with respect to lawful behaviour and performing acts that are grounds for arrest;
- Demonstration of deceit by repeated lying, use of aliases and conning others for personal profit or pleasure;
- Acting impulsively and fail to see the consequences of their actions;
- Being irritable and aggressive as indicated by repeated physical fights, assaults or verbal battles;
- Showing reckless disregard for the safety of self or others;
- Being consistently irresponsible and failing to retain jobs.
- Failing to honour their financial obligations;
- Lacking remorse by being indifferent to or rationalising having hurt, mistreated or stolen from others;
- Belonging to gangs and cliques that do not only appear in school-aged children, but at the highest executive level in business.

Psychopathic and Sociopathic Behaviour

A *Sociopath* is an individual with many characteristics of APD and expresses his/her violence psychologically through constant criticism, sidelining, exclusion, undermining, etc. Sociopaths are usually highly intelligent, have higher socio-economic status and often come from middle-class families.

Many serial bullies would also meet many, if not all, of the clinical criteria for being termed a psychopath. Psychopaths lack remorse, guilt and conscience. Most, but not all, psychopaths meet the diagnostic criteria for antisocial personality disorder. Similarly, not all people with antisocial personality disorder meet the criteria for a psychopath. Industrial psychopaths can thrive in business and many are found in management or executive positions.

Abuse and Narcissistic personality disorder

The serial bully displays behaviour congruent with many of the diagnostic criteria for *Narcissistic Personality Disorder*. This is shown by a pervasive pattern of grandiosity and self-importance, the need for admiration and the lack of empathy. People with this disorder overestimate their abilities and inflate their accomplishments, often appearing boastful and pretentious. In addition, they have fantasies of unlimited success and/or power, while correspondingly underestimating and devaluing the accomplishments of others.

They are contemptuous, envious and impatient with others and take advantage of others to achieve their own ends. They need power, prestige, drama and enjoy manipulating others. These qualities draw them to top leadership positions, but at extreme levels of narcissism, the results can be disastrous.

Narcissists can become intolerant of criticism, unwilling to compromise and frequently surround themselves with sycophants (groupies, bootlickers, flunkys, flatterers – a self-seeker who attempts to win favour by flattering influential people). While narcissists often appear to be ideal choices for leadership positions, they may fall victim to the distortions of their narcissistic tendencies that are reinforced by their position. Some will fraudulently claim to have qualifications, experience, affiliations or associations that they do not have or are not entitled to.

They have low self-esteem and need constant attention and admiration. They fish for compliments, expect superior service and for others to defer to them. They lack sensitivity and empathy especially when others do not react in the expected manner. They expect to receive before and above the needs of others and overwork those around them. They may form romantic or sexual relationships for the purpose of advancing their purpose or career, abuse special privileges and squander resources.

The Psychotic condition of an abuser

The term *"psychosis"* is applied to mental illness and the term *"neurosis"* to psychiatric injury. The main difference is that a psychotic person is unaware they have a mental problem whereas the neurotic person is aware of this fact, often acutely. The serial bully's lack of insight into his/her behaviour and its effect on others has the hallmarks of a psychosis, although this obliviousness would appear to be a choice, rather than a condition. They show these behaviours:

- Are very controlling of others. If someone resists, they are vicious in their attack to regain control.
- They do not listen to others, lack conscience, show no remorse, are drawn to power, are emotionally cold and flat, dysfunctional, disruptive, divisive, rigid and inflexible, selfish, insincere, insecure, immature and lack interpersonal skills.
- They are vicious, criticising and vindictive in private but charming in front of witnesses. Only those closest to them get to see their real nature.
- Are very convincing or compulsive liars. They are thus able to fabricate authentic-sounding reasons for their behaviour when confronted.
- Are charming and convincing, qualities they use to make up for their lack of empathy.
- Hiding under their charming exterior is often sexual harassment, discrimination and racial prejudice.
- On the surface they seem very self-assured, but inside they are very insecure people.
- They excel at deception, have a vivid imagination and are often very creative.
- They encourage feelings of shame, embarrassment, guilt and fear. That is how all abusers, including child sex abusers, control and silence their victims.

- Show inappropriate attitudes to sexual matters or behaviour.
- Refuse to acknowledge value or praise others.
- When others describe their uncaring nature, they respond with impatience, irritability and aggression.
- Often have an overwhelming, unhealthy and narcissistic need to portray themselves as a wonderful, kind, caring and compassionate person, in contrast to their behaviour and treatment of others.
- Are oblivious to the discrepancy between how they like to be seen and how they are actually seen.
- Are unaware of the differences between leadership qualities such as maturity, decisiveness, assertiveness, trust and integrity and the immaturity, impulsiveness, aggression, distrust and deceitfulness of bullying.
- When called to account for their actions, they aggressively deny everything and then counter-attack with distorted or fabricated criticism and allegations. If this is insufficient, they quickly feign being the victim so as to evade accountability by manipulating others through the use of guilt.

Passive-Aggressive behaviour in bullies

Some serial bullies show signs of passive/aggressive behaviour. These people can be very dangerous. They have a pathological reaction to authority and those they perceive are in positions of authority. They channel their aggression into passive behaviour by slowing down efforts of others and stonewall progress. They are very hard to detect and others often feel frustrated when dealing with them but do not always understand why.

As most of us grow up, we are faced with restrictions that are normal and necessary. People with this tendency have often been controlled excessively, so the person learns to control others without confrontation. They love the thrill of insubordination and it sometimes does not matter if they win, as long as their opponents appear to lose. They love to play win-lose games and put something over on others.

They use excuses such as: *"It's not my fault this didn't work, it's yours."* They show frequent signs of helplessness; the simplest of things seems beyond their comprehension. They provoke a feeling of defensiveness when others are dealing with them. Most tasks are performed late or not at all. When prodded they become argumentative. They are backstabbers, gossipers and are often so good at it that others believe their falsehoods.

Most people display the above signs at one time or another. However, if this develops into being their normal behaviour, these people are likely passive-aggressive and others will have to remain on guard when dealing with them. Confront them using facts when you catch them in the act. Make sure they understand the consequences of their actions, *"If this happens again, I will ..."*

Some serious passive-aggressives have criminal tendencies. Although they insist that others adhere to the rules of society, they have an unwillingness to conform, believing these do not apply to them. These people get a thrill out of speeding, of drinking and driving - and getting away with it. In some, this tendency keeps accelerating because they require higher and higher levels of danger, thrills and excitement to keep them appeased. Additional characteristics are:

Deny Everything

"This is so trivial it's not worth talking about ..."

"You're over-reacting."

"I don't know why you're so intent on dwelling on the past," and

"Look, what's past is past. I'll overlook your accusations and we'll start afresh."

This is an abdication of responsibility by the bully and an attempt to divert and distract attention by using false conciliation. They then go back to bullying the victim! Imagine if this line of defense were available to all criminals *("Look, I know I've just murdered twelve people, but that's all in the past. We can't change the past - so let's put it behind us and concentrate on the future so we can all get on with our plans.")*

Counter Attack:

After denial comes an aggressive counter-attack. A further advantage of the denial/counter-attack/feigning victimhood strategy is that it acts as a provocation. The target, who may have taken months to reach this stage, sees his/her tormentor getting away with it and is provoked into an angry and emotional outburst after which the bully says simply, *"There, I told you s/he was like that."*

Others do their dirty work:

Frequently targets are asked why they didn't report the abuse before and they will usually reply, *"Because I didn't think anyone would believe me."* Sadly they are often right in this assessment. Because of the Jekyll and Hyde nature of the bully, no one can - or wants to believe it. Abusers confidently and arrogantly, rely on this belief. Targets of bullying in the workplace often come up against the same attitudes by management when they report a bullying colleague. In a workplace environment, the bully usually recruits one or two colleagues (sometimes one is a sleeping partner) who back up the bully's denial when called into account.

Pretend they are the victim:

They manipulate people through their emotions, especially by giving guilt. They show indignation, pretending to be devastated that they're the one being picked on with false accusations. They claim they're the one being bullied or harassed and portray themselves as the injured party and the target as the villain of this harassment. By using this response, bullies avoid accepting responsibility for what they have said or done.

Provoke others:

Bullies seem incapable of controlling themselves and confront or provoke their victims until there is either an unpleasant physical interaction or a loud and derogatory verbal interaction.

Non-Valid testimony:

Because of the serial bully's Jekyll and Hyde nature, compulsive lying, charm and plausibility, the validity of this person's testimony cannot be relied on in disciplinary proceedings, appeal hearings and under oath at tribunal and in court. Mediation with this type of individual is inappropriate. Serial bullies regard mediation (and arbitration, conciliation, negotiation etc.) as appeasement, which they ruthlessly exploit. Negotiation allows the bully to give the impression in public that they're negotiating and being conciliatory, while in private they continue the bullying.

Effects of Bullying

The range of physical, emotional and other effects of bullying is very wide. Helping those who have been bullied or recognising that we are being bullied requires that we consider all of these effects.

Physical Effects:

- The victims' constant high stress level interferes with their immune system causing frequent illnesses such as the flu, ulcers, irritable bowel problems, skin problems such as eczema, psoriasis, athlete's foot, shingles, colds, coughs, ear, nose and throat infections. Their body's batteries never have an opportunity to recharge.
- They suffer from aches and pains in joints and muscles or have back pain with no obvious cause that will go away or respond to treatment.
- They are disempowered such that they become dependent on the bully to allow them to get through each day without their life being made hell.
- Initially they are reluctant to take action against their bullies and report them knowing that they could accelerate the abuse. Later this gives way to a strong urge to take action against the bullies so that others do not have to suffer a similar fate.

Emotional/Psychological Effects:

These are many and varied. They affect the target's relationship with the bully, with others and with themselves. Targets of bullying have:

- An overwhelming desire for acknowledgement, understanding, recognition and validation of their experience and strong motivation for justice to be done;
- An unusually strong desire to educate their employer and help the employer introduce an anti-bullying policy;
- Levels of guilt are abnormally high and may preclude an individual from negotiating fair rates of remuneration for their bullying experience or with future employers;
- Work becomes difficult, often impossible to undertake and the workplace holds such horrific memories that it becomes impossible

to set foot on the premises. Many targets of bullying avoid the street where the workplace is located.

- Their world and self-view is shattered and they may find it impossible to function normally or effectively in *any* work environment. Research indicates that often those who suffer most from workplace bullying behaviour are those with the most to give – those with high expectations of themselves and those who are prepared to go the extra mile because they believe that what they are doing is meaningful and important;
- An unwillingness to take stress leave because the person doesn't want to believe they are sufficiently unwell to merit it;
- An unwillingness to talk or interact with the bully;
- An unusually strong sense of vulnerability, victimisation or persecution;
- An overwhelming sense of betrayal and an inability or unwillingness to trust anyone;
- Headaches and migraines;
- Shattered self-confidence and low self-esteem;
- Become seriously depressed, especially upon waking;
- Become tired, exhausted and lethargic;
- Found their levels of guilt are abnormally high which may prevent them from starting new relationships;
- Found themselves constantly fatigued, similar to Chronic Fatigue Syndrome or sweating, trembling, shaking or having heart palpitations;
- Suffered from panic attacks triggered by any reminder of the experience;
- Physical numbness on the toes, fingertips, lips and emotional numbness, especially the inability to feel joy;
- Impaired memory that is due to suppressing horrific memories;
- Found they are constantly on edge mentally, have a short fuse and are irritated, especially by small insignificant events;
- Often been highly upset by the amount of anger they feel towards their abuser and are horrified by the mental pictures of creative, cruel, torturous ways they could pay back their abuser;
- Constantly been on alert because their fight or flight mechanism has become permanently activated;
- Become hypersensitive and inappropriately perceive almost any remark as critical;

- Found that work becomes difficult, often impossible to undertake;
- Become obsessed with the abusive experience that takes over their lives, eclipsing and excluding almost every other interest;
- Believe that their abusive problems are hopeless and that their efforts to stop it will be futile;
- Been sleepless, have nightmares, constantly relive events, wake early or wake up more tired than when they went to bed;
- Poor concentration and become forgetful especially with trivial day-to-day things;
- Experienced regular intrusive, violent visualisations and flashbacks and can't get the abuse out of their minds;
- Become emotional, bursting into tears regularly over trivial matters;
- Become uncharacteristically irritable, have angry outbursts, are hypersensitive and feel fragile;
- Feelings of withdrawal and isolation, want to be on their own and seek solitude;

Other effects of abuse

Post Traumatic Stress Disorder, (PTSD), depression, stress breakdown and self-injury may result when a person is abused over a prolonged period. These effects are examined below.

Post Traumatic Stress Disorder (PTSD):

Post Traumatic Stress Disorder (PTSD) is a natural emotional reaction to a deeply shocking and disturbing experience. Post traumatic stress following victimisation is largely due to the shattering of basic assumptions victims hold about themselves and the world. These basic assumptions are that:

- The world is kind, caring, compassionate, generous and giving;
- The world is meaningful;

For the targets of abuse, their world and self-view is shattered and they may find it impossible to function normally or effectively. Research indicates that often those who suffer most from unacceptable abusive behaviour are those with the most to give, that is those with high expectations of themselves and those who are prepared to go the extra mile because they believe that what they do is meaningful and important.

One researcher has estimated that at any time, around one per cent of the population are experiencing PTSD. Within some groups of society, such as those who lived in conflict zones during the post-election violence in early 2008, the incidence of PTSD is expected to be much higher than one per cent.

There is growing recognition that PTSD can result from many types of shocking experiences including an accumulation of small, individually non-life-threatening events. These situations are called Complex PTSD. The individual experiencing trauma feels s/he is unable to escape the situation. Traumatic situations of domestic, school and workplace abuse can be extremely difficult to get out of.

Sometimes those who are abused think that they are going mad. They are not, as PTSD is an injury, not an illness. The silent suffering could be considerable, but those who suffer, mostly unnecessarily, are prevented from realising their potential and contributing fully to society and to industry. Many sufferers of Complex PTSD are hard workers who are reluctant to seek help.

Depression:

Stress or more appropriately *'distress'* occurs when an individual believes that the demands or perceived demands of a situation outweigh his/her ability or perceived ability to cope with the situation. The coping mechanisms under challenge include those the person needs to resolve the problem, be it emotional, familial, work-related or otherwise. From a psychological viewpoint, depression occurs when individuals feel their world is consistently unpleasant, punishing or deprives them of the opportunity for a positive and satisfying life. Their negative experiences may be compounded by feelings of being unable to change their situation - a process of learned helplessness.

Individuals with depression expect and predict that their unpleasant and distressing experiences will continue into the future. Guilt-ridden perceptions of being responsible for their own distress, either through the things they have done or not done or negative thoughts about their inability to cope, add to the depressed feelings. The combination of a negative view of their lives, the expectation that it will continue, the self-criticism or self-blame for the situation, coupled with the inability to cope, are the characteristic psychological processes of depression.

Stress Breakdown:

Stress breakdown differs from a nervous breakdown or mental breakdown that are the consequence of mental illness. Stress breakdown is a psychiatric injury, which is a normal reaction to an abnormal situation. The two types of breakdown are distinct and should not be confused. A stress breakdown is a natural and normal conclusion to a period of prolonged negative stress. In a stress breakdown, the body is saying:

"I'm not designed to operate under these conditions of prolonged negative stress so I'm going to do something dramatic to ensure that you reduce or eliminate the stress. Otherwise, I may suffer irreparable damage and I must take action now."

A stress breakdown is often predictable, sometimes days or weeks in advance. The person's fear, fragility, obsessiveness, hyper-vigilance and hyper-sensitivity combine to evolve into paranoia. If this happens, a stress breakdown is only days or even hours away and the person needs urgent medical help. The risk of suicide at this point is heightened. Research says that young men are committing suicide at five times the rate of females.

Self-Harm:

Self-harm is the intentional causing of harm to one's own body. Self-harm is linked to abuse and cover these actions:

- Cutting;
- Burning skin by physical means using heat;
- Burning skin by chemical means using caustic liquids;
- Punching hard enough to cause bruises;
- Head banging;
- Hair pulling from head, eyelashes, eyebrows and armpits;
- Poisoning by ingesting small amounts of toxic substances to cause discomfort or damage;
- Insertion of foreign objects;
- Excessive nail biting to the point of bleeding and ripping cuticles;
- Excessive scratching by removing top layer of skin to cause a sore;

- Bone breaking;
- Gnawing at flesh;
- Wound interference to prevent wounds from healing thus prolonging the effect;
- Tying ligatures around the neck, arms or legs to restrict the flow of blood;
- Medication abuse without intention to die;
- Alcohol abuse;
- Illegal drug use;
- Smoking.

Cutting and burning are among the most common forms of self-harm. Those who are smoking and drinking are not consciously harming themselves; they are taking part in a socially accepted lifestyle. It is only once these actions become excessive that problems can occur. There is also a strong correlation between eating disorders and self-harm. This is due to the fact that starvation, binge-eating and self-induced vomiting and overuse of laxatives and diuretics are forms of self-harm.

Conclusion

Bullying springs from deep-seated psychological problems, which need to be identified in each case and treated. Victims of bullying also suffer many negative effects. The lives of these victims need to be carefully examined for these negative signs and provide help as appropriate.

Chapter 4

WORKPLACE BULLYING

Workplace bullying is the deliberate, repeated and hurtful mistreatment of one person by another. Others refer to it as harassment, emotional abuse, targeted aggression or abuse of power that undermines self-confidence and causes stress. It's constant, inappropriate, overt and covert behaviour that criticises, belittles, isolates and undermines the victim. It involves humiliation, sabotage, spreading gossip, overwork, unnecessary pressure, delaying tactics and it can escalate into physical and verbal assault, sexual assault and arson. Evidence shows that bullying is normally repeated and can escalate in intensity over time.

Have you ever wondered how the bullies you saw at school are now? Chances are they are still making someone's life hell, but this time in the workplace. An employee's worst nightmare may be that one of them might be their direct supervisor. It almost seems that those young sandbox bullies (male and female) grow up, trade in their cute little shorts for fancy business suits and a slick hairdo and continue to apply their bullying behaviour to ensure their career success.

New studies indicate that childhood bullying leads to workplace bullying, that children who are victims of bullies, often become victims as adults. Bullies themselves also tend to be unpopular, both in schools and later in the workplace. They maintain relationships (not friendships) by displays of strength and by inducing fear to gain respect.

Cultural influences may play a part in bullying. Some women feel powerless when relating to men, which may prevent women from taking action to stop the bullying. Others have been brought up to respect their elders and people in authority. As a result, they may find it difficult to confront bullying if perpetrated by an older person or authority figure.

Workplace bullying is not limited to bosses. It can come from peers, especially those who are jealous or are threatened by their colleague's abilities and/or success. Finally, workplace bullies are differentiated by gender. Women can be equally as vicious as men in spite of using more verbal techniques.

Should their target assert his/her right not to be bullied, a paranoid fear of exposure compels the bully to perceive that person as a threat and hence neutralise and dispose of him/her as quickly as possible. Once that person has been eliminated, there's an interval before the bully chooses another target and the cycle begins again.

Guidelines issued by the Commonwealth Public Service Commission describe workplace harassment as a form of employment discrimination, consisting of offensive, abusive, belittling or threatening behaviour directed at an individual worker or group of workers which may be a result of some real or perceived attribute or difference. However, these *Guidelines* are not backed up by specific laws.

The workplace epidemic

Bullying is spreading through the workplace like an epidemic. Whereas twenty years ago most people could reasonably have expected to go through their working life without a serious bullying incident, today almost everyone seems to be at risk of being severely bullied during their career, maybe more than once. Bullies torment, browbeat and harass others to hide their weaknesses and inadequacy and to divert attention away from their incompetence. If employers took the time to determine the cost of high sick leave, staff turnover, low employee morale, poor productivity and customer service they would realise the cost of allowing bullying to continue in their workplaces.

Because workplace bullying doesn't always leave physical evidence, it's not well documented and since it rarely erupts into open confrontation, it's also the most tolerated of all workplace behaviour. Verbally harassed workers don't express their feelings, fearing what they reveal will be used by their tormenters to 'prove' their instability. Many employees who speak up are isolated and suffer greater harassment or their co-workers erect a wall of silence. Some insist the episode didn't happen the way it did. For all harassed workers, a tight job market adds to the dilemma, so they adapt - try to handle it - and just cope. But the diminished self-esteem, the energy that's consumed day after day going back to that kind of emotional beating, takes its toll.

If enough people do not defend the victim - the person begins to believe they're crazy, feel guilty or that they could be magnifying the situation. Victims also fear retaliation, ridicule and harassment if they complain. On-the-job harassment could be compared to the battered wife syndrome: the emotional effects are the same. There are parallels between family violence and violence against women in the workplace, including the fact that in both cases violence usually represents an abuse of power.

Most employers have distinguished themselves by their inaction - even when bullying has been reported. In a competitive business environment where profit often takes precedence over personnel, self-monitoring may be insufficient.

Some describe their office as toxic because of the toll they take causing stressed, overworked employees to become sick or to leave the company. Turnover in many companies has risen to epidemic proportions. Many companies are downsizing or merging with other companies who use different styles of leadership. After a takeover, this can lead to a loss of up to 75 per cent in work productivity. Or companies promote managers who may have high technical knowledge, but their people-skills must have been taught at the Saddam Hussein School of business.

Cost to companies

Bullying in the workplace has proven to be one of the most costly disciplinary matters a company can deal with. If not dealt with swiftly and aggressively, it can result in loss of productivity and de-motivation of any staff that have either observed or been subjected to the bullying. It can cause high absenteeism, loss of job satisfaction and often involves the loss of good employees who will not tolerate such seemingly condoned behaviour by their companies.

Hidden direct costs include those associated with pursuing formal grievance procedures, other staff time in addressing bullying-related incidents and workers' compensation costs. Lost productivity costs include not only those costs arising from reduced performance by victims while at work, but also lower initial efficiency among replacement employees until they reach the same level of performance as those replaced. This also can apply if the victim or bully is transferred to a new position within the organisation. It also includes productivity loss among co-workers who are affected by the bullying. Then there are the consequences of bullying and its stress as it impacts on worker innovation and creativity. There may also be detrimental effects on company image where the organisation is involved in a highly publicised case, with resultant impact on shareholders.

If the employee leaves in disgust because of inaction by the company to deal with the bullying issue, they might find that the company gives them a bad or no reference. If they pursue the issue and take the harassment and victimisation charges to court - they will likely need a big purse to cover the cost of the legal expenses. Most don't bother and go on to better things and the bullies win again.

There are many consequences for organisations. They include direct economic impacts such as the costs of paid sick leave, replacing staff and the legal and compensation costs arising from complaints and grievances. Absenteeism and staff turnover rates have been reported at very high rates in some overseas studies, up to 87 per cent absenteeism and 82 per cent staff turnover.

Workplace bullying has serious economic effects on Australian organisations. In one Australian study 34 per cent of bullied victims took time off work. The average time taken was 50 days, including 28 days on paid sick leave. Almost one-quarter resigned or retired and organisations incur costs in replacing those staff as well as losing valuable experience.

A recent impact and cost assessment calculated that workplace bullying costs Australian employers between $6 and $13 billion dollars every year when hidden and lost opportunity costs are considered and when using a very conservative prevalence estimate of the extent of overall victimisation and up to $17 and $36 billion per year when a somewhat higher estimate of 15 per cent prevalence is applied.

Serious bullying costs an average of $17,000 per case, but most Australian managers don't realise the cost of bullying, so pretend it isn't happening in their businesses. My research has identified that the majority of supervisors in Australia have not received even basic supervisory training so are blundering their way in business and making costly mistakes.

Most managers view people who complain of bullying as sissies or poor team members who don't play by the rules to meet performance measures. Some people just expect to get pushed around and others expect they will be able to push other people around. People being bullied often resign from their jobs instead of reporting the bullying, which hides the problem even more. The victims fear they won't be believed or that they will get a bad reference if they "make waves." So they simply leave and go elsewhere. This is why businesses should conduct exit interviews to determine the reasons why their employees leave their company. Many companies, instead of censuring the bully, transfer him or her to another department and the cycle continues in the new department.

New attitudes towards supervision

Until recently, psychologically violent people in the workplace were regarded as tough managers or difficult people or at worst a "pain in the neck." These attitudes are changing as the dysfunction, inefficiency, cost and severe psychiatric injury they inflict on others is revealed. The serial bully in the workplace is often found in a job that is a position of power, has a high administrative or procedural content, but little or no creative requirement which provides opportunities for demonstrating a caring or leadership nature.

Many managers fear the stigma of being branded a bully and then having to defend such allegations in a stress claim. An employer or manager has the right to instruct an employee on how the work is to be done in the workplace, but are not allowed to carry it to the level where it could be considered bullying. Many find that the blurring of the line between performance management and harassment has made it harder for managers to manage.

Workplace harassment may be distinguished from legitimate comments on the work performance of a subordinate employee by his or her supervisor. It's acceptable and indeed good management practice requires, that supervisors inform their subordinates of what is expected of them, the extent to which they meet those expectations and where they do not and what can be done to overcome perceived problems. It is not workplace harassment for managers to manage.

So how do managers decide when that line has been crossed and what does bullying behaviour look like? Typically, it comes from a boss to a subordinate in the form of verbal or emotional abuse. It includes yelling, swearing or ridiculing, continual and trivial fault-finding, chronic unjustified criticism, berating, intimidation, public humiliation or sabotaging of achievements. But the workplace bully can also be the silent snake-in-the-grass who cruelly bullies through manipulation, isolation, exclusion and gossip. Or they set an employee up to fail by overloading them with work, inconsistently and unjustifiably changing work responsibilities and even cancelling scheduled holidays.

What do the experts have to say?

So, how do you deal with a person who is a compulsive liar with a Jekyll and Hyde nature, is charming and glib, excels at deception and evasion of accountability? Diagnosis of such an individual is challenging. This is especially difficult should that person's superiors behave in a similar manner, give him or her glowing reports and deny everything. Let's see what the experts have to say:

Adelaide-based *Working Women's Centre* director, Sandra Dann said the extent of bullying uncovered was "pretty horrifying." She described the practice as "highly entrenched," in large organisations with a hierarchical management approach. She said bullying was a "symptom of a sick workplace - not of gender," noting male bullying was more likely to have violent or sexual undertones. She denies the number of women bullies was increasing, saying they were just more identifiable. But whoever the perpetrator, the cost to society is significant. The WWC survey found more than half of respondents reported the incidents to their managers, but did not receive adequate support or help. She says, *"Knowing there are penalties if you break the law, is a good incentive to start doing the right thing by workers."* She also called for "accessible" legal redress for victims.

The following *Occupational Health and Safety* regulations were updated as follows:

- South Australia: 1972 and 1984-1987
- Tasmania: 1977 and 1995
- Victoria: 1981 and 1986
- New South Wales: 1983 and 2000
- Northern Territory: 1984-1987
- Western Australia: 1989
- Queensland: 1995
- Australian Capital Territory: 1991 (Commonwealth employees)
- Australian Capital Territory: 1993 (Maritime industry)

[**Note:** However, none of the Occupational Health and Safety regulations in Australia cover workplace bullying, harassment or violence in the workplace.]

An Australia-wide survey conducted by the *Morgan & Banks* recruitment firm shows more than 10 per cent of respondents report bullying is increasing at work. At least half the cost of work-associated stress is directly attributable to bullying.

The *North West Adelaide Health Service* alone loses about $5 million a year in bullying-related costs. A new program aims to cut that figure in half.

Drake Personnel chief Diane Utatao said that workplace bullying affects one-in-four Australians and costs employers up to $12 billion a year and that the antics of one serial bully had the potential to reduce the performance of his/her victim in half and that of other employees by up to 33 per cent. Because the bully is bullying, they too are a productivity drain. She said that permanent employees in fear of losing their jobs were more likely to put up with bullying.

When a worker tries to attribute the injury to workplace bullying, workers compensation more often than not reject the claim (unconfirmed reports claim 95% of all stress-leave claims are initially rejected). In the meantime, the victim and bully often continue to work together - and the bullying may continue. Because of this, many workers are forced to go on stress leave, rather than continue to work in the same vicinity as their bully. Unless the company deals with and settles the issue within a short period of time - the victim's stress level can increase - rather than be alleviated. The longer the process takes to be resolved, the more chance that the victim will resign or go on stress leave. And the bully might go unpunished.

Claims that are accepted by workers compensation may take six to nine months to process. All that time, the bullying could be continuing or the claimant could be away from work on stress leave. Mediation is often recommended but mediation involves the victim and the offender facing each other. Mediation can be so distressing for some victims that it's cruel. Bullies can be very persuasive and end up making the victim feel bullied during the mediation. It might be necessary to bring the bully to account more directly under the enterprise bargaining agreement or their employment contract.

Young doctors were found to be falsifying work records, dropping out of their specialist courses or abandoning their medical profession. Although bullying is of epidemic proportions, many accept it as a rite of passage to become doctors. Some see it as survival of the strongest. Senior specialists are bullying juniors to a point that some suffer from depression and may have thoughts of or attempt suicide. This entrenched culture of medical bullies is diverting millions of dollars from the cash-strapped public health system by sick leave and lost productivity. Surveys found that 10 per cent of staff felt bullied, but new training programs and complaint systems aim to slash the problem.

And there's trouble in our courts and legislative assemblies too. As **Queensland District Court, J. Dodds** states, *"In today's Australian community it is not acceptable (if ever it was) for a person in authority over another in a workplace to harass, belittle or demean that other as a method of enforcing his authority or relieving his frustration."*

Unfortunately in our legislative assemblies bullying is a way of life that sets a dangerous precedent for the rest of business society. For too long, strong leadership in politics and in the corporate sector has been equated with table-thumping, shouting and dressing-down - especially in parliamentary debates. Politicians need to look closer to home when setting laws for their states and ensure they abide by them as well!

A **TMP Worldwide Survey on Bullying** said that of the 5,000 Australian employees questioned, 18 per cent said their boss bullied them and their co-workers, with 29 per cent reporting that employers are more hostile towards their employees than they were ten years ago. The survey shows that the biggest bullying bosses emanate from the legal sector with a massive 33.3 per cent of respondents in that industry type saying they were experiencing bullying tactics from their employers. Government sector bosses were not that far behind in the bullying stakes with 21.6 per cent of personnel in that sector saying their bosses were bullies.

Mr. Geoff Qurban of TMP Worldwide says, *"Times get tough, sometimes the tough get going and forget about the niceties and good manners expected of them in the workplace.*

"A downturn in the economy always brings about the worst in bosses' interpersonal skills. The pressure is on them to make the bottom line look good. They need to make sure that everyone in their operation is pulling their weight and they probably are at the brunt of external factors too, like looking for new markets, developing new products and maintaining a financial even keel.

"Most employees, i.e. 34.8 per cent, said the number one factor that makes their bosses belligerent is the inability to communicate and only 34.8 per cent said it was the pressure to produce. 12.9 per cent of respondents said it was their bosses inexperience to cope with the job

and 11.25 per cent said it was the difficulty in obtaining a good work/life balance that made their boss belligerent."

Workplace Stress Management

There are many areas where managers can work to reduce stress in order to create a workplace environment where there is higher productivity and fewer stress-related claims, sick days and accidents. To do this, managers should:

- Identify all the possible causes of stress;
- Eliminate harassment in the workplace. Conduct an assessment of all areas of workplace life that could contribute to stress. Determine the frequency and duration of stressors and the health impact on employees;
- Find ways of controlling stress levels by modifying the workplace, work systems or management style.

This process should be on-going. Frustration through lack of control can lead to a steady build-up of stress. Those who rate their jobs as demanding, but who have little control, are more likely to suffer from workplace stress. A workers compensation claim for stress should be managed in the same way as all other occupational injury or illness. *Unfortunately most claims for occupational stress are initially disputed by the insurance company.* Those who have been subject to workplace harassment and have been forced to take stress leave will have to be diligent in their efforts to prove their case.

Griffith University Workplace Bulling and Violence Project Team's information sheet on workplace bullying states that there has been no Australian research surveying the general population or large representative employee groups, so that we do not yet have reliable statistics on the number of Australians experiencing workplace bullying.

The best international research shows between 25 and 50 per cent of employees will experience bullying at some time in their working lives (although in some occupations, the figure is up to 95 per cent) and 4 to 20 per cent of people have been bullied in the past six to twelve months. Best estimates based on international research extrapolated to the Australian population is that 10 to 15 per cent of the Australian labour force will experience workplace bullying in a given year. This means about one million Australians have experienced the direct effects of workplace bullying during the past twelve months and about five million Australians will have experienced it at some point during their working lives.

Recent research shows that workplace bullying affects not only those directly victimised, but also other workers who witness bullying incidents as well as the families of victims. Therefore, a much larger number of Australians are affected each year by the consequences of workplace bullying than the actual number of victims.

Implementing an anti-bullying policy

An anti-bullying policy can be implemented with minimal cost within an organisation's existing anti-harassment, equity and conflict resolution procedures. As such, it offers a cost-effective way of minimising risks of the costly impact of bullying. Implementation of the policy sends a positive message to staff, clients, investors and other key stakeholders that negative behaviours that disrupt productivity and quality and undermine customer service will not be tolerated. In these terms an anti-bullying policy signals that the organisation is responsible and ethical and cares about maintaining motivated committed staff and good customer relations.

Conclusion

Australia must upgrade its laws so that all its workers are properly protected against workplace bullying, harassment and bullying. *"Codes of Practice"* and *"Guidance Notes"* are useless unless Acts relating to workplace bullying, harassment and violence have regulations with some teeth. Occupational Health and Safety regulations appear to be the most logical Acts to include this coverage.

Chapter 5

THE SERIAL BULLY

Serial bullies are those who are not happy unless they are bullying others. Most have been bullies all their lives and it has become a way of life for them. Vulnerability of others is their major stimulant. Their need to control can reach obsessive heights. They hoard information and can be evasive when asked for information by their subordinates. They form or join committees to look busy and important, but never achieve anything of significance or value. They abuse disciplinary procedures by using criticism and humiliation in the guise of addressing shortcomings in others' performance. Their real aim is to control or subjugate others - not to obtain performance improvement. They don't trust others, which partly explains their compulsion for excessive monitoring. Their departments are dysfunctional and inefficient and their behaviour prevents staff from performing their duties.

Being a bully is the primary identity of the serial bully. Most serial bullies have unhappy and unsatisfactory private lives that are characterised by a string of broken relationships and domestic violence. Others stay in a marriage, but batter their wives and children.

Serial bullies commit mostly non-arrestable offences such as:

- Incompetence;
- Neglect or dereliction of duty;
- Misappropriation of budgets;
- Enhancing expense account records;
- Falsifying time sheets;
- Pilfering;
- Stealing, diverting, skimming or "losing" clients' money and investments;
- Embezzlement;
- Fraud;
- Deception;
- Malpractice;
- Misrepresentation;
- Conspiracy;
- Using the employer's resources to run their own business on the side;
- Moonlighting for employer's clients or competitors;

- Awarding contracts to family and friends;
- Leaking information to people who should not be in possession of that information;
- Failure to fulfill obligations;
- Breaches of health and safety regulations;
- Breaches of rules and regulations;
- Breaches of codes of conduct;
- Indiscretions;
- Impropriety;
- Inappropriate sexual conduct or language;
- Being the target of previous grievance or disciplinary action;
- Being the target of previous legal action (unfair dismissal, harassment, personal injury, etc.);
- Fraudulent qualifications and misleading or bogus claims of professional affiliation;
- Collusion;
- Corruption;
- Being fired or asked to leave their previous job(s); and/or
- Recruitment through nepotism or favouritism rather than ability. In some cases serial bullies have been found to have criminal convictions for fraud or have been compelled to attend therapy or counselling for their habit of compulsive lying.
- Arsonists;
- Rapists (also date rape) and those who commit acts of sexual violence;
- Violent offenders including organised serial killers.

The psychology of the serial workplace bully

A particularly common type of bully in the workplace is the serial bully. This type of bully deserves special mention. The serial bully is essentially a master of deception. They also hold deep prejudices. Their background tends to have certain patterns that serve to explain their current behaviour, while not justifying it.

Manipulation and deception:

Serial bullies commonly use workplace affairs as strategic alliances to gain power, control, domination and subjugation. They excel at deception and a surprising number of people are fooled by their behaviour because most have exceptional verbal facility and will out-manoeuvre most people in times of conflict. They are unusually skilled at being able to anticipate what people want to hear and then saying it plausibly.

While their language and intellect may appear to be that of an adult, the bully is emotionally retarded and most perform poorly in academic or professional roles. Their intelligence excels when it is focused on deviousness, cunning, scheming and manipulation of others.

Some have an aura of invulnerability and untouchability and sometimes display a seemingly limitless, demonic energy. They cannot be trusted or relied upon and fail to fulfil commitments. They are unable to maintain confidentiality, often breaching it with misrepresentation, distortion and fabrication.

They are convincing and practised liars; are always takers and not givers. Serial bullies select and harass any person they believe will be a threat to them. This threat is the exposure of the bully's inadequacies, which will in turn threaten the bully's job, promotion prospects or standing within the hierarchy. They are control freaks that have a compulsive need to control. They also despise anyone who enables others to see through their deception and their mask of sanity. Serial bullies act randomly and impulsively.

They are evasive and have the ability to escape accountability and are quick to discredit and neutralise anyone who might otherwise collate incriminating information about them. They live forever in the present and show no remorse. Blaming others is their means of avoiding responsibility for their behaviour and the effect it has on others. When questioned or called to account, they show impatience and irritability and then become aggressive or launch a psychological assault. They rarely stay in one workplace for long and show no loyalty to anyone except themselves. They are financially irresponsible and often have a poor credit rating.

Unusual sexual attitudes

They can exhibit unusual and inappropriate attitudes to sexual matters, sexual behaviour and bodily functions. Underneath the charming exterior there are often suspicions or hints of sex discrimination and sexual harassment, perhaps also sexual dysfunction, sexual inadequacy, sexual violence or sexual abuse.

They see people as objects, in the same way that child sex abusers and rapists see their targets as objects for their gratification. In a relationship they are incapable of initiating or sustaining intimacy. Many hold deep prejudices against the opposite gender, people of a different sexual orientation, people of other cultures and religious beliefs, foreigners and so on. However, serial bullies go to great lengths to mask their prejudices.

The person who uses corporal punishment (especially male) will later use the memory of administering the punishment as part of his visualisation during sexual activity, including masturbation. Anyone who advocates corporal punishment and especially anyone who practices it, is almost certainly - and unwittingly revealing their propensity towards sexually abusive behaviour.

One of the most serious bullies is the serial bully who accounts for over ninety per cent of the five thousand plus cases reported to the UK National Workplace Bullying Advice Line and Bully OnLine over five years. Over two thirds of all calls were from the public sector. In almost half the cases, the bully was having an affair with another member of staff. The affair had little to do with friendship and a lot to do with strategic alliance to gain power, control, domination and subjugation. In another quarter of the cases, there was a suspected affair and the remaining quarter, there was often a relationship with another member of staff based not so much on sexual attraction but on a mutual admiration for the way each other behaves. Sometimes the female junior was identified by her special treatment - promotions or being put in charge of an area (whether she was qualified or not).

Projection:

Bullies project their inadequacies, shortcomings, behaviours and so on onto other people. Investigation usually reveals they have either left their jobs or partners unexpectedly or under suspicious circumstances.

They do this to avoid facing up to their inadequacies, for learning about oneself can be painful. This projection also helps to divert attention away from themselves and their inadequacies. This is achieved through every criticism that the bully makes about the target. *What they are actually doing is admitting or revealing these behaviours in themselves.* This knowledge can be used to identify the bully's misdemeanours. For instance, if the allegations are of financial or sexual impropriety, it is likely that the bully has committed these acts.

A failure to grow up:

Adult serial bullies were invariably bullies at school. The serial bully has bullied before, is doing it now - and will do it again. Investigation usually reveals a string of predecessors who have either left unexpectedly or under suspicious circumstances (their positions have been made redundant, they've been unfairly dismissed, involved in disciplinary or legal action or have had stress breakdowns).

When the bully makes allegations of abuse (which tend to be vague and non-specific) it's likely to be the bully who has committed the abuse.

The serial bully is an adult on the outside, but a child on the inside. S/he is like a child who has never grown up. One suspects that they are emotionally retarded and have a level of emotional development equivalent to that of five year old. The bully wants to enjoy the benefits of living in the adult world, but is unable or unwilling to accept the responsibilities that go with these benefits.

Conclusion

Employees must be constantly vigilant when working with serial bullies and corporations need to ensure that these people are promptly fired and prosecuted for their behaviour.

Chapter 6

HOW OTHER COUNTRIES DEAL WITH WORKPLACE BULLYING

UNITED KINGDOM

Research shows that between fifty and seventy-five per cent of workers are likely to experience bullying at some time during their career. In a study of 3,500 UK workers by *Mercer Human Resource Consulting* found more than one in five had been bullied at work at least once during the past year. Almost one in ten reported bullying on more than one occasion, with two per cent saying they have been bullied five or six times.

The UK has one of the highest adult suicide rates in Europe; around 5,000 a year. The number of adults in the UK committing suicide because of bullying is unknown. In the UK, suicide is the number one cause of death for 18 to 24 year-old males. Females also attempt suicide in large numbers but tend to use less successful means. There are more than a million violent incidents at work each year in England and Wales. About a quarter of these involved physical assault resulting in injury. High-risk professionals are the police, social workers, probation officers, security guards and bar staff. Nurses also face increasing violence, as do teachers.

Often the cause of negative stress in an organisation can be traced to the behaviour of one individual. Many see bullying as the main - but least recognised cause of negative stress in the workplace today.

Some bullying comes in the form of discrimination. A study completed by the *Medical Practitioner's Union* found that senior hospital doctors are denied salary distinction awards simply because of the colour of their skin. The awards are given to recognise exemplary performance within the NHS, such as innovation or outstanding clinical and managerial skills.

White consultants were three times more likely to receive a distinction award compared to colleagues from ethnic minorities. White doctors working in obstetrics and gynaecology, dermatology and general surgery were ten times more likely to be given the bonus and orthopaedics and trauma staff were thirty times more likely to receive a bonus.

The Department of Health rejected the claim. They are planning to replace the current distinction awards with new clinical excellence awards in 2004.

Staffroom Bullying:

Did you know?

- One teacher in three claims to have been bullied at work;
- More than 90 per cent of reported cases of workplace bullying are caused by a serial bully;
- Bullying is not a gender issues, but women make up 75 per cent of victims who seek help;
- In 1998, a Northumberland primary teacher won £100,000 in an out-of-court settlement after he'd been bullied by his head.
- There is no legislation that directly addresses bullying.

NORWAY

Norwegian research into workplace bullying presented a paper at the *Adelaide Workplace Bullying Conference - Skills for Survival, Solutions and Strategies in 2002*.

Norway expert **Dr Stale Einarsen** presented some interesting research, which focused on "who is doing what to whom, where and why and with what kind of consequence." His paper brought together a number of elements from Norwegian research into workplace bullying. Einarsen defined bullying as, *"A situation where one or more persons persistently over a period of time, perceive him/herself to be on the receiving end of negative actions from one or several others in a situation where the one at the receiving end has difficulties defending against these actions."* He noted that, *"Typically, a victim is constantly teased, badgered and insulted and perceives that he or she has little recourse to retaliate in kind."*

Einarsen differentiated between 'direct bullying' consisting of open verbal or physical attacks and 'indirect bullying' comprised of subtle acts such as excluding or isolating a victim from his or her peer group and notes that bullying is not "the everyday struggle and conflicts that are part of all human interaction."

In Norwegian research 5 per cent of workers reported bullying at work. Such bullying usually occurred in large, male-dominated organisations and to older workers with males offending more often than women.

"Bullying seems not to be an either or phenomenon but a gradually evolving process" often triggered by a work-related conflict which escalates. In early phases the victim seems to be attacked only now and then. As the conflict escalates however, the frequency of the attacks becomes higher and the behaviour harsher.

Research quoted by Einarsen indicates that bullies are frequently self confident, impulsive and do not suffer from any lack of self-esteem. They frequently demonstrate a general aggressive reaction pattern in many different situations.

Einarsen also noted that victims of bullying at work are often conscientious, literal-minded, often over-achievers who have high expectations of themselves and their work situation.

Norwegian research demonstrated substantially different responses to bullying by targets. Such responses ranged from the "seriously affected" those who reported a range of emotional and psychological problems, to the "disappointed and depressed" who demonstrated a tendency towards becoming depressed and suspicious of the outside world.

A "common group" was also identified. This group demonstrated a "normal personality in spite of having experienced the largest number of specific bullying behaviours."

Einarsen suggests that a number of structural factors in the working environment may encourage the development of bullying behaviour. Such structural factors include:

1. Deficiencies in work design;
2. Deficiencies in leadership behaviour;
3. Socially exposed position of the victim and
4. Low moral standard in the department.

He further notes that, *"The tension, stress and frustration caused by a job situation characterised by high role conflict, lack of self monitoring possibilities and poor performing supervisors may in itself be perceived as harassment when attributed to hostile intentions."*

A high degree of ambiguity or incompatible demands and expectations around roles, tasks and responsibilities may have created a high degree of frustration and conflicts within the work group, especially in connection to rights, obligations, privileges and positions.

Einersen notes that bullying:

- Impacts negatively on the productivity of the organisation;
- Undermines the psychological, psychosomatic and muscle skeletal health of workers; and may result in;
- Post traumatic stress disorder for some workers.

For these targets that become victims of bullying, their world and self-view is shattered and they may find it impossible to function normally or effectively in the work environment. This research would indicate that often those who suffer most from unacceptable bullying behaviour in the workplace are those with the most to give - those with high expectations of themselves and those who are prepared to go the extra mile because they believe that what they are doing is meaningful and important.

UNITED STATES

In the US workplace, there are two million violent victimisations a year, including assaults, rapes and robberies; and an average of 1,000 workplace murders a year, according to *The National Crime Victimisation Survey* conducted in the early 1990s (the most recent figures available). The *US Campaign Against Workplace Bullying* (CAWB) survey in 2000 found both men and women guilty of bullying, with women being three quarters of the targets. More than 80 per cent of bullies are bosses.

The CAWB found 41 per cent of bullying victims were diagnosed with depression and one in five men and one in three women suffered from post-traumatic stress disorder. Eighty per cent left their jobs. Those who stayed, admitted that they were under-performing because of their level of anxiety and sleeplessness. So the result of bullying for employers involves under-performing staff or they lose staff – both very expensive results of bullying.

According to a US study, one in six workers is affected by workplace bullying. *"It's like a cancer that gets into your system and keeps eating away at you,"* says one man who quit a job because of a malicious boss.

"I went from a fully functional, productive person to a nervous, paranoid, depressed individual," wrote one woman.

CANADA

In a recent study, the number of employees seeking help for work-related conflict had increased by 29 per cent from 1999 to 2001. Many companies still do not have formalised workplace violence policies. Often when management are asked to intervene - they don't handle complaints properly. Their message is loud and clear - we aren't going to do or say anything to someone who makes a lot more money than you do. Most employees throw up their hands in disgust and leave the company.

Most wish they had called a lawyer when their harassment started. Fortunately, there are lots of strategies and legal remedies a victim of harassment can pursue when their boss won't defend them.

The first thing a person should do is research how prevalent or persistent the problem is within their workplace. Also try to rally other victims or witnesses behind you. Determine whether others will back up your complaints. Gather evidence that proves the company knew about the abuse, but refused to act. While a paper trail helps, it's not an absolute necessity. In reality, if you don't have it - it will become a case of "s/he said" versus "you said." Credibility will be called into question.

Employees can sue for constructive dismissal by trying to prove the company breached its contract by imposing terms and conditions that weren't originally agreed to. But these cases are harder to win. From the onset there's a power imbalance. The company will often say that the employee resigned and that they're entitled to nothing.

Another legal remedy includes suing for intentional or negligent infliction of nervous suffering.

In both cases, the employer can be found liable if you can prove through medical evidence that there was a direct link between what you suffered and what the employer didn't do. When an employee starts a civil action, most employers decide to settle it out of court. The vast majority get resolved before a statement of claim is issued.

In its employers' guide to anti-harassment policies, the Canadian Human Rights Commission notes that, "disrespectful behaviour, commonly known as 'personal' harassment, is not covered by human rights legislation. While it also involves unwelcome behaviour that demeans or embarrasses an employee, the behaviour is not based on one of the protected grounds. These grounds include race, national or ethnic origin, colour, religion, age, sex, marital status, family status, disability, pardoned conviction or sexual orientation.

If people want to avoid a costly lawsuit, they can try to seek help by using provincial or federal occupational health and safety legislation or workers compensation. Federal and provincial legislation is finally starting to recognise workplace violence as an occupational hazard. Most jurisdictions recognise that the employer has a duty to maintain a safe workplace. But workplace violence experts say the law still doesn't adequately address violence perpetrated between co-workers. Despite these shortcomings, it's much more informal and less costly than going through the courts.

Canada won't get meaningful legislation on this topic until one or two very public lawsuits have been tried and won in court.

In Canada's Labour Code (which covers federally regulated employees) the definition of danger has been broadened. This could allow for protection against bullying, say lawyers, although it has not yet been tested. In addition, a draft policy of the Workers' Safety Insurance Board includes stress-related illnesses, which, if adopted, could allow bullied employees to claim any illness that resulted from the bullying as a compensable injury, says labour lawyer *Jeffrey Goodman* of Heenan Blaikie.

Glenn French, the national director of The Canadian Initiative on Workplace Violence, a non-profit research group in Toronto says that while physical violence in the workplace tends to come from external parties - customers or maintenance workers, for example - psychological violence comes from within. *"You have a better chance of being a workplace fatality in the United States,"* he says, *"Whereas in Canada, you have a better chance of being bullied, harassed and abused."* Studies suggest psychological violence in the workplace is widespread. In a 2000 survey of Canadian labour unions, more than 75 per cent reported incidences of harassment and bullying.

This problem is not a strictly Canadian phenomenon. A study in 1997 by the *International Labour Organisation* showed that 43 per cent of international civil servants believed bullying and verbal aggression was a problem at work.

Most people think of violence as a physical assault. However, workplace violence is a much broader problem. It is any act in which a person is abused, threatened, intimidated or assaulted in his or her employment. Workplace violence includes:

Threatening behaviour - such as shaking fists, destroying property and throwing objects.

Verbal or written threats - any expression of an intent to inflict harm.

Harassment - any behaviour that demeans, embarrasses, humiliates, annoys, alarms or verbally abuses a person and that is known or would be expected to be unwelcome. This includes words, gestures, intimidation, bullying or other inappropriate activities.

Verbal abuse - swearing, insults or condescending language.

Physical attacks - hitting, shoving, pushing or kicking.

Rumours, swearing, verbal abuse, pranks, arguments, property damage, vandalism, sabotage, pushing, theft, physical assaults, psychological trauma, anger-related incidents, rape, arson and murder are all examples of workplace violence.

Workplace violence is not limited to incidents that occur within a traditional workplace. Work-related violence can occur at off-site business-related functions (conferences, trade shows) at social events related to work, in clients' homes or away from work but resulting from work (a threatening telephone call to your home from a client).

How do you recognise workplace emotional abuse?

It's using words or actions of a psychological nature that create and/or take advantage of an imbalance of power. A pattern of behaviour that undermines, sabotages, interferes with or influences the career of another employee. It includes repeated, intentional, offensive comments or actions that demean and belittle an individual or cause personal humiliation.

How do you know you're exposed to a bully?

- Are you introduced in terms that are belittling or patronising?
- Do supervisors or colleagues always put you down or ignore you?
- Are you constantly made to feel that what you do is not acceptable or up to par?

- Are you allowed to do what you were hired to do or given demeaning tasks?

Do you receive:

- Unsolicited or unwelcome references to ability or conduct;
- Comments that reflect on unwarranted intrusion on one's dignity as a person (eg. Treating you as a child or "as cute");
- Unwelcome advances that interfere with one's work;
- Intimidating or hostile behaviour;
- Adopting your ideas without recognising your creativity and efforts;
- Consciously/unconsciously excluded from the decision-making process;
- The only comments you receive are about your appearance or dress - rather than ability.

[**Note:** I checked the Canadian Occupational Health and Safety Act (10/17/2013) and did not find any reference to workplace bullying, harassment or violence, but did find a section protecting workers against sexual harassment.]

EUROPE

There are similar figures for Europe - about 8 per cent of EU workers (or 12 million workers) have been bullied, according to a European Union survey in 1996.

However, there is far less research quantifying the impacts on organisations of high absenteeism, staff turnover rates, diminished work performance by affected employees and the loss of good employees who will not tolerate such seemingly condoned behaviour in their companies. The costs to companies is high and include absenteeism, staff turnover, costs of legal advice and support in relevant court and tribunal actions, compensation payouts in court contested and mediated cases and redundancy payouts.

The *Mobbing Report* from Germany's Ministry of Labour suggests that bullying is worse in Germany than any other European country. The report estimates 800,000 people were suffering - intolerable abuse - every day and that 1.5 million workers suffered sickness caused by bullying. Suicide has also been identified as a consequence of bullying and the German government is considering legislation. Big industrial unions such as IG Metall have departments dealing solely with workplace bullying and courts have begun making large payouts to people who have complained of systematic harassment. In Saarb-cken (a clinic to treat psychiatrically injured targets of workplace bullying) has been opened where patients can receive treatment free from the state or through private insurance policies.

And Russia is getting tough with workplace bullies. Last year 2,000 Russian soldiers were convicted of bullying, which results in thousands of suicides and desertions a year. Families pay thousands of roubles in bribes to buy their sons out of military service.

A soldier serving with President Vladimir Putin's ceremonial bodyguard was sentenced to two years in a punishment battalion after being found guilty of bullying a recruit so mercilessly that his target slit his wrists with a razor blade in an attempted suicide. The soldier repeatedly forced the recruit to do pull-ups and beat him with a belt when he could not continue. On one occasion he also forced him to drink four pints of water without stopping, which made him vomit.

Faced with a mounting toll of violence afflicting on average one of every two health workers worldwide, a joint program of labour, health and public service organisations on 24 October, 2002 launched a new initiative aimed at helping health professionals fight fear, assault, humiliation and even homicide where they work.

The joint task force - comprising the International Labour Office (ILO), the World Health Organisation (WHO), Public Service International (PSI) and the International Council of Nurses (ICN) - has launched a set of "Framework guidelines for addressing workplace violence in the health sector" during a meeting at ILO headquarters in Geneva.

The initiative comes in the face of a mounting problem in hospitals and other health workplaces worldwide, both in developed and developing countries. Research shows that nearly 25 per cent of all violent incidents at work occur in the health sector and that more than 50 per cent of health care workers have experienced such incidents.

"The current knowledge is only the tip of the iceberg," adds international safety and health specialist **Vittorio di Martino**, who has studied violence in the workplace for the task force. *"The enormous cost of violence at work for the individual, the workplace and the community at large is becoming increasingly apparent."*

The study notes that violence in the health sectors goes well beyond assaults or affronts to the individuals, threatening the equality of health care as well as productivity and development. Says di Martino: *"The consequences of violence at work in the health sector have a significant impact on the effectiveness of health systems, especially in developing countries."*

Women are especially vulnerable. While ambulance staff are reported to be at greatest risk, nurses are three times more likely on average to experience violence in the workplace than other occupational groups. Since most health workers are women, the gender dimension of the problem is evident.

In accordance with the European Commission, the guidelines define workplace violence as "incidents where staff are abused, threatened or assaulted in circumstances related to their work, including commuting to and from work, involving an explicit or implicit challenge to their safety, well-being or health." Although workplace violence has become a serious problem in all service sectors, reports show that health workers are among those particularly at risk:

In the United States, health care workers face a 16-times greater risk of violence than other service workers. More than half of the claims of aggression in the workplace in the US comes from the health sector.

In the United Kingdom, nearly 40 per cent of the National Health Service (NHS) staff reported being bullied in 1998.

In Australia, 67.2 per cent of health workers have experienced physical or psychological violence in 2001.

Widespread violence at work against health personnel is not limited to the industrialised world. More than half of the health personnel in Bulgaria (75.8 per cent) South Africa (61 per cent) and Thailand (54 per cent) and 46.7 per cent of health workers in Brazil have experienced at least one incident of physical or psychological violence in 2001.

Research also shows that psychological violence in the health sector - including verbal abuse bullying and mobbing - is more frequent than physical violence and between 40 and 70 per cent of the victims report significant stress symptoms.

Workplace violence affects all professional groups, genders and work settings in the health sector. The highest rates of offences, however, were reported by ambulance staff, nurses and doctors. Large hospitals in suburban, densely populated and high crime areas, as well as those located in isolated areas, are particularly at risk.

In many countries, reporting procedures are lacking and perpetrators are not persecuted. Strategies to combat workplace violence in the health sector still have a long way to go, starting with raising awareness and building understanding among health personnel and other parties concerned at all levels.

The guidelines are intended to support all those responsible for safety in the workplace, be they governments, employers, workers, trade unions, professional bodies or the general public. In particular, the guidelines show how health workers can approach the problem of violence in the health sector while considering all types of intervention and involving all parties concerned in a coherent, non-discriminatory, culturally and gender sensitive manner; identify, assess and reduce the risks through preventive action; and minimise the impact of violence and prevent its recurrence.

The guidelines prioritise the development of a human-centred workplace culture based on dignity, non-discrimination, equal opportunity and cooperation, including a clear policy statement on violence at work from the top management and awareness raising initiatives at all levels. The ILO is expected to adopt a *Code of Practice on Violence and Stress at Work in Services - A Threat to Productivity and Decent Work* in October, 2003. (For more information, contact International Labour Office, Department of Communication, communication@ilo.org.)

Conclusion

It appears that workplace bullying thrives in all countries. Unless employees and progressive companies lobby their policy makers, this will continue to harm not only employees, but affect the gross economic stability of those countries.

Chapter 7

SEXUAL HARASSMENT AND DISCRIMINATION

What constitutes sexual harassment?

Sexual harassment can be a male harassing a female; a female harassing a male; a male harassing another male; or a female harassing another female. Most sexual harassment is males harassing females. Unfortunately most women have been harassed since they entered the workplace and think "it comes with the territory." Well *No*; it doesn't.

This is one work problem that's bothered women for centuries. However, the situation is changing slowly as laws are updated. Most laws that include sexual harassment come under Anti-Discrimination Acts and Regulations.

There are many ways in which sexual harassment can be expressed, from the very subtle to the most overt. Sexual harassment can include one or more of the following:

- Unwelcome sexual remarks - i.e.: jokes, innuendoes, teasing, verbal abuse;
- Taunts about a person's body, attire, age, marital status;
- Displays of pornographic, offensive or derogatory pictures;
- Practical jokes that cause awkwardness or embarrassment;
- Unwelcome invitations or requests, whether indirect or explicit;
- Intimidation;
- Leering or suggestive gestures;
- Condescension or paternalism that undermines self-respect;
- Unnecessary physical contact - i.e.: touching, patting, pinching, punching or physical assault.
- Sending sexually explicit e-mails.

Verbal:
- Telling dirty jokes with sexual connotations;
- Asking for sexual favours;
- Comments about one's sexual anatomy;
- Pursuing an unwanted relationship;
- Unwanted compliments with sexual overtones;

- Condescension or paternalism that undermines self-respect.

Visual:

- Staring at someone's sexual anatomy;
- Holding uncomfortably long eye contact giving sexual messages;
- Flirting non-verbally;
- Pornographic pictures.

Physical:

- Unwanted touching and making physical contact;
- Standing too close.

No longer can others in positions of power "look the other way" and ignore that sexual harassment is occurring. For instance, if I'm a supervisor and do nothing when I see another person sexually harassing an employee, it's believed that I've condoned the action. If the employee knows that I observed his/her harassment or know about the situation (and did nothing) s/he can charge both the harasser and me with sexual harassment. Co-workers, as well as superiors may be responsible for acts of sexual harassment and can be charged.

There are many myths about sexual harassment:

Myth #1: Sexual harassment is not very common.
Reality: Sexual harassment is much more common than you might think. One survey found that 75 to 95 percent of all working women had been exposed to sexual harassment and a shocking 52 per cent of women had left a job because of sexual harassment.

Myth #2: You invite sexual harassment by your behaviour or your dress.
Reality: Sexual harassment is an expression of power. It is usually practiced with little regard for appearance or behaviour. Sexual harassers often pick vulnerable victims. Harassers may misinterpret behaviour or dress as being enticing in order to justify their aggressive actions.

Myth #3: If you object, you have no sense of humour.
Reality: Sexual harassment is not a laughing matter! Some people confuse sexual harassment with flirtation that can be harmless and fun if

it's mutual and there is no intimidation or humiliation involved. Sexual harassment is no joking matter when one's job, working conditions, career opportunities, health or happiness are affected. There is no humour in the anxiety, anger, fear, guilt and frustration it causes.

Myth #4: A firm *"No"* is enough to discourage anyone.
Reality: In most cases the harasser has greater physical, social and economic power, which is often accompanied by the power of reprisal. This enables the harasser to override the firmest *"No."*

Myth #5: A woman's *."No"* means *"Yes."*
Reality: *"No"* means *"No!"*

If ignored, sexual harassment will not usually stop. Instead, it worsens. Trying to be subtle with, polite or nice to the harasser does not usually work. The offending behaviour should be specified along with a request or demand that it stop. Putting it in writing is often much more effective than just verbally. The woman may wish to tell the harasser how his behaviour makes her feel. She may wish to include or threaten a particular consequence (that his actions are against the law) if the harassment is not stopped. In serious cases the police may be involved, especially if charges for assault, sexual assault, extortion or harassment by telephone are involved.

Workplace Discrimination

Workplace discrimination can take many forms. Some of them could be classified as bullying. Here are some actual cases:

1. The workplace common room was full of pornographic material and lacked a women's toilet.
   Complaint: Sexual harassment and sex discrimination by female working in job traditionally classified as "men's work" in the automotive industry. Constant verbal abuse and sexual harassment led to a workers compensation claim being lodged after visits to doctor and psychologist. Employment terminated six months later.
   Result: Court order of $80,000 compensation payment by employer covering both workers compensation claim and separate sexual harassment.
2. The bar manager touched her gratuitously and intimately.
   Complaint: Sexual harassment by hotel co-worker who ignored employer warnings.

Results: Bar manager ordered to pay $4,000 compensation. Employer ordered to pay $10,000, choosing not to admit any liability.

3. *"It doesn't look very nice with you doing table service while you are pregnant."*

   Complaint: Sexual harassment, pregnancy victimisation of recreation club worker.

   Result: Employer ordered to pay $7,500 and a written employment reference.

4. A company manager told her that flirting by male colleagues goes with the territory.

   Complaint: Female employee of a communications company against her employer and four male colleagues in which employer offered to pay $20,000 compensation if she left the company or $15,000 if she stayed and accepted a different job role. Both declined by complainant.

   Result: In court, the company ordered to pay $20,000 damages and written work reference.

5. The sex discrimination consisted of offensive and derogatory remarks made by the site manager, shift supervisor and co-worker.

   Complaint: Sex discrimination of female security officer in shopping centre.

   Result: Warnings given to offending parties. Shift supervisor and co-worker transferred to another site. Site manager required to attend conflict resolution and harassment training course. Complainant promoted to shift supervisor's position.

In seminars where I discuss sexual harassment, I'm often challenged by male employees - especially those who work in male-dominated environments - who say, *"Why should I have to clean up my act for a female. If she wants to come into my domain - she has to live by our rules!"*

My answer is, *"How many of you have daughters, wives, lovers, sisters or mothers who are out in the workplace?"*

I then ask, *"What would you do if one of them came home from work crying because she had been sexually harassed at work?"*

Most of them would reply, *"I'd punch his lights out!"*

"Well then, what do you think the father, husband, lover or brother of the woman you're harassing is feeling about your actions?"

End of discussion.

In the UK, women who suffer sex discrimination at work have a better chance to fight it. Women who are passed over for promotion by their male colleagues or receive less pay for similar work will no longer be forced to prove that they were discriminated against. This new regulation will have severe repercussions for employers.

The Burden of Proof Directive came into force in the UK in October 2001. It will make it easier for applicants to win sex discrimination cases; so more employers are likely to settle more cases out of court. It means that the burden of proof in claims of sex discrimination now lies with the employer rather than with the employee.

Workplace bullies targeted by ACTU Campaign (Queensland)

In Queensland, a workplace survey conducted by unions as part of an ACTU campaign to stamp out workplace bullying revealed that 77 per cent of the bullying was done by employers, managers and supervisors. The results of the survey show that over 54 per cent of workers experience intimidating behaviour at work that can only be described as bullying. Bullying is under-reported. Almost 70 per cent of those reporting bullying said more than one victim was involved. More than half said nothing was done about it.

QIEU's participation in this survey has revealed that bullying is also common within the non-governmental education sector. The results of this survey were available in 2001 as follows:

Intimidating behaviour such as shouting ordering, belittling, threats, abusive language, demands to perform tasks without adequate training, impossible targets an oppressive/unhappy workplace and fear of speaking up about conditions are of most concern to employees.

Bullying has resulted in employees experiencing a considerable amount of anger, depression, high blood pressure, digestive problems, stress, headaches and sleeping problems. Bullying is an occupational health and safety issue and should be treated with concern by both employees and employers. Employers have a legal duty to control all health and safety hazards in the workplace including structures and behaviours that may lead to bullying.

Note: The above article covers bullying that involves sexual harassment and discrimination that are covered under Human Rights and Equal Opportunity and Anti-Discrimination Acts. This does ***not*** protect employees from other kinds of bullying and harassment situations.

Differences between workplace harassment and sexual harassment

Sexual harassment: is unwelcome behaviour of a sexual nature. If the person's behaviour towards you is unwelcome and unwanted and there are sexual overtones, then you are being sexually harassed. Touching is only one form of sexual harassment. There are other forms of sexual harassment that may not involve physical contact. Any behaviour or conduct that makes your work environment intimidating, hostile or offensive can also be sexual harassment.

What is seen as sexual harassment by one person may not be by another. Just because the harasser is treating one of your co-workers the same way and that person doesn't mind, doesn't mean you aren't being harassed. This is why it's important for you to let the harasser know that you do not welcome the behaviour and that it makes you feel uncomfortable. If the behaviour persists despite your objections, then it's sexual harassment.

Good-natured flirting or jesting which both parties find acceptable or an office romance to which both parties willingly consent, are not considered to be sexual harassment.

If you think you are being sexually harassed, you may feel embarrassed, confused or intimidated. Don't ignore your feelings. You did not ask to be harassed and you have a right to work in an environment that's free of sexual pressure of any kind.

Sexual harassment is usually an attempt by one person to use power over another. The issue, then, is not what you did to invite the harassment. Harassment is behaviour that the person ought reasonably to have known would be unwelcome. It's important, though, for you to let the person know that the behaviour is, in fact unwelcome.

Workplace harassment: also includes harassment of a person due to their race, ethnic background, religion, physical or mental capabilities or gender. It is possible for a person to experience both types of harassment at the same time. For example, a person who is being sexually harassed may be treated that way because of his or her race.

Workplace and sexual harassment are both unwanted and offensive. They both leave the person feeling demeaned, intimidated or embarrassed. They both go beyond the bounds of normally accepted behaviour. While one has sexual overtones, the other is a form of discrimination resulting from prejudice. The behaviour is one-sided and not wanted by the victim. The victim may be male or female. The harasser ought to reasonably have known that the behaviour would be unwelcome.

Many times people do not commit workplace harassment maliciously. Some people use the guise of good-natured teasing to isolate someone who is different. What they consider good-natured teasing may hurt or embarrass the other person. In those cases, it is important to let the person know you do not appreciate his/her behaviour. In most cases of unintentional harassment, the behaviour will stop. However, if it continues, turn to someone in authority for help.

Are ethnic jokes a form of workplace harassment? It depends on the situation. Sometimes people tease each other back and forth about their ethnic background. No offense is meant by the teasing and none is taken. What is considered offensive may vary from person to person. The easiest way to find out what offends a particular person is to ask them. If you're unsure about a certain term or gesture, ask them how they feel about it. Often, though, the jokes only go one way. Sometimes, members of a group that is being made fun of tolerate and just laugh off the comments. However, most often jokes and other comments about specific groups are offensive. They reinforce negative stereotypes and contribute to ethnic or racial discrimination.

Workplace harassment is unwelcome conduct based on race, religious beliefs, colour, gender, physical or mental disability, marital status, age, ancestry or place of origin. Harassment may negatively affect job performance and decrease job satisfaction. It may also create physical problems such as headaches, nervousness, insomnia and anxiety attacks.

Harassment is wasteful. If an employee has to spend time and energy dealing with harassment, it takes time and energy away from the job. Harassment often leads to absenteeism and high staff turnover. This includes:

- Being coerced into leaving the company through no fault of the victim; by constructive dismissal, early or ill-health retirement due to stress of the bullying etc.;

- Supervisors disciplining their staff in front of workmates or clients;
- Labelling their staff's behaviour as stupid or dumb or making sarcastic remarks, instead of trying to correct the actual behaviour of the staff member;
- Reprimanding the victim for breaking company rules when there are no set policy and procedures manuals available that define the rules and regulations of the company;
- Attempting to get the target to do unethical things and when they refuse to do so, threatening them with gross insubordination charges;
- Keeping the person "in the dark" - leaving him/her "out of the loop" when distributing information, then belittling the person because of his/her lack of knowledge;
- Overloading them with work, setting unrealistic goals, giving menial tasks or not enough work to make them feel like valued employees;
- Refusing to grant annual, sick and compassionate leave;
- Refusing to give the necessary training which holds the victim back from promotional opportunities;
- Changing deadlines for assignments with little or no warning;
- Conducting disciplinary proceedings with verbal or written warnings for trivial or fabricated reasons and without proper investigation.

The Company's responsibilities:

To keep a work environment free from workplace and sexual harassment, companies must:

- Ensure that all managers promptly resolve harassment complaints referred to them, including telling employees their options in a harassment situation;
- Ensure that complaints are handled confidentially;
- Appoint a person to receive and immediately investigate formal harassment complaints
- Ensure that disciplinary action is taken if investigative findings warrant such action;
- Take steps to prevent the recurrence of harassment;
- Take steps to protect an employee who makes a harassment complaint in good faith from retaliation.

The Supervisor's obligations:

Supervisors have an obligation to provide a harassment-free workplace by:

- Being a role model. Never engage in or condone behaviour that could be interpreted as harassment.
- Walking through the workplace to monitor the working environment. Inappropriate pictures or posters, insults or offensive jokes may indicate a harassing environment. Remove them.
- Showing you take the issue seriously. Post the policy and discuss it at meetings.
- Watching for signs that harassment is taking place. Rumours, sudden changes in turnover or illness, decreased motivation and lower job performance may indicate that harassment is taking place. Ensure that exit interviews are done with every staff member who voluntarily leaves your company.
- You have an obligation to treat every harassment complaint seriously.
- You must respond to any complaints made to you immediately, without delay.
- You must also treat them discreetly, with respect for the sensitivity of the situation.

Your department may have specific procedures for dealing with formal harassment complaints. Check with your Human Resources Manager for advice on the best way to handle the situation. It's to everyone's advantage to resolve the situation informally. If an employee brings an informal complaint of harassment to you, you can act as a mediator between that person and the harasser. Discuss the situation with the two people and determine what type of solution will work for both parties.

If the problem can't be resolved informally or if the complainant wishes to make a formal complaint immediately (which may be the case if the harassment is severe) then call your Human Resources Manager or other individual appointed to investigate harassment complaints.

What do you do if you see sexual harassment occurring in your workplace?

In instances that involve crude language, jokes, name-calling or leering, the harasser's behaviour is apparent to more people than just the victim.

If you see someone behaving in a way that could be called harassment, tell them in private that their behaviour is inappropriate. This gives them the opportunity to stop behaving in that manner and may prevent a formal complaint being made against them. If the behaviour continues, you have a responsibility to report what you have seen.

Discuss the situation with the victim. Be supportive and understanding if the person discusses the situation with you. Encourage him/her to take steps to stop the offending behaviour. If the target is too intimidated to take action, offer to accompany him/her in taking the matter forward to a supervisor or Human Resources Manager. If you have relevant information, be willing to share it. This will help the target if an investigation takes place. If you have witnessed harassment and a formal investigation is conducted into the incident(s), you will be interviewed by an investigator to find out what you saw. You may also be asked to testify at a grievance hearing, a board of inquiry or in a court of law, depending on which route the complainant has chosen to pursue.

What will happen to the harasser?

If the situation is resolved informally and the harasser stops the behaviour, nothing will happen. If a formal complaint is made and the person has been found to have committed harassment, s/he will be disciplined. The discipline taken will depend on the seriousness of the misconduct and the circumstances surrounding the harassment. It can range from a reprimand, to suspension without pay, to dismissal and the person's personnel file will be documented in the same way that it would be in any disciplinary action.

What should you do if someone accuses you of harassment?

Make sure you understand the exact behaviour that is making the person uncomfortable. Apologise and stop the behaviour immediately. If you think there has been a misunderstanding about the behaviour between you and the person, ask your supervisor to work with you to resolve the situation on an informal basis.

If you have always acted like this with your staff - why all of a sudden is your behaviour called harassment? What is harassment to one person may not be to another. Such actions as a supervisor putting his/her arm around an employee or a co-worker telling an ethnic joke, may be acceptable, but others may consider this harassment. The person who is uncomfortable with the behaviour has a responsibility to let you know his/her feelings. However, you also need to notice how an individual reacts to your behaviour. Look for body language that indicates the person is uncomfortable with what you are saying or doing. If you are unsure of their reaction, ask the person if your behaviour is unwelcome.

Situations of more obvious harassment (such as touching of a more sexual nature or physical assault) will be viewed on the basis that you ought reasonably to have known that your behaviour was unwelcome.

The consequences of making a false accusation can range from a reprimand, to suspension without pay, to dismissal. But if the person is found to have made the complaint in good faith, then no action would be taken against them.

QIEU's participation in this survey has revealed that bullying is also common within the non-governmental education sector. Intimidating behaviour such as shouting ordering, belittling, threats, abusive language, demands to perform tasks without adequate training, impossible targets, an oppressive/unhappy workplace and fear of speaking up about conditions are of most concern to employees.

Bullying has resulted in employees experiencing a considerable amount of stress, anxiety, tension, anger, depression, high blood pressure, digestive problems, stress, headaches, backaches, sleeping problems and deteriorated work performance. They often have feelings of social isolation, a fear that they will lose their job, loss of confidence and self-esteem. This loss of self-confidence, along with repeated criticism about their work performance can convince someone that the bullying was their own fault. People can find themselves trapped in a very distressing situation.

Bullying is an occupational health and safety issue and should be treated with concern by both employees and employers. Employers have a legal duty to control all health and safety hazards in the workplace including behaviours that may lead to bullying.

Sexual and workplace harassment is offensive, degrading, inappropriate, threatening and illegal. It is any unwelcomed behaviour which is sexual in nature and directly or indirectly, adversely affects or threatens to affect, a person's job security, prospects of promotion or earnings, working conditions or opportunity to secure a job, living accommodations or any kind of public service. Sexual harassment is usually an attempt by one person to exercise power over another.

Employees may experience harassment in any situation involving the employment relationship, whether at or away from the worksite. The harasser should reasonably have known that the behaviour would be unwelcome or unacceptable to the recipient. People who have been harassed speak of feeling humiliated, ashamed, degraded, embarrassed and angry.

Often workplace bullying can't be dealt with under existing Australian laws. However, where bullying involves sexual harassment or discrimination on the basis of things like disability, gender, race or age, a claim may be made under the Human Rights and Equal Opportunity or Anti-Discrimination Acts.

Under Occupational Health and Safety law, an employer has an obligation to protect employees from all acts of violence. Verbal abuse, intimidation and humiliation are seen as occupational violence. A complaint can be lodged with the health and safety representative at work or with a Health and Safety Inspector in your region.

[**Note:** **This is *not* found anywhere in Queensland Occupational Health and Safety legislation.]

Conclusion

If you are forced to resign because you are being bullied, you may be able to claim this as an unfair dismissal. If you become unwell as a result of inappropriate management action in relation to the bullying, you may be able to claim worker's compensation.

Many Awards and Agreements contain grievance procedures to follow in an attempt to resolve a situation. This usually means taking your complaint to a more senior person at work. If you are not sure about how the grievance procedures operate, request a copy of it. If you are a union member, you have the right to union representation at all stages of the grievance procedures. Ask for confidentiality.

Where a grievance procedure does not exist and you are a member of a union, that union can be contacted to act on your behalf.

Chapter 8

CASE STUDY - TIM FIELD

This is the story of Tim Field. Sadly, he died of cancer in 2006.

Tim worked with and has saved many people who were bullied in the workplace - not only in the UK but world-wide. His story of bullying was the catalyst for him to channel his energies into helping those who had been bullied - not only at work, but at school as well. He was the author, co-author and publisher of:

Bully in sight: how to predict, resist, challenge and combat workplace Bullying (1996);

Bullycide: death at playtime, an exposé of child suicide caused by bullying (2001) (that he co-wrote with Neil Marr).

His company Success Unlimited also sells *Post Traumatic Stress Disorder: the invisible injury (2001)* (written by Dave Kinchin).

Tim also managed the *Bully OnLine* website at www.bulyonline.org

As expected, this brave man rattled some chains and the National Union of Teachers (NUT) lodged a 100,000 UK pound High Court web libel claim against him. Former National Union of Teachers (NUT) area representative and now Oxfordshire County Council education (personnel) officer Tom Long sued Tim Field for an article he published on his web page.

Here's Tim's story about the bullying he endured: (written in 2003 by Tim Field).

I enjoyed fifteen successful years with my employer, starting in computer systems support and development, including user support and training and graduating to customer services. I had a series of good managers. In early 1991 I moved to a new department that developed, sold and supported scientific computer software worldwide. A highly talented and motivated team had been assembled by the department manager who was an excellent "people" person. All went well. At the end of 1992, this manager suddenly and unexpectedly resigned. A new manager took over and within 3 months, morale had noticeably declined. As Customer Services Manager, one of four section leaders reporting to the department manager, I was responsible for ensuring fast, accurate delivery of bespoke software to companies worldwide, together with rapid response to customer queries. The success of the business hinged on this operation which was a team effort in which everybody played a full role.

Within three months, I noticed the following, which intensified with time, although I was only able to identify and articulate many of these in retrospect:

- Constant nit-picking and often non-specific criticism, which did not match my or colleagues' or customers' views on the service levels being achieved;
- Simultaneous and persistent refusal to recognise, acknowledge or value my role, work and achievements;
- Being undermined and sidelined, with opinions ignored, requests declined, decisions overruled and resources refused;
- Being ignored and overruled in meetings;
- Being excluded from management meetings concerning the running of the department;
- Having information withheld;
- Having contributions dismissed, reports and statistics disregarded;
- Having my responsibility increased, but authority taken away;
- Being forced to seek approval from peers for almost every action;
- Being unable to pin my manager down on what was "wrong;" when challenged, he became impatient and aggressive, often making.implied threats: *"perhaps you'd be happier at a lower - grade in another department," "perhaps we made a mistake promoting you,"* etc.
- Being coerced into taking on additional, unnecessary and superfluous work;
- Being overburdened with work - in the end I was doing the work of three people;
- Nevertheless, despite all the hoops I was increasingly being forced to jump through, I continued to fulfil the responsibilities of my job. In retrospect, this made things worse; the more I achieved, the more he seemed determined to destroy me.

Achievements and a list of duties (2 pages of closely-typed A4) were repeatedly deemed "irrelevant." Confusion reigned but the demands of the job kept growing. By November 1993, injury to my health had taken its toll and my confidence and self-esteem was destroyed. I was working in a management vacuum. I couldn't understand what was wrong (knowing nothing about bullying at this stage) and began planning my escape. In January 1994, I received the first written criticism that *"I was not fulfilling expectations ..."* (Later, I realised that he never defined what his expectations were, nor would he have done.)

In order to achieve a "satisfactory" performance, I had to take on an additional job. I was now doing the work of three people. The customer base had increased five-fold, we (the whole team) had cut delivery times and improved accuracy by a factor of at least ten since I started, but there was "no possibility of taking on any new staff." I discovered later that at that moment, my manager was actively recruiting staff for the other three sections of the department. This was not the only time he lied to me.

My section was then abolished and moved underneath one of the other sections, with a refusal to clarify the status of my "section," to the consternation of all who had worked so hard to make it a success. It was called a "merger" but it was a calculated move to eliminate me. At the same time this manager managed to get himself promoted. Stress levels, already through the roof because of impending privatisation, rose even further.

Stress levels within the department were so high that the manager arranged for everyone to attend a "stress awareness seminar." This was cheaper - much cheaper - than a stress management course or stress counselling and consisted of a quick chat by an occupational health adviser plus a video on stress which caused some amusement when the manager featured in the film was called Stephen but who liked to be known as Steve.

I questioned my manager about his criticism and whilst he was "always available to discuss anything," every attempt to discuss what was wrong was "not relevant." Pinning him down was like nailing jelly to a tree. In March 1994, I applied for voluntary redundancy. My manager, on hearing this, stated that he was "fully behind" me. Brutus was an honourable man.

On 2 June 1994, I watched the BBC2 programme, *The Business: Bullying at Work*, featuring Andrea Adams and her identification of workplace bullying. The penny dropped. I started working with personnel (the juniors were supportive at a personal level but had no policies or procedures to fall back on) and occupational health (very supportive but powerless) to make them aware of what was going on.

Initial scepticism waned as more and more came out. A journal swelled to 40 pages within 48 hours.

I made it clear to my manager that his behaviour was unacceptable. His reaction was interesting - he appeared confused and made implied threats, *"This isn't going to do your career any good."* Having regained control, this had no effect, which he couldn't handle. The threat was repeated and sensing loss of control, he became garrulous and shifted uncomfortably on his chair. I realise now he decided at that moment to get rid of me altogether. I had become the threat he feared.

On 28 July 1994, I came to work feeling very strange. I had been stressed and emotionally numb for so long that I barely noticed. With hindsight I can see that I had been walking round like a zombie for six months - I have no idea how I survived in that state for so long. On sitting down at my desk, a colleague came in and remarked how awful I looked. After eighteen months of enormous stress, my brain finally collapsed under the strain.

I burst into tears and sat there, trembling, repeating for nearly ten minutes *"I can't cope, I just can't cope."* Shortly after this, my manager seized the opportunity to relieve me of my position. A colleague was appointed in my place and not long after, the section was re-instated with her as section leader. She was horrified and embarrassed to find out what was going on, as were the rest of the department. *"It stinks,"* confirmed a colleague. They were good people, but under enormous pressure themselves and unaware of what had been happening.

Six months later I was invited to the departmental Christmas party and by a quirk of fate ended up sitting opposite the bully. He dominated the conversation, talking mostly about his bonus and how big it was going to be. He ignored me, not even asking how I was.

A consequence of stress breakdown is reactive depression, a new experience for me. Wild swings of mood, from thoughts of suicide to occasional euphoria, overwhelming negativism, anger, irritability, aches and pains, fatigue, constant infections, disturbed sleeping and eating patterns - over forty symptoms, with half still present a year later. For months, all I wanted to do was curl up and die. The reason I didn't pursue the suicide option was the thought of my two young children - plus some excellent counselling.

I estimate the cost to my employer (at that time still the taxpayer) to be in excess of £250K, comprising redundancy, pension, administration, personnel and occupational health time, six months sick leave, re-recruitment, loss of knowledge, experience, wasted training investment, etc. Not one penny was charged to the bullying manager's budget. I know he's been implicated in other employees' stress breakdowns, including a spectacular stress breakdown six months before mine which the company hushed up.

I summarised the experience and asked the personnel manager to put it on my manager's file. She refused to record anything about what had happened. This woman was subsequently awarded a prize for "managing change" and her photograph appeared in People Management. The bully was protected and promoted although the company finally fired him for incompetence in the summer of 1999, five years after I reported him. His empire quickly collapsed and it comes as no surprise that the company is now in financial difficulties, the share price has plummeted and the department in which I worked is now downsizing faster than it was growing during my time there. The reason is simple: the bully built no foundations for the business. I recall several conversations with him about building foundations for long-term strategic growth and his dismissive responses at the time now make sense. Despite being a former business development manager and despite being glib and plausible on the surface, he knew almost nothing about business. He was a fraud but I was the only person at the time who saw through him – and he knew that I could see through him, hence his need to destroy me.

A recent Advice Line call and contact with former colleagues reveal that morale at the company is still at rock-bottom and still falling, just as it was a decade ago. Every employee I meet now is focused on the same objective: getting out. The company's motto should be "We've hit rock bottom – now we're drilling!"

The personal cost has been a stress breakdown, terminated career, a year of initial recovery (on benefit) four years of stress at home and a family breakdown. Following the stress breakdown in July 1994, I spent six months on sick leave, after which I accepted a voluntary redundancy package. A further six months was spent at home in recovery. I considered self-employment (I will never be employed again) and in July 1995, one year and three days after the breakdown, I felt well enough to attempt a day's work - mainly shuffling paper, nothing serious. I now know that the stress breakdown was a psychiatric injury, not a mental illness. Legal action was a non-starter - one has to apply to tribunal within twelve weeks of leaving and *there's no law against bullying anyway*. A personal injury claim has to be started within three years and it was four years before I felt well enough to read the forms. This would have tied me to a further five years of litigation and of repeatedly reliving the nightmare. Only after the Long case in May 2001 would I have stood a chance of success anyway.

For a further six months I gradually increased the amount and content of my work at home and eventually set up the UK National Workplace Bullying Advice Line in January 1996. The following month, I gave my first training workshop. It took me ten days to recover from the effort of giving this one-day workshop. By this time, work on my book was proceeding steadily and calls were beginning to come in on the Advice Line.

This set the pattern for 1996 and by the end of November, over 400 people had come to me looking for advice and support; most of these cases were at the severe end of the spectrum, with many callers near or in breakdown, many having thought of suicide and some having already attempted it. Remembering Andrea Adams' kind letter and words of support just after my own breakdown, I sent each caller a package of information to help them turn the corner in their experience. A pattern emerged early, with most callers in their mid-to-late 40's, at the top end of the pay scale. About 75 per cent of callers are female and over 50 per cent of reported bullies also female. The three worst affected sectors seem to be teaching, nursing and social workers - the caring professions. Since 1999 there's been a noticeable increase in cases from the voluntary/charity/not-for-profit sector.

1996 culminated in the publication of my book *Bullying in sight: how to predict, resist, challenge and combat workplace bullying.* As no publisher would touch it, I typeset and published it myself under the imprint Success Unlimited. Diana Lamplugh OBE kindly wrote a foreword. The book has sold over 9,000 copies in 30 countries and has been reprinted three times. Feedback is phenomenal.

Seven years after the stress breakdown, I am now about 98 per cent recovered mentally and about 75 per cent recovered physically, with an improvement rate of about 0.5 to 1 per cent a month. From my experience and from talking to over 5,000 people in similar situations, I estimate it takes between two to five years to affect recovery and only if one has support. Some people never fully recover from such an abusive experience. Physically I may never recover fully.

Interest from the media has increased steadily and on average someone from the media contacts me every day. Appearances on TV, radio and in newspapers and magazines are increasing as the issue of bullying - of children, adults, partners, the elderly and in the uniformed services - comes out into the open.

I published David Kinchin's book *Post Traumatic Stress Disorder: The invisible injury* in January 1998. David has updated the book to include a chapter on PTSD [Post Traumatic Stress Disorder] caused by bullying. A new revised edition was published in September 2001.

During 2000 I co-wrote, with international journalist Neil Marr, a book on children who have committed or attempted suicide because of bullying at school. I published *Bullycide: death at playtime* on 30 January 2001. The Times Educational Supplement described it as "an excellent book." I plan more books exploring bullying and its causes.

Demand for the UK National Workplace Bullying Advice Line is constant. During 1997 I realised I couldn't meet the level of demand indefinitely and in January 1998 I made my insight and experience available on the world's leading Internet web site devoted to bullying, *Bully OnLine* at www.successunlimited.co.uk which is now my preferred first point of contact.

Update, January 2003

The last twelve months have been a year of intensive personal development. Spurred on by and embracing the teachings of Brian Tracy and Rhonda Britten, I've focused on neutralising and eliminating the remaining negative thoughts and feelings to finally make it back into the real world - whatever that is! My bullying episode started in January, 1993 and it feels like my life has been hijacked for the last decade. It's taken 8.5 years of recovery to get to this stage and for the first time in ten years, I'm back in charge and at last life for me is getting better and better. 2003 sees many challenges, the first of which is to move out of the spare bedroom and into a "proper" office – this was achieved on 1 March. Sharing my knowledge and insight with public seminars, moving all my support work under the wing of a non-profit organisation (later to become a registered charity) and employing people to help with the workload are high on my list of objectives for the remainder of this year. The most exciting challenge for me this year is the development and delivery of an innovative new seminar

"Recovery and re-empowerment from bullying and abusive life events" which enables people to get their lives and careers back on course by recovering from an abusive experience in less than half the time it would normally take.

[**Note:** Tim was instrumental in helping me obtain much of the information and many of the case studies in this book. He will be sorely missed for all the effort he put into making bullied people's lives better. I fully believe that he died from cancer because his body had suffered so much from the stress he dealt with for almost a decade.]

Chapter 9

CASE STUDY - FINANCIAL SECTOR

[**Note:** The following Australian case study had the most significant amount of information in it, so I have given it a chapter of its own.]

I was the owner of three successful human resource management firms, but was tired of the amount of travel involved in running my international companies. So I was tempted, when I was head-hunted by an up-and-coming company for the executive position as Head of Human Resources. The organisation desperately needed my help to overhaul their human resources systems so they could comply with government regulations that were necessary for obtaining a licence. My responsibilities included upgrading the company's human resources policies and procedures and running the human resources, employee relations, training and payroll functions of the company.

The position reported directly to the CEO (a relatively young man named Andy). When Andy interviewed me, he assured me several times that I would have full autonomy to run the Human Resources Department. Andy also advised me that he wanted me to be his "right hand man" to be his eyes and ears and root out problems and give him advice on solving them. I would be part of the executive team. When I was offered a large salary plus bonuses, I decided to accept the position and closed down my companies.

I was impressed to see that my offer letter included the following information:

{Company} believes it is the right of all staff to work in an environment free of harassment. Sexual harassment, which is a form of offensive behaviour and is detrimental to staff morale, is unlawful sex discrimination and constitutes unacceptable conduct in the workplace. It will not be tolerated under any circumstances."

The job proved to be very gruelling. Although the company advocated a work/life balance, the five-month deadline for upgrading the policies and procedures manuals was an almost impossible task. For the first four months of my employment I did not take a day off - working weekends and more often than not brought work home to do in the evenings. I felt it was worth it though, because both Andy and the government licensing authority approved the policies and procedures and I met my tight deadlines. In July (five and a half months after I was hired) the company obtained approval from the governing body for their license.

In many areas Andy sabotaged my achievements and did not give me the autonomy that was promised. Many of Andy's stalling tactics reflected upon the smooth-running of the HR department and made me appear incompetent. He excluded me from the decision-making process and did not allow me run the HR department the way I believed it should be run. The new policies and procedures could not be implemented until supervisors obtained training on how to use them. When I scheduled training sessions for the managers Andy cancelled the training with little explanation.

Shortly after the HR Policies and Procedures were approved, they were put on the company intranet so managers and employees would have access to them. However Andy made comments to me several times, that he did not believe that the job descriptions needed upgrading. He did not allow me to upgrade the position descriptions nor provide training to the managers on how to do so for their staff.

I also became aware of the high incidence of nepotism in the company. Not only were family members working in the same department, but most of the executive were personal friends of the CEO.

Just before the licence was granted Andy began making comments to me about reverting back to the original performance appraisal system when they came due in September. It was at this time that I became aware that the initial stage of performance appraisals that identified the objectives for each employee (that should have been completed in September of the previous year before I started with the company) had not been completed. I reminded Andy of this and he decided to complete the initial part of the Performance Appraisals in June - only three months before the employees would be evaluated on their performance for the entire previous year. Even at this late date - instead of using the government approved performance appraisal system, he decided to use the company's old ineffective score card system. This contravened what had been agreed upon when we obtained our government licence.

During my employment, I noticed that Andy did not follow many of our other company policies and procedures. Several times Andy used language unsuitable for the workplace making such comments as; *"No f*

.... ing way." I believe that gutter language has its place - in the gutter. Most who use that type of language come from lower-class environments or are badly educated. Such language offended our employees, especially coming from our CEO.

Andy showed many signs of narcissism and seemed to lack the emotional intelligence required of a leader. He tended to see relationships in terms of superior-inferior and dominant-submissive. He constantly interfered with other executives' decisions, even though he was not an expert in their areas. His need to control resulted in many poor decisions being made. For instance, until I mentioned it to him, he didn't seem to recognise that his sales and marketing department did not have anyone who specialised in marketing - only sales. He seemed to believe that sales and marketing were the same.

He left me out of the loop, making crucial HR decisions without my input or knowledge. For instance he made employees redundant rather than go through the properly documented disciplinary process. One employee disagreed with him once too often and the next day the announcement was made that his position was being made redundant. Andy explained that anyone who did not follow the company vision would have to go. I interpreted this to be that if employees didn't follow *his* way of doing things, they would be asked to leave. I learned after-the-fact that he had made the man's position redundant - with no consultation with me before doing so. As Head of Human Resources I should have been consulted before action was taken.

Even though the company was rapidly expanding, only one employee had been terminated because of inappropriate behaviour - but over ten employees had been "let go" because of "restructuring" or "redundancy" of their positions. Most of these employees were poor performers and should have been put through the disciplinary process. These redundancies were done without my involvement or approval. Within a short period of time Andy would replace those positions - whereas by law he should have re-hired the redundant employees.

One woman had worked in the system for thirty years. Her position before her redundancy was as personal assistant to Andy. She was replaced by another woman who did essentially the same work, but with a different title.

Upon monitoring the absenteeism of employees I noted that several departments had extremely high levels of sick leave. I now realise that it was likely because of the level of abuse they were subjected to by their supervisors, managers and executives who used the CEO as a benchmark for acceptable corporate behaviour.

Andy was not consistent in the discipline he meted out and showed favouritism to an employee (a personal friend) who had severely broken the company rules, but received no written warning on his file.

He used bullying tactics with his direct reports (the executive of the company). Our meetings became a matter of him taking strips off the executive members. I cautioned Andy that this was something that just wasn't done in public. Andy agreed that it wasn't right - but continued to do so.

The executives were invited to a three-day retreat where the facilitators tried to enhance the group's leadership skills. It became apparent (especially to me) that Andy broke most of the established leadership rules.

We started each day by either having a twenty-minute walk or jog. Each morning Andy arrived back at the lodge running full out in competition with one of the other executives who had been a marathon runner. He *had* to win at any cost and it was obvious from his physical exhaustion the toll it took on him to win.

During a teambuilding exercise - Andy immediately took over the role of leader (no executive challenged this - including me) and inevitably the team effort failed. The facilitators must have realised the kind of person he was and that his executive were terrified of going against his way of doing things, so the retreat was a total failure.

Much of Andy's harassment involved other executive members. Bill, the head of Group Risk, was instrumental in the company obtaining its licence because he insisted that Andy follow the compliance requirements. Andy objected to many of his suggestions and resisted vigorously. Three days after the company received its licence, Bill was given a redundancy package. I had been on a well-earned holiday when this happened and did not learn about it until I returned to work. Andy's unofficial reason for this redundancy was that Bill had been making advances on female employees and that Bill had come into work under the influence of alcohol. I seriously question that these accusations were true.

The next day, Bill came to the Human Resources Department to sign some papers and I took him aside to ask him what had happened. Bill explained that he had received no warning about his demise - was just told that his position had been made redundant and to clear out his belongings. During this conversation, Bill warned me that my own position was probably next and described the signs I should watch for. The first sign of trouble would be if Andy started taking some of my responsibilities away from me and the second would be that he would start degrading me in public.

It didn't take long to happen. That same afternoon Andy told me that he would be moving the payroll function into the finance department. One week later he came to my open-area office to have me sign off on several new Human Resources Policies and Procedures. I was startled to see that Andy wanted the company to return to using its old antiquated job description and performance appraisal systems that were contrary to those accepted when the company obtained its licence. I tried to make Andy see that the old system simply didn't work, but he wouldn't listen to me and tried to force me to sign off on the new system. Andy kept stating how much he had given in relating to the new system and that I should be willing to bend as well.

I knew that if I agreed to the changes, it would go completely against the government licensing regulations (which would be illegal). I told Andy I couldn't approve the revised policy, but suggested that he do so instead. I didn't want to become the "fall guy" that could happen if I signed the documents and the governing body questioned the changes. Andy completely lost it. His face was beat red and he became so frustrated at my refusal that he publicly humiliated me by shouting so loudly that my entire staff and others nearby heard what he said. I contemplated taking Andy into a nearby private office, but decided not to when I smelled alcohol on his breath. Shortly after his outburst Andy left my work station and spoke to the Human Resources Manager (who sat behind my station).

At 5:40 p.m. as I was leaving the office, my staff was still working. Two of my staff asked me if I was okay. They explained that the whole floor had heard Andy yelling at me. They were very upset at how Andy had treated me and said they could clearly hear the confrontational aspects of the session. They also mentioned that others who were not working in the Human Resources department had overheard Andy's angry words. The Training Manager stated that he thought it was a case of harassment - that the CEO was out of control. I later learned that the Training Manager had not heard the confrontation, but was just concerned when the other two employees discussed the situation with him. The next morning, the HR Manager confirmed that she too had smelled alcohol on Andy's breath.

That morning I discussed the incident with my staff and asked if they would be willing to testify about what they had witnessed. All three who had been in the area at that time agreed to do so, however, later only one put her comments in writing. Her report read:

'On Wednesday, (date) I overheard a discussion between Rebecca and Andy regarding the company's performance appraisal system. The tone of voice and manner in which Andy spoke to Rebecca was quite aggressive. He was raising his voice and was clearly annoyed with the content of the discussion. It made me feel quite uncomfortable to hear the CEO talking in such a manner to a senior member of staff.'

The next week was a traumatic one for me. At an executive meeting the next day Andy asked two of his executive to work with me to finalise the company performance appraisal plan. Neither of the executives who were chosen had any background in human resources. The next Monday the three of us met and I was amazed when the executive (who was a very close friend of the CEO) took over the meeting. He explained how he felt the process should work and outlined his beliefs on a whiteboard. The other executive agreed with his information. I sat amazed, because they had fully endorsed the system that had received government approval! I told them this and we agreed to meet in two days to finalise the policy (which would be identical to that already in place with the licensing body).

When we met two days later, the executive did a one hundred and eighty-degree turn-around (he must have discussed it with the CEO). The other executive member nodded his assent. I glared at them both as I stated, *"He got to you didn't he?"* and disgustedly walked out of the meeting.

Every time I saw Andy, I seethed inside at the way I had been treated. I contacted a lawyer to see whether I could charge the company with breach of contract because I was not being allowed to do the job I had been hired to do. I also looked into how I could take action to fight the bullying I'd received from my superior. I realised that as Head of Human Resources, if I condoned such behaviour, the rest of the staff would not have protection from bullying and felt I must set an example.

Normally I would be the one investigating such claims as is shown by the company policy on the issue:

Head of Human Resources' Responsibilities

If employee wishes to place a formal complaint, Line Managers and/or Harassment Advisers will contact the Head of Human Resources to pursue the complaint.

Complainant may go directly to the Head of Human Resources to ask for help in resolving the problem.

Ensure complainants and witnesses are not victimised in any way.

Head of Human Resources will interview all parties and make a ruling.

Documentation of investigation taken will be securely stored by the Human Resources department on a special file (not employee's personnel file).

If disciplinary action is taken against an offender, a brief note will be placed on his/her personnel file containing a summary of the nature of the complaint, the outcome and the action taken against him/her.

Because I couldn't investigate my own situation of bullying, I planned to have a representative from the Equal Employment Opportunities Board conduct an investigation - preferably in-house. To do this, I would need access to recording equipment that was used for all serious disciplinary interviews. George (a former police officer who worked in the group risk department) stored the equipment, so I asked him to show me how to use the equipment. George made me explain why I needed the equipment.

Later that same morning, George asked me to have lunch with him (first time). During lunch, he explained that the Fraud Policies and Procedures had a clause that stated that if the CEO was involved in a grievance, that George had the responsibility to mediate. (I later learned that the policy had been formulated *after* I had spoken to George about getting the equipment. I now believe that George had gone straight to the CEO after I had requested the equipment. I believe that Andy had urged him to do whatever he had to do, to keep the investigation in-house).

After several sleepless nights George's coercion worked and I allowed him to do the investigation. My complaint would be made to the

Chairman of the Board, who was Andy's boss. I felt that because the Chairman of the Board was well known throughout Australia, that he would be fair in his evaluation of the issues. With my lawyer's help, I wrote a letter to the Chairman of the Board of Directors charging Andy with bullying, not only for my own incident, but also for the bullying of the other executive members. I also believed that the smell of alcohol on his breath left him open to be charged under our policy on Serious Misconduct. Our company policy stated:

Serious Misconduct Includes:

Reporting for or returning from breaks or company appointments under the influence of alcohol; and physical assault or harassment.

Everyone involved was to be interviewed. This included the executives who had been harassed at meetings, my staff who had witnessed the bullying and the Human Resources Manager who had also smelled alcohol on Andy's breath. After submitting the letter, I felt so sick that I threw up my lunch and had to go home at 4:00 pm.

George interviewed me the next day and did a follow-up interview five days later. At the second meeting, George went over the information from my earlier interviews. I got the impression during this interview that George had lost his neutrality - that he was slanting his questions from Andy's point of view. I felt I had to be careful of every word I said. He stated that he would be speaking with Andy that afternoon and would call me at home that evening with his findings.

When he phoned, he told me that his interviews could not prove any of my allegations - in fact I was told that I would be lucky if I wasn't charged with slander or defamation of character (another example of the bullying). This traumatised me, but I decided to wait until the investigation was over before doing anything further.

Six days later I asked George for a copy of transcripts of the interviews. He flatly refused to give any of them but my own. I saw no transcript that proved my accusations were false. I asked him when I would get a report outlining his findings and was told they were in the hands of the company lawyer (who were the top employment lawyers in the city). At our initial meeting, the Chairman of the Board had promised that lawyers were not going to be involved in the investigation. It was at this time that I learned that George was monitoring all my e-mails.

My stress rate skyrocketed as I waited for action. Three weeks after my bullying episode, I had to see my doctor about another matter. My doctor was so appalled at my appearance and my story about the bullying; that he promptly put me on two week's sick leave that he thought would be sufficient time for the company to resolve the issue. In two weeks nothing had changed - so he placed me on one month's stress leave under WorkCover.

I waited - and waited for the report relating to the interviews with the executives and witnesses and had to extend my stress leave. All I wanted was for Andy to receive a reprimand; that he apologise and promise that he would not use such bullying actions in the future. The most devastating thing for me was that during this period not one person from the company called to see how I was, even though most had been told I was away on sick leave. I received only one call from a member of my staff who wanted to discuss a business-related question.

Seven weeks later, the company finally sent a letter requesting a meeting in the company boardroom with George and the Chairman of the Board. The morning of the meeting, I had a panic attack and found it very difficult to enter the building. However, I gave myself a pep talk and prepared myself for the onslaught.

George began by reading a report outlining the harassment allegations I had made and the responses to it. I asked why I had not been sent a copy of the report so I could have prepared for the meeting. George said I would *not* be receiving a copy of the report he was reading. He resumed reading his report that stated everyone interviewed had denied that harassment had occurred or that alcohol was involved. To me this could only mean that the executive team and my staff had lied about the harassment incidents. When I again asked for copies of the investigation interviews - I was denied. I felt that the company was accusing me of imagining the situation - that none of the things I'd accused Andy of had occurred.

Throughout the 75-minute session, both George and the chairman kept asking me if I had any comments to make. In the report I was chastised for not moving the meeting that took place to a more private setting. I replied, *"Why would I do that? I was concerned about my safety. If you were a woman, would you take a man who was out of control and under the influence of alcohol into a private room?"*

The Chairman of the Board asked me how I thought the situation could be resolved. I replied that if the bullying and alcohol incident had happened to *any other* employee, I (not George) would be doing the investigating. Because I knew the facts were accurate and the investigation would have been fair, I would have suggested that a written warning be placed on Andy's file stating that if the bullying incidents did not stop - he would be terminated.

I then asked the Chairman of the Board how he thought the situation could be resolved. The only thing he could suggest was to employ a company-appointed mediator. I asked what there was to mediate, because apparently all my allegations had been denied! We were deadlocked.

I had been advised by my lawyer to just listen to what they said - not to rebut the information. However at one stage I shook my head and the Chairman questioned me about the gesture. At this point, I decided I'd had enough and said, *"I'm shocked to see what kind of power the CEO has over his staff that they are too terrified of losing their jobs that they lied during the investigation. How could I work in such a hostile atmosphere or trust the integrity of the other executives when they would not back up my allegations about the bullying by the CEO at executive meetings? And how could I deal with my staff who think it was me who threatened to charge them with insubordination if they didn't testify."*

I also added, *"I'm concerned that George has not mentioned anywhere in his report about his phone call where he threatened me with slander and defamation of character."* George adamantly denied having made such a comment. I looked George in the eye as I replied, *"Because George has lied about that phone call as well - how can I possibly believe that this investigation has been fair and above board? Not only will he not give me a copy of the report he's reading to me today, but he won't give me copies of the transcripts of the investigation. Would you believe this investigation if it was you who had lodged the complaint? Until I see both of them - there's no way I can believe this has been a fair hearing."*

I also looked the Chairman of the Board in the eye and said, *"You know, I used to respect you, but your inaction during this fiasco proves that you had no intention of being impartial. You know my allegations are true, yet you let that bully get away with his harassment! Taking the side of the bullyagainst me make you a bully by proxy."*

I felt that I had the following choices:

1. Do nothing.
   a. This was completely unacceptable to me because I would have no assurance that a repeat of the bullying wouldn't happen in the future to other staff or me.
   b. How could I do my job when Andy could override all the work I'd done with the Human Resources Policies and Procedures?
   c. And then there was the problem of having to face Andy's wrath that I wouldn't accept Human Resources policies that contravened those given to obtain the company's licence?
   d. If the company ignored the bullying, I felt I couldn't effectively do my job as Head of Human Resources.
   e. How could I trust the other members of the executive?
   f. How could I trust my own staff if they lied during the interviews?
   g. How did I know that the company hadn't told lies to the staff that made Andy look good and me look bad?

2. Quit my job. I had done nothing wrong and had nothing to be ashamed of, so why should I quit? I also realised that my situation could fit the company policy that stated:

   Duress: The term 'duress' refers to 'undue pressure' applied to an employee to 'force' a resignation and is typically used as a means to argue for a claim of unfair dismissal against an employer. Pressure on an employee to resign takes many forms, from overt threats of dismissal 'as the only other option' to the more covert suggestion that the employee should start looking for an alternative external position.

   Any substantiated claim of 'duress' leaves (company) open to the possibility of a claim for unfair dismissal and the subsequent 'remedy' or reinstatement and/or damages.

   Therefore an employee being investigated for misconduct must not be threatened in any manner or given the 'option' to resign ahead of or as an alternative to, being dismissed.

3. Take the company to court for breach of contract, wrongful dismissal and/or for harassment and victimisation.

   Victimisation: Anti-discrimination laws provide protection against victimisation. An individual is victimised if s/he is threatened with or subjected to, any form of detriment because of a complaint of discrimination or harassment.

   (Company) recognises that complaint procedures must ensure that all reasonable steps are taken to ensure that complainants and those involved in the complaint process do not suffer further disadvantage, retaliation or threats. [Telephone threat of slander]

4. Go to the government regulatory board with my findings that the company had not abided with the agreement they had made when granted their licence.

5. Hope for a severance package - at least six months to make up for the fact that I would need time and money to re-launch my companies.

I ended the meeting by expressing my disgust at what a sham the investigation had been and stated that I would be consulting my lawyer.

I spoke with my lawyer and was advised that if I took the company to court - I would likely have to pay an additional $50,000 to $100,000 for legal fees and possibly spend years in court - with no guarantees that I'd win enough to pay for my expenses let alone get any settlement. I had already spent nearly $10,000 on legal fees. I realised that my nerves could not tolerate that alternative and I wanted to get on with my life and re-start my companies. However, I felt that if I quit my job - Andy would win and would continue his bullying.

I decided to have my lawyer try for a severance package and consider lodging a wrongful dismissal and/or breach of contract charge later. This was done and I settled for three month's severance pay. To do so, I was forced to sign a "gag" order stating that I would say nothing disparaging about the company or Andy.

A few months later I learned that George had applied for my job as Head of Human Resources (he was turned down). I felt that George had been in Andy's pocket throughout the investigation and that he'd had an eye on my Head of Human Resources position from the onset of the investigation.

I've learned that a bullying policy is only words on paper. Its effectiveness is in the commitment of senior staff to see that it is enforced. I also believe that what comes around - goes around and the CEO will be paid back for his unprofessional and bullying acts.

When I received my severance pay, it should have been the end of my story, but my story doesn't end there. I also learned that the company refused to give any kind of reference at all - which left those who had made enquiries believe that I had done something wrong and/or had been fired. My next battle was to obtain payment for my stress leave from my company's WorkCover insurance firm - CGU. They denied my claim for stress leave, even though I did not have a meeting with them. They had obviously used George's biased and untrue information as the basis for refusing my claim. So instead of receiving three months severance pay I received only three weeks pay.

It's ironic that they did this, because as Head of Human Resources, I had just received CGU's magazine called *"Cover to Cover."* Their September 2001 issue had an article entitled: *"Say NO to workplace violence."* (See Chapter 8 for more information). Here are relevant comments from the article:

Any form of physical <u>verbal or psychological intimidation</u> is classified as violence, according to "Violence at Work, Queensland Workplace Health and Safety Guide 1999." The Guide says that the experience of violence is <u>subjective</u>, so that <u>what is perceived to be violence for one person may not be so for another</u> and people who witness acts of violence can also be affected.

(Andy yelled at me in front of my staff and smelled of alcohol while he did so - a very threatening experience. I felt Andy was out of control. My staff was affected by the CEO's outburst and one smelled the alcohol on his breath.)

'Abuse' is any unreasonable behaviour that involves the misuse of physical or psychological strength or power.

(Andy abused his position of power. He wanted me to break the law by changing the human resource policies that had been accepted by the government licensing body.)

Managers may victimise employees through inappropriate methods of supervision.

(Andy disciplined me in front of my staff and others and tried to make me do something unethical. Although he had hired me for my human resources expertise, he let others less qualified [including himself] decide how the system would work.)

It is an implied part of the employer's duty of care under each State and Territory OH&S to prevent workplace violence.

(The abuser was the CEO of a company. He of all people should have been setting an example for behaviour in the company).

Employers should adopt a zero-tolerance attitude to any form of violence.

(Andy was out of control during the incident and did not set a good example for the rest of the company. He was not reprimanded for his actions even though there was a company policy on harassment and bullying).

Some employees may not report acts of insidious violence perpetrated against them. They may feel intimidated or embarrassed, powerless due to their position in the organisation, bound by cultural constraints, not aware of their rights and prone to peer pressure. The employer needs to make efforts to prevent this scenario from arising.

(Not only has the company and board of directors condoned this behaviour, but have not taken any steps to stop it from occurring in the future. Employees have seen a senior executive of the company completely ignored when a complaint was formally made to the Board of Directors. What kind of protection does the rest of the staff have against this kind of behaviour happening in the future?)

When the employer is the perpetrator of workplace violence, it can make the situation even more difficult for the victim. In these situations, employees must go straight to the local OH&S Authority.

(I recognise that I should have gone directly to OH&S instead of expecting a fair investigation by my biased company in-house investigator.)

Management needs to investigate less serious allegations. It is the responsibility of the employer to determine how the violence occurred and in all cases of violence, to implement prevention strategies to avoid it happening again.

(The management investigated and ignored the incident even though alcohol was involved. The CEO was not reprimanded in any way, so will likely continue to harass/bully others.)

Fear of returning to work, anxiety, stress, depression, grief and guilt may all be part of the reaction to a violent event. If symptoms are not treated, they can worsen and leave the victim feeling threatened, vulnerable and worthless.

(Three weeks after the incident, I went on sick leave, then stress leave under WorkCover due to stress because the company was still dragging out the investigation and I was required to interact with Andy on a daily basis. I did not obtain the results of their investigation until almost seven weeks later and remained on stress leave until that time. Even though there were three witnesses, the company refused to reprimand Andy for his behaviour. WorkCover dismissed my claim for stress leave because of the biased report the company had submitted to them.)

In some circumstances, employers may be vicariously liable for the conduct of the perpetrators and, along with the alleged perpetrators, may also be charged for breaching OH&S laws. Employees can also sue their employers, claim worker' compensation and make complaints to the Anti-Discrimination Board or the Federal Human Rights and Equal Opportunities Commission.

(I did ask for compensation, but was refused coverage by CGU).

When CGU (the company WorkCover insurer) refused my claim they wrote the following: *"After careful consideration, the claim has been rejected because:*

Your employment was not a significant contributing factor to the claimed injury.

Your claimed injury was caused by stress of a type, which does not create an entitlement to compensation under the act.

They quoted:

Relevant legislation:

"Compensation is not payable in respect of an injury consisting of an illness or disorder of the mind caused by stress, unless the stress did not arise wholly or predominantly from

a) Reasonable action taken in a reasonable manner by the employer to transfer, demote, discipline, redeploy, retrench or dismiss the worker; or

b) A decision of the employer, on reasonable grounds, not to award or to provide promotion, reclassification or transfer of or leave of absence or benefit in connection with the employment, to the worker; or

c) An expectation of the taking of such action or making of such a decision.

Reason for giving this notice:

Your employment was not a significant contributing factor to the claimed injury. Your claimed injury was caused by stress of a type, which does not create an entitlement to compensation under the Act.

An internal investigation into the matter conducted by.......................... of .... found that the incident on .... did not involve the breaking of company policies or harassment."

I feel that WorkCover (CGU) listened only to the employer's side of this issue by not interviewing me personally.

What comes around - Goes around:

By September, 2008, the company was seriously faultering financially and by May, 2009 (like in the case of Tim Field) the CEO left the company and was replaced.

Chapter 10

CASE STUDIES - AUSTRALIA

Not for profit Organisation

My experience of profound and systematic bullying by my General Manager occurred when I was hired as part of the senior management team for a not-for-profit organisation. My role was focussed on strategic Human Resources. While I was employed by this company for three and a half years, the management team of five had eight changes of staff. Most of those managers were pushed out of the company by the General Manager's incessant bullying.

My predecessor was the first manager to go - forced to resign after 33 years of service to the company. This was followed by the Operations Manager who simply walked out. The Finance Manager was then systematically humiliated and harassed. Statements were made publicly focussing on his incompetence. In meetings 'errors' in budget reports were highlighted. Revenue problems were blamed on the Finance Manager. On the day that he was called in for a performance counselling session - he resigned. At the time, I genuinely believed the GM's assertions that the Finance Manager was incompetent. Later, I learned that the GM had stopped talking to the Finance Manager and had left him out of the loop on some crucial decisions.

When our Marketing Manager began to privately express his frustrations about the General Manager, I became aware that the growing unease I was experiencing was more widely felt. He left the company frustrated at the situation and the bullying target shifted to the Corporate Relations Manager. After 15 years of service with the company, this cool, composed, highly professional woman found herself embroiled in shouting matches in the workplace, thoroughly demotivated and job hunting. Her emotional outbursts in the face of relentless bullying were labelled as "mid-life issues." She eventually resigned. It was during the time I found myself in the midst of a relentless barrage of attack.

His style was "passive-aggressive." In one-to-one conversations he would either shout me down or imply violence with statements such as, *"If I wasn't at work, I'd take you out and hit you."* Publicly, he'd bait me and make statements questioning my ability to function. Discussions would rapidly degenerate into arguments. His final tactic was to cry. The sight of a 50-year-old managing director weeping at board rooms and management conferences was so embarrassing and disquieting that it ensured subjection in as effective a manner as the shouting was threatening. People learned not to ask questions, challenge or rock the boat in any way. Staff meetings became silent.

Questions were raised around my ability to meet targets. This was despite my department achieving all of its performance goals. In one meeting with all of the management of our company and our New Zealand subsidiary present, my GM publicly declared during a presentation I was giving, that there was significant concern about my ability to manage a budget. I calmly refuted his comments. His comments were greeted with stunned amazement by my colleagues and those of the NZ company who sought me out to commiserate and express concern for what they had witnessed. The truth was that my department during my entire employment period met budget targets even when they were reduced during the budget year.

At staff meetings, it became more and more obvious to others that I was being challenged and baited. I was also a support for others who experienced his belittling. This included members of the Board who were themselves feeling intimidated.

After two and a half years, I lodged a formal complaint with the chair of the Board. I stated that there was a pattern of bullying behaviour that I was witnessing and personally experiencing. While there had been informal discussions, this was the first time anyone in the company had lodged a formal complaint. The outcome of this was a series of facilitated meetings to address the issues and the consequence was a rapid deterioration of my personal situation. My department's budget was cut significantly and staffing levels reduced by fifty per cent. The public and private insinuations increased and other staff were instructed to monitor my e-mails (they refused and advised me of the situation). Our supervision sessions were suspended and weeks would pass without him speaking to me.

My esteem and morale plummeted. Any behaviour that demonstrated my emotional turmoil was seized upon as examples of my unreliability and inability to cope with the size of my role. While I was determined to complete the projects I had started, I felt compelled to clean my office of personal effects.

The Board instructed the GM and the Management Team to attend a management development program in an attempt to build the team and assist our leader to evaluate his behaviour. During the program, it became clear that our GM's view of the company and our own team dynamics were significantly at odds with how the rest of the team viewed the issues. The exercise highlighted an alienation each of us was experiencing and strengthened us as a group.

Some Board members attempted to pass a motion of no confidence in him. His bullying, delaying tactics impacted on the Board so significantly that the motion was postponed and the leader of the faction resigned after developing a stress-related health condition.

Management meetings descended into shouting matches with participants walking out in mid-meeting on a regular basis. Staff morale plunged while absenteeism, illness and the need to work from home all increased.

At the start of 2002, the General Manager determined that my role was redundant and I was retrenched. As I was actively seeking a new position, I was relieved. Less than a month later the marketing manager was sacked. To forestall the Board from sacking him - the GM then resigned.

Aged Care:

My experience with this company was by no means unique. The position I was employed for had been previously occupied by a person who was very familiar with the industry, however he was sacked after just four weeks. Following my departure, a chap with many years experience in the industry was "head hunted," employed for just eight weeks and apparently resigned as he had not been allowed the scope to do what he'd been hired to do. I believe this fellow had sold his home in another state to take up his position.

[During my interview with her, I asked questions and was given the following answers:]

a. What happened during the bullying/harassment?
    CEO expected that I would behave outside of the conditions of the Aged Care Act to encourage potential residents to "buy" into the company properties. When I refused and cited reasons for my

refusal, he stated that he had asked other company members and they supported his methods of "encouragement."

CEO calling me on mobile telephone frequently and screamed questions at me.

Not listening to my point of view or to reasoning over targets set (and achieved).

Accosting me in the foyer of the company building and speaking to me through clenched teeth about his lack of faith in me.

b.   Who was involved?

CEO of the company and his wife, whose position had no name. She seemed to put herself into whichever position she fancied filling at the time. Both characters seemed to hold no trust in any employee.

c.   What kind of company?

Provision of residential accommodation for over 55's. This includes retirement villages, high care and low care residential accommodation.

d.   What were the repercussions from the bullying?

I had been "head-hunted" for this position and was interviewed four times, three of which interviews were with the CEO. A generous package was offered and I found the offer of the challenge irresistible. I resigned from my former position to join this company and expected to "give my all" and blaze a new career for myself. However, after only three months with the company I realised that despite having exceeded goals which he'd set for me and having made great inroads on my new career, he was going to make my position untenable for me. I felt cheated of the opportunity to prove myself in this environment and also felt unfairly treated.

e.   What action was taken by the company?

I resigned, giving one month's notice. However, I was told to leave immediately. I realise that this is common practice - however sales were lost as a consequence of my early departure. After my resignation I was asked to report to the company accountant to hand back company equipment and documents. This I did and found myself escorted around the building in the manner that a criminal might be.

f.   Cost to the company?

The cost to the company in lost productivity, absenteeism and my termination were:

- *My termination of employment.*
- *The cost of replacing me.*
- *Lost sales which I had been working towards.*
- *Loss of reputation for the company.*
- *Continuity with clients could not be maintained.*
- *Loss of morale to colleagues of mine who believed in what I was doing.*

High School:

At first Fiona thought it was the perfect job - and it was for a year - until Laura arrived. After twelve months as a senior co-ordinator at a South Australian State high school, Fiona felt she was making a difference and developing strong ties with the students and fellow teachers. Then Laura was appointed to a more senior position in the school and the first hint of the coming traumas was in the form of hand-written notes to Fiona - usually involving trivial matters. The demands and the frequency of the notes escalated, as did Laura's behaviour.

Fiona soon found herself being dressed down by Laura in front of other staff and students, mimicked by her in the staff room and the subject of hostile verbal attacks from her in regular performance assessment meetings.

With her self-confidence destroyed after formal complaints went nowhere, Fiona left the job she loved before her five-year contract expired. She felt she had no choice if she was going to maintain her sanity, her ability to reason and be rational. She is now considering her legal options.

Correctional Centre:

Marion worked as a welfare officer in Australian correctional centres for more than ten years before becoming a victim of bullying. Marion says her supervisor began a campaign of bullying and intimidation against her after she failed to complete an additional task she was given, apparently due to a lack of time and resources. Her supervisor immediately pulled in the facility's acting governor and the acting chief welfare officer. Marion says her supervisor made sure that he had the weight of the department behind him when he confronted her about her inability to follow instruction. Their joint confrontation - dressed up as a mediation session left her little hope that she would have a fair hearing.

Soon after and amid escalating demands being placed upon her, Marion was ordered to relocate her office. She was ordered to move to a part of the prison where she would be the only worker present on most days. She was fitted with only a fire alarm to ring in case she needed assistance. Other than that, it was largely just she and the inmates, she says.

Marion says her ongoing treatment by this stage had eroded her faith in the internal complaint mechanisms and left her with little choice but to go external - to her union and WorkCover - with her concerns. She lost her appetite, was unable to sleep and dreaded going into work. But she says two of the worst things were not knowing whom to turn to for support and feeling as though nothing she could do would change the workplace culture enough to stop it from reoccurring in the future. Marion is now on stress leave while, for the person who initiated the bullying - her direct supervisor - business continues as usual.

Warehouse packer:

In a disturbing case of bullying, a warehouse packer was repeatedly chased by a forklift truck, skewered by its fork and left with a disfigured leg and unable to play sport.

Store Assistant:

A store assistant, 27, suffered back burns after a colleague set his shirt on fire with a cigarette lighter. The victim had been repeatedly verbally abused and subjected to practical jokes.

Victoria labourer:

A labourer shot his colleague after being pushed to the boiling point by 18 months of workplace taunts. Li You He, 47 was charged with causing grievous bodily harm after allegedly pulling up in his car beside his 34-year-old colleague as they were leaving work and shooting him.

Call Centre:

I have worked in a call centre for eighteen months and really started being bullied almost from the start of my employment, but I can only see that in retrospect now. After about three months of employment, I was moved to a new team as my team leader resigned suddenly. My new team leader seemed very friendly and helpful to start off with. Without reason she started to attack my Scottish accent (I work in a call centre in Australia). She started saying things like *"I cannot understand you so God help the customers if we cannot understand you."* These comments became more and more frequent and they got to the stage where they became very upsetting.

I spoke to a union rep (even although I was not a member) for advice. She told me that these were racist remarks and to take it to HR. On her advice this is what I did. HR decided to tell the call centre manager who promptly sent me an e-mail asking me to, *"Withdraw my allegation as this could ruin someone's career."* I felt intimidated by the e-mail and as I had only been in the job for six months thought it better to withdraw my complaint in case I lost my job. Apparently HR spoke to the team leader in question who said she was not aware she was making comments about my accent. Funnily enough though, after HR spoke to her the comments stopped.

I felt very uncomfortable being in her team and she was nit-picking about small things in my performance and was now saying my tone with customers was inappropriate as when I get a difficult call my tone rises. I tried to tell her this was a normal reaction that everyone's tone rises when stressed or upset but I was told this was not the case. I asked for a transfer and was told that they were not happy about this but would give me it this time but there had better not be any more problems.

Anyway, I thought this would be the end off my problems but unfortunately worse was to come. I had jumped from the frying pan into the fire so to speak. On my first day in my new team my new team leader told me that she was my last chance, if I did not make it work with her I would be out the door and this had come from the call centre manager. I was reminded of this on a daily basis for eight months. I felt intimidated and stressed by this but no matter how well I did at the job it was never good enough. Between them, my call centre manager and team leader manipulated every situation and even lied between them to support their stories. I have been belittled, have constant derogatory comments made about my accent and culture and am constantly threatened about losing my job. This has made me very stressed and my blood pressure very high. I cannot sleep and feel physically sick in the morning about the thought of going to work.

It is having a terrible effect on my husband as he also works in the same company and he sees the constant abuse I am subjected to. I recently wrote a 14-page report about my team leader and lodged a formal complaint. I was off work on stress leave at the time as my doctor was very concerned for my health. I was assured by the HR department that my complaint would be investigated. I have been moved to a different team but none of the issues I raised in the complaint have been addressed. I am back at work now and am now being intimidated by the call centre manager and HR. My union rep knows what is happening but is powerless to stop it. I am scared, frustrated and stressed. I do not know when this is going to end and my health is really suffering.

At the moment, I am in the process of lodging a complaint with the Equal Opportunities Commission about the racial abuse and comments but I don't know how much good it will do, as the company will manipulate the situation into me being the problem not the victim.

Local government: (a)

I'm a single woman in my mid-30s, working in Australian local government. I experienced bullying in my last job, but didn't recognise it until fairly late - after it had taken its toll on my psychological health. The short version: The organisation was *very* conservative and hierarchical (e.g. secretarial staff, all female, were consistently referred to as "the girls" regardless of their age). The community was small, insular and homogenous. I arrived fresh from a leading-edge big-city organisation overseas and though I am Anglo-Saxon and English-speaking, I was still seen as very much the foreigner. So there was a clash right from the beginning. My bosses felt compelled to "put me in my place" by disregarding my achievements - e.g. obtaining $150 000 funding from external sources - and focusing on minor errors - e.g. coming in 10 minutes late once in a three-month period.

The first year or so of my job went fairly well and I had an opportunity to heal somewhat. I was aware of a weird dynamic between my boss's

114

boss (a woman in her mid-40s) and me, but for a long time it was just a latent thing that had no real impact. However, this began to change. The first incident occurred when, in the middle of a work-related discussion, she suddenly asked whether I was currently in a relationship. She then went on to discuss *her* recent experiences with men (which I think was her real aim) and to extrapolate from her experiences some advice for me. I tried to end the conversation tactfully by moving towards the door of her office, but she got up from her desk and walked towards me, getting really aggressive, like she wanted to force me to stay and listen to her.

Further incidents involved some very negative generalisations about my personality *("You're sneaky.")* and my future *("You'll never be a manager.")* In each case, the comments were unrelated to the discussion at hand. Unsurprisingly, all of this occurred behind closed doors with no witnesses. The final straw came when she insisted that some positive feedback from a State government minister on a major aspect of my work had to be excluded from a progress report to senior management. I saw this for what it was - an effort to undermine my professional standing.

Fortunately, I was able to apply what I learned (too late) in my last job. I joined the union, talked to relevant agencies and prepared a formal complaint. The HR department handled it adequately. They seemed sure that it was just a misunderstanding and not actual bullying (this was after the HR representative mentioned that she didn't know much about workplace bullying as it is a "new" issue). It's still too early to see what repercussions there will be, if any, but the bully has certainly changed her approach with me.

I feel very empowered by my actions. I know I handled myself professionally. I have learned a lot about interpersonal relationships and this knowledge will help me to be more effective in my career. I also used this information to help a friend who observed a bully-and-target dynamic at her job (she passed the information on to her manager, who thought it was a revelation and moved to deal with the situation). So in a small way I have become an anti-bullying campaigner.

I share this story to make the point that one can heal from bullying and even become a stronger, better person. Remember: it's not you - it's them. And you *will* survive.

Local government: (b)

I was a Local Government Officer in a senior position. My boss (who had never liked me) generally let me get on with things but in 2000 he began to bully me. All the usual things like praising others for work, which was 90 per cent, mine, constant criticism, shouting at me if I dared approach him when others weren't around etc etc. This seemed to coincide with a change in the sickness monitoring procedure, which meant that I "triggered" all the time since my medical condition causes me to have frequent odd days off. Eventually, I began to crack and ended up sounding off to a colleague. This minor misdemeanour was blown up out of all proportion and I was subjected to "informal" disciplinary procedures "for my own good." Eventually I gave in and left.

On Friday (15th Feb 2002) I received a letter from the Employment Tribunal telling me that the initial hearing will be on the 18th March (2 days before my son's 18th birthday.) Also in the letter was the delayed reply from my ex-employers to my tribunal application.

They denied everything. Absolutely everything. They said that I had not made any complaint about my boss, either formal or informal *even though I have a letter from the Assistant Director inviting me to a meeting to discuss my allegations of being bullied!* They said that they never discriminated against me because of my disability, but even if they had, it was more than three months before my complaint so I am out of time anyway. In short, I must be prepared to prove everything and fight very hard even though my boss's bullying has left me barely able to cope with the part-time work that I now do. My house is a mess and I am on strong medication for depression (for the first time in my life.)

I know that only 1 in 10 "constructive dismissal" cases succeeds and the Union have already told me that I have little or no chance of success so why am I going on? Because I am this man's fourth victim (that I know of.) The others all left with their tails between their legs but I want to draw attention to what he is doing. OK, the management appear to condone his actions so far, but if people start taking them to Tribunal they might just consider him too hot to handle and his days 0f power then might be over. *It is not a question of revenge but of justice.*

Public service:

I'm a 27-year-old male who once worked for the Australian Public Service. In the first half of 1997, I was working for a large government agency and had accepted a temporary promotion to a small, self-managed team within the same organisation. My duties were mainly to process the travel-related paperwork of the team's members as well as helping arrange meetings both in the main campus and at external sites.

A man who had been recruited from another federal government department headed the team. The team was to be a pilot for a major reorganisation of the agency and it was our task to ensure that it went smoothly. It was not long before his bullying [of his staff] began.

When he was calm, he would be extraordinarily patronising and condescending. When he wasn't getting his own way on something, no matter how trivial, he would throw the most appalling tantrums in the office. These tantrums would often involve screaming fits, verbal abuse, name calling and threatening gestures towards his current target.

In one instance, he called our office from a mobile phone while he was interstate. I answered the phone as the person he wanted to speak to was not at her desk. The connection was very poor and so I asked who was calling.

He then exploded into a rage, screaming foul-mouthed abuse down the line at me. I would have hung up had the person he wanted to talk to not returned to her desk. His behaviour was in direct contravention of agency regulations regarding misuse of communication equipment.

He was incapable of treating anyone who was not his superior with basic respect and dignity. This alone makes him virtually unemployable, as it is impossible in this day and age to conceive of a workplace where this is not a minimum requirement. Around his superiors, he would put on an Oscar-winning performance of civility and affability, sometimes bordering on pretentiousness. This effectively disguised his true nature.

He would not allow anyone under him to perform well in their jobs, as it would have shown up his own incompetence and inadequacy. At team meetings, he would often make a big fuss about some minor issue, while paying scant attention to matters of substance. Although he often claimed to be playing 'the devil's advocate,' with hindsight I believe that this was a ploy to conceal his own inability to manage.

On one occasion, I had to organise a high-level meeting with about five minutes notice because he had failed to notify me until almost the time it was about to start! Working right through my lunch break, I had to book a room, arrange refreshments and make sure the location was sent out to all participants. Although the meeting was a success, he never once thanked me for my efforts in making it so.

The worst incident occurred about a fortnight prior to my departure. I had already found out that he didn't want to extend my position there. He called me into his office under the pretext of discussing why he wasn't extending my tenure. As soon as he sat down in his chair, he dramatically spun around and began berating me. I was taken aback at first, not expecting this kind of treatment. I attempted to reply, but he kept cutting me off with more accusations.

A few weeks earlier, I had attended a training seminar on assertive communication. I applied my skills to this situation. I remained calm and stated my case. This clearly rattled the bully. He reacted by exploding into another 'grand mal' tantrum, hysterically screaming all sorts of abuse at me and babbling incoherently about some totally unrelated issues.

At one point, this bully became so aggressive and irrational towards me that I genuinely feared that he was about to become physically violent. I will never forget the filthy, evil look he shot at me as I gratefully departed his cubicle at the conclusion of his abusive tirade.

I was in a state of shock afterwards. I wound up back at my old job in another section, with an accompanying pay cut. I did complain to personnel and I was able to extract a written 'apology' from the bully. It was scarcely worth the effort, though, because in his 'apology' he reiterated his opinion (should that be 'fantasy'?) that it was my entire fault anyway. I was left with a psychiatric injury (depression) that lasted about eighteen months and a stress-related skin condition, which has only recently cleared up, as a result of my experiences. The bullying, however, didn't end there.

My ex-leader would continue to make smart-alec comments whenever we passed each other on the campus. When he stalked me one weekend in a local shopping mall, I decided to seek legal advice on a restraining order. The lawyer I consulted was quite surprised that I had been able to extract a written apology from him. He informed me that most people in my position didn't even get that far.

I was stunned to discover that he had an appalling history of misbehaviour and misconduct at his last workplace, including sexual harassment as well as verbal abuse and tantrum throwing - they certainly weren't sorry to see him go! When I appealed to them for help, in full accordance with their own guidelines, I was instead betrayed, belittled and patronised. In effect, they said that I was just young and stupid and didn't know what I was talking about. And then they wonder why all their good people are leaving.

I've pretty well made a full recovery, thanks in no small part to Tim Field [of Bully OnLine in the U.K.]. I am now a full time IT student, having taken a generous redundancy package about a year ago. Never again will I allow myself to become an unwitting victim of a workplace bully.

Legal profession:

Reading some of the case histories reminded me of a two-year period early in my legal career while employed in a Government Solicitors Office. I had heard that the general manager had a reputation as a bully. Naively I thought I could handle it, as my previous experience with bullying had been at school and the Army and dealt with it OK.

I had not really experienced the Office bully. Reading your selection criteria, this guy was an expert and I am positive that he knew exactly what he was doing - his bullying was to keep order. He would pick someone in the office - someone who did not fit his world view of the grey public servant and start a campaign of putting that person off his or her work. It would start small scale - the occasional critical comment on a piece of advice, but then built up. An advice prepared a month previously would turn up on your desk with "please discuss" on it. An appointment would have to be made to see him. Then, at your appointment he would read out passages of the advice, out of context and ask why it had been expressed that way - and that he was not sure that the law was correct - and no matter how you expressed yourself, he would not see your view.

As one of the senior government lawyers said, he was never more right than when he was wrong. The "please discuss" treatment would last, on average, two to three months. Once he had locked on though, no one in the office wanted to know you. It was known as having the "kiss of death." No more invitations to coffee or lunch. Complete isolation while the little (short man) creep had his fun.

Without really being equipped, I stood up to him. The pressure got worse and worse. I got to the point where I had to see him once a month to basically tell him what I'd done the previous month. Go through my advices and other work, explain why I had done things a particular way - all of which he subjected to ridicule - often in front of my supervisor (who, of course, privately sympathised, but did not hesitate to put the boot in when the boss was around - or in any of these meetings).

In those meetings I felt myself withdrawing, curling up to make myself a smaller target. It didn't work, as the bully he was he just went harder. I was threatened with disciplinary action and was told that he'd had other legal officers removed from duty by "breaking them" and that is what he was going to do to me.

What I did do was get some help in realising what it was that let this man affect me - and I realised that nothing had prepared me for this sort of power relationship. Even in the Army, a bullying superior can be circumvented (normally the ones at the same or higher rank sort this out). I had to identify what this guy got off on in the bullying and take that away. I found out he got a buzz out of the fear he caused and that as long as you were frightened of him, he was always going to go after you.

And so I learned to not be afraid. This came about as part of rebuilding my self-confidence via completing a course of martial arts to the level of 1st Dan Instructor. This was done through personal training with a Kung-fu Grand Master. He was aware of what I was going through and he literally taught me not to fear anything.

I was called into see my boss after a weekend where I had, after a very torrid grading, achieved the rank as above. It was torrid, as it was very physically demanding. I was sporting some cuts and bruises, but I felt like I had not felt in a long time. I walked into his office feeling ten foot tall. Instead of hunching over, I sat in the chair bolt upright and looked him dead in the eye and did not look away.

"Well," he said, *"Would you like to tell me how you're going?"*

"Why don't you tell me," I said, *"as yours is the only opinion which matters."*

"Are you feeling all right?" he asked, sneering. Very matter of fact I told him I'd never felt better. He quizzed me as to my cuts and bruises and inquired whether I had been in an accident. I informed him I had been doing some Kung fu with some friends on the weekend. In his most mocking tone he said:

"Hohoh, are you some sort of black belt?" Fixing the little bastard dead in the eye, I leaned forward and said very quietly: *"I am now."* That moment was priceless. Instantly the power relationship changed. He shrank back and look of real fear crossed his face. I told him to relax and: *"I guarantee, you are in less danger today than you were last week. I am fully in control of myself. You don't frighten me any more and this is the last meeting we will have on these terms."* And it was - and I was left alone - and he didn't start on anyone else until I had moved out of his Branch.

I wish, however, I had known about Bully OnLine back then - because everything you say about bullies and how to deal with them is true - for my case history points out something unfortunate - to be left alone I had to have him fear me - and that is not right - no matter what the little creep did to deserve it.

Utility company:

Three stress breakdowns in one little office and what have management done about it? I was angry then and I find I am still angry. Perhaps this is the time to put our office's case history on the record.

I worked for almost twenty years for a large utility in a technical capacity. Our section had fifteen staff, many of whom had worked together for decades. We had much good will among workers and not very many layers of management. I was and am still proud of the company, which is extraordinarily efficient and usually tries to be humane. But the company, like so many others, fell prey to the management mania - efficiency! seminars! slogans! In spite of this nonsense, we took up the slack when new practices and software were imposed on us. Slowly, the pressure increased, with experienced staff retiring but not being replaced. When we asked about raises or promotions, we got laughter in response. (Really.) We carried on for several years, becoming more cynical and learned that management never meant what they said, no matter how pretty it sounded. Morale took a dive.

One day our section head and department head decided to hire a guy to do the front-end planning for our jobs. A great idea. But they screwed it up - they did not hire one of the three or four sensible choices for this job - they hired "Gulo." They knew what they were getting. For thirty years, Gulo's management style had never varied: Trample and smear subordinates, suck up to superiors. He was a very loud man with an abrupt manner and no people skills. Faced with complaints, his superiors would always excuse him, saying he had learned his behaviour in the armed forces. We often wondered whom he might be blackmailing to keep his job.

Two women who had worked for him had taken a lateral move to my section just to evade him. These gals were both very proud of their work and identified strongly with their jobs. Once hired, his original job description was abandoned. Instead of planning our projects to make our work easier, Gulo was put in charge of micro-managing us and doing our evaluations. He took over all liaison functions, breaking our ties to people in other departments and telling them it was our fault when there were mistakes or late deliveries, painting us as stupid and lazy.

Disaster came within two years. For many months, we made frequent complaints to our superiors, ranging from fury to tears to cold detailing of Gulo's socially destructive behaviour. These complaints were all ignored. Then, in the space of a few months, three staff members, one man and the two women, suffered stress breakdowns so severe that they are still under medication, almost three years later. One of them collapsed at my feet, in the office. When the ambulance arrived, I rode with her to the hospital.

I was whistleblower and spokesman - if I hadn't sent a letter detailing the breakdowns and abuse to several layers of management, the union and HR, I suppose nothing would have been done. Finally management took action, if you want to call it that. They hired a mediator to sort it out and then on her recommendation, put the three on sick leave, forced them and Gulo to retire and gave me a small buyout package in return for my silence. They did nothing else, did not apologise and give the impression that it was just an unfortunate personality conflict.

I have been out of the office two years and I'm still angry. The men who heard all our complaints have been promoted. The corporation probably spent, in buyouts and lost time and mediator fees, several hundred thousand dollars on this "unfortunate personality conflict." The remaining staff (some still my friends) have lost any ambition or enthusiasm and are just marking time.

I know there must be good managers in the world, but I only remember the men who cut three work lives short, with terrible emotional pain and suffering. Yet the pain inflicted and money wasted has been buried, hidden, rationalised away. Shame!

National Mortgage Company:

I have been the victim of a vicious bully whom I have worked for seven years. I am an Underwriter for a national mortgage company. Over the time I have worked for the firm, the bullying has become more pronounced and acute. I work in an office of about thirty people.

To a person, everyone knows that our supervisor is tyrannical, petty, abusive, incompetent and inconsistent. We all do what we can to help each other get through instances of abuse. Everyone so far has continued to stay with the firm mainly due to the financial benefits that would likely not otherwise be available. My boss is a Serial Bully and rotates victims. We all joke about whose turn it is and will be next. She even has the emotionally needy cohort who executes her agenda - although the cohort also complains about the abuse she suffers at the boss's hands and then snaps back into submission when she loses her spine. I, however, am the most frequent and favourite victim. Until very recently I have been able to "put the beast to sleep" by pretending that her regular petty assaults aren't happening and telling her what she wants to hear. I have tried not to challenge her and have endured many public assaults. Things started heating up about three months ago when she was forced by our corporate office to hire a Sales Manager.

Her focus immediately shifted from victimising me to abusing him. She felt threatened by him and began berating him in front of other employees, especially those who reported to him. He went to an offsite meeting at our corporate office and mentioned to her superiors that our office is under-staffed and has management issues. When he returned, she took him in her office and verbally abused and humiliated him. He was so injured by her assault that he contacted superiors at the corporate office and complained about her. He even left the office in tears on one occasion. I felt sorry for him and tried to explain that she is the one with the problem and that everyone has suffered at one time or another at her hand. He eventually lined up another employment opportunity and went into her office to resign and confronted her with her abusive behaviour. He let her know that our whole office is intimidated and afraid of her. She gleaned from their conversation that I must have been his information source and has since stepped up her abusive attacks on me.

She has humiliated me in a group setting with a visiting consultant, although she ended up looking really irrational; she changed my work schedule which was geared towards reducing my productivity and also income; she completely came uncorked on me a few days ago and among other things accused me of being irrational, having problems relating to co-workers, playing both sides of the fence and being duplicitous.

She then became very paranoid and asked me to put my comments to her in writing (which I declined to do) and indicated we would continue the conversation when there was a third party present (her terrorised cohort). I told her that I had no interest in ever continuing the conversation and that I would not feel that her cohort was any sort of unbiased third party since the cohort is afraid of her, as am I. Since that day, she tried to pretend the conversation didn't happen and be chummy with me. I have been professional but distant and avoid communication. She then called a meeting with the sales staff in the office, who have in the past been her weapon of choice.

She has told me repeatedly that they all complain about my being difficult to work with, which they do not. She is projecting. In the meeting, to a person, the entire sales staff let her know that I have been nothing but excellent, helpful, knowledgeable and consistent. They inquired as to why she changed my work schedule and let her know how this has adversely affected them. While I am very happy that my co-workers are standing up for me, I know that this has infuriated her. I am positive she will desperately search for another "flaw" in my personality or work habits and manufacture some other "problem" that I am causing.

I wanted to tell this tale because I read so many case studies where the group didn't stand up for the victim. I am fortunate that the people I work with will to a degree stand up for me when they can. My Serial Bully doesn't have the latitude to do the damage to me that she would like to. I do plan to seek other employment when it makes financial sense. The mortgage market is volatile and a downturn is coming. I have seniority and will likely still have a job when a lot of people in the business won't. I have to plan my escape but have no intention of letting this petty tyrant win. I will prevail, but on my terms. In the meantime, our Sales Manager is working his last week with the firm and plans on being very specific about why he is leaving the company when he gives his exit interview.

Primary school:

I am a 43-year-old Primary School Teacher in Australia and when I transferred to a remote country school some seven years ago, my life was turned upside down. I have been teaching for over twelve years now. I also worked for many private companies during my life from which I always received glowing references. This was also the case when I went to University for three years. I received many letters from the Dean congratulating me on my performance and eventually topped my final year. I had never been bullied in the workplace so I had no idea what was going on until I became so ill that I could no longer face going to work. I won't detail every incident but, if you want more, I'll happily provide same.

During a lunch two bullies sat beside me (unusual I thought - then I got it) and vividly described a frog dissection seen on a computer. I asked them could they talk about it after lunch which was ignored until another staff member asked the same thing not two seconds after me.

During a dinner, one bully described the removal of a road kill kangaroo's testicles. I also own a pet house rabbit - I actually saved her when she was four weeks old and she is now nearly five and a much loved little friend. My bullies knew of the rabbit. In one day, one bully described vividly three times how she had cut her finger whilst chopping up a rabbit - each time in my presence. One bully laughed hysterically as she heard the description. As cutting one's finger is not usually a laughing matter, I can only assume the laughter was because I was there. All of the above occurred during a one month period and pretty close to my final demise.

This is not everything - having put up with it on a daily basis for six years, it's hard to remember. I guess it follows the usual bullying behaviours - find weaknesses and go for the throat! I even blacked out momentarily during two bullying episodes and even today I can't remember what was said or done. I have never experienced a black-out in my life.

About two to three years ago, a doctor asked me was I depressed. I dismissed this though looking back, had I addressed the problem then the symptoms wouldn't be so bad today. I have major depressive illness now with anxiety attacks so bad that I lay and groan on the floor or bed. I have night time enuresis that worsens when highly stressed. I have tried to commit suicide; I have become a recluse and am a shadow of my former once confident self. Still fighting for Worker's Compensation - the confusion and bewilderment has now turned to fury and anger upon enlightenment of bullying information.

Lastly, do government schools in Australia really want to address bullying in the playground? It seems not, they are far too busy doing it themselves!

Learning disabled adults:

I've worked in the care of disabled people for fifteen years. For the last six years I've been part of a small team providing care for a group of adults in their own home. About eighteen months ago, a married couple joined the team and since then I've watched most of the original team members being picked off, one by one, by them. Over the last few months, I too have become a "victim" and I am now off sick and unable to see a time when I will ever feel comfortable and safe working in my usual job again.

I've experienced malicious gossip, about fellow staff and myself; I've seen the people we provide care for treated in a totally unacceptable manner; I've been on the receiving end of insulting, derogatory remarks about myself and women in general; fed the wrong information about tasks involved in my job, leading to mistakes; I've had a fellow professional wag her finger at me and shout extremely abusive comments on my work in front of the bullies and others - even though I'd only met her a short while before. I later found out that this couple had spent a considerable amount of time telling her what an awful person I was, prior to her even meeting me; I've been isolated and ignored - I could go on and fill pages with the incidents and events that I've seen and experienced.

To make matters worse, my new line manager is obviously very friendly with and supports these bullies and the one or two other new staff that are now part of their gang.

Since making a formal complaint, my line manager has threatened me with disciplinary action if I dare to meet or speak to my former workmates even socially, she has spent a lot of time warning me of all the nasty repercussions that await me if I proceed with my complaint and worse still, has kept the bullies informed of everything I have said and done, despite my being assured that confidentiality would be maintained, resulting in one of the "gang" actually making threats and leaving me terrified not just for my own safety, but that of my family.

The impression I've had from the reaction of senior managers is that to act on this now would be an admission of their failure to deal with this situation when others first reported it and rather than risk it becoming known that they have failed miserably in upholding their own policy on bullying, they are going to try and sweep it all under the carpet.

Like most of my workmates, I have a family and can't afford to leave my job. Also, like all my workmates, I am now sick with work related stress, which is hardly going to enhance my prospects of finding alternative work. Nor can I ever imagine feeling confident or safe in my usual work place again. For the first time in my life I am receiving counselling and on medication to help me cope. We are looking into legal steps that we can perhaps take, but in reality all of us are so shaken in confidence and so weary and sick of the whole business, that we don't really know where to go from here.

My employers are supposedly investigating the situation, but have already told me I will be expected to go back to work in the same environment, with the same people, when its 'sorted,' telling me in advance that they will take no action. I've got together with five other staff that have had the same experience as myself - they have also made complaints - and we are seeking legal advice - though whether we can get our union to support in that, we don't yet know. I can't believe that at the age of 37, with years of experience in my work, that I am in this situation.

I have now found out that at least five others, who have raised the same complaints/concerns as myself, have been subjected to the same treatment from this manager. I wish there was some sort of independent body to support the victims of bullying in the workplace, something that could put pressure on employers to uphold their own policies in dealing with this sort of situation.

Doctor bullied by secretary:

It is five years since I left my dream job due to bullying. I am still a doctor but my life has changed since then as I now work in a different type of job which I have no formal training for. I studied for seventeen years, seven years in medical school and ten years of post graduate training and exams. I no longer work in my chosen specialty.

I have a court case pending and I long to sit in the dock and tell my story. It took me fifteen months after I left the job to realise I needed to do something about what happened. My GP diagnosed me as having post-traumatic stress and it was then I went to a solicitor. I passed through four solicitors before I met one who would take my case. One solicitor was so shocked by what I told him he actually said to me, *"If you are making this up, you are psychiatric."*

My case is complicated in that the secretary who bullied me was supported by my boss, who at the time was my husband. He supported her because they were having an affair. They knew that I knew, even though I had no proof.

It was an impossible situation for me. The secretary was so brazen because she knew she would not be reprimanded for her behaviour. She would scream at me and run after me cursing at me. She would refer to me as "that bitch" to other members of staff. She would openly laugh at me in front of others. She was the head secretary, so she made sure I could not get access to any secretarial back up. She would openly brag about what a good time she was having with my husband. She told me I was the problem and said I treated people badly because I couldn't hang on to my husband. It was like the worst episode of the tackiest soap and there I was right in the middle of it.

Somehow they managed to get a serious complaint made about me. I was not allowed to know why I was complained about or who made the complaint. I told the overall boss what was happening and he laughed at me. He ignored my allegations. He subsequently promoted the bully to his Personal Assistant. At this stage, four people had made serious complaints about this secretary and yet she was still promoted.

When I tell my story people don't believe me. Some people have even said I am a scorned woman and that is why I am taking a case. Can you imagine how difficult it is to deal with a situation like this? I left my husband and I left my job. The secretary stayed on and as I said, got promoted. Yes I want my day in court and maybe then people will see that what I experienced was horrendous, deliberate, emotional hurt.

I am highly qualified and good at what I do. At times I pity the bully as she must have been so jealous of me she even took pleasure in having an affair with my husband and flaunting it in my face - even though she was married herself. To this day I have never told her husband what she did. He is a good man and I don't want to hurt him.

As a doctor I feel this secretary has an antisocial personality disorder. She is a serial bully. She bullied two other women in the same place and they are helping me with my case. I saw this secretary in action and she is textbook material. I have never experienced such a public display of dysfunction. Of course, I only realised all this after I left. At the time I was punch drunk. I just buckled under the pressure of it all.

Now I am strong and I will tell my story in court. After my court case, I will spend some time helping people who are or who have been bullied. Thank you to Tim Field for his book, which shed a light of hope in my darkest moments. It was through reading his book I began to understand why I was bullied and why I had PTSD and what a serial bully is. I wish it had never happened.

Bullied medical trainee

The tears ran down my face, hidden by my surgical mask. My consultant continued relentlessly, *"Why can't you do this? It really isn't hard. Are you stupid? Can't you see how to help me?"*

I hated myself for crying. I avoided her eyes so she couldn't see my tears and the deep hurt in my eyes, but I couldn't speak without betraying myself. I managed a few one-word answers. The criticism continued, if not with words, then with sighs and angry tutting.

The atmosphere in the operating theatre was tense. The staff had all seen this happen many times before - hard working, pleasant trainees reduced to non-functioning wrecks in the space of an operation. I looked helplessly at the scrub nurse, another trainee. She saw my distress immediately and gave me a supporting glance. But she too was suffering. *"No, not that one. Why do we have to have trainees in my operations? Not like that,"* she lashed out at the scrub nurse, another hard-working, competent trainee, now shaking and anxious, her self-confidence fast diminishing.

I didn't know what to do. I felt uncomfortable continuing in such distress. Either my consultant didn't notice or she didn't care. I wondered what would happen if I asked to leave and decided that it would probably just make things worse. I stayed. Three hours of hostility and criticism. At the end, I ripped off my mask and gloves and turned, only to find her standing behind me. She registered my swollen eyes and tearstained face in complete silence. I have never seen such a cold, emotionless stare and I hope never to again.

Her behaviour was always the same on the ward rounds, in clinics and in theatres. She was hostile, critical and discouraging. I continued in this post for the complete six months, becoming increasingly anxious and depressed. I left my post feeling suicidal.

I am now taking a year away from medicine. The past year has been hard, coming to terms with what happened to me in my last post. I had naively hoped that bullying stopped at school. Now I know that bullies continue to bully people throughout their lives. The bullying I endured has left me traumatised. Despite being told that she treated everyone this way, I believed it was my entire fault.

I couldn't believe that such an intelligent and talented surgeon should need to make herself feel better by making those around her feel terrible. I couldn't believe that this was the basis of basic surgical training. This behaviour is often seen as traditional in surgery and when I brought it to the notice of consultants at my routine assessment and to the post-graduate dean, it was ignored; further abuses of power.

As I look back on this time, I wonder why I felt so helpless. While trying to come to terms with the fact that I effectively let myself be bullied, I read about the experiments in which learnt helplessness was described. A dog was put in a cage and given electric shocks through one side of the floor of the cage. The dog quickly learnt to stay on the other side. The same happened when the other side was used, the dog avoiding the shocks. Then the dog received shocks from all parts of the floor at random. Initially, the dog tried to avoid them, but when unable to, it gave up and lay down and received the shocks. After this the cage door was opened. The dog did not escape but stayed on the floor of the cage receiving shocks. I realised that the feeling of being unable to escape is all part of the torture.

I don't know why bullying is still a part of medical training. It does not encourage learning and certainly does not bring out the best in members of a team. In the past, I have been cared for by kind and encouraging seniors. I am now a disillusioned junior doctor, not only because I was bullied by my consultant, but also because she is considered suitable to train junior surgeons and because evidence of her bullying is ignored by those who should help and protect junior doctors from such inappropriate behaviour.

Perhaps some doctors should ask themselves whether they are part of the caring profession at all.

[**Note:** Perhaps this is why we have such a terrible shortage of qualified doctors – the good ones have been bullied out of the health system.]

Graphic designer:

"She could never be positive about the achievements of other staff. All she could say was, 'well, you'll just have to do better.'"

Dave has worked as a graphic designer in television for twelve years. After leaving a television station interstate, he got work with a company that had recently won several large design contracts.

His was in a fairly senior position where he had some control over his own work. It was highly creative work and thoroughly enjoyable. The clients were happy with the ads being produced and the team got on well.

Right from the start Dave was bullied by another worker, the head of his unit whose job it was to delegate work to the other designers. Dave wrote, *"She seemed to be envious of my experience. I was more original, more innovative than she was. But she couldn't accept that. If I came up with an idea, she's made a catty remark like, 'Where'd you copy that from?' I know she rode the other staff hard too but she really had it in for me. She also knew that I had some of the sales people in my office from time-to-time. They'd come down to me, crying, after she'd sent them off. She could never be positive about the achievements of other staff. People would turn themselves inside out for clients, for the company and all she could say was, 'Well, you'll have to do better.' The girl in my job previously had done fantastic work. I saw some of it, really original, but she left because of the way she was treated."*

Dave was determined that no one would have a chance to criticise his work. He often worked late, not leaving until 7 or 8 pm. In one week Dave was late for work on several occasions, just through sheer tiredness. The head graphic designer reported him. *"I received a letter from the manager saying, 'If this happens again, you will be sacked.' No mention of the twelve hours or more of unpaid overtime I was doing every week! Or that one person did the work of three in that place."*

Making matters worse were events in Dave's personal life. His former flat mate had been charged with embezzling a large sum of money from the television station at which they had both worked. Dave was stunned by this turn of events. Rumours flew around the office that Dave was the 'mastermind' behind the embezzlement. *"There were stories that TVs and videos had started to go missing when I joined the TV station. I was supposed to be some sort of Mafia boss. There was even a rumour that I was a heroin addict. Mind you, I looked pretty awful by then because I was so exhausted by the whole business. I didn't seek legal advice because I'd had nothing to do with the stealing but that didn't stop the accusations."*

After that Dave withdrew from contact with others in the office. *"I felt ragged but I worked twice as hard to stop myself dwelling on the problems at work."* The head designer felt confident enough to make open personal attacks on Dave. *"I was screamed at in meetings. Once, she came into the pub where the design unit and I were having lunch and tore a strip off me there. She even managed to get my holidays delayed for a month on the grounds that it wasn't convenient for the company. She took pleasure in insulting me in public. If a client praised my work, she saw it as an opportunity to make derogatory comments about my creativity. She was angry and jealous. She was that aggro, she'd even pay out the general manager!*

"I just internalised it all. Everything around me seemed so dark. Initially I approached the line manager but he just denied anything was going on. I was told to be 'professional.' By that he meant keep your head down and shut up. I started to have violent dreams, especially about being shot in the head. It was also around the period of the conflict in Bosnia where my family comes from. Very bizarre. I got to work one day to find that someone had fired bullets through a window. That really rattled me. It was around that time I started to see a psychiatrist for depression."

The final straw came when Dave was on leave. The head designer rang and abused him for using a courier to deliver urgent work to a client. Dave rang his line manager to complain about the abuse. When he was unresponsive, Dave wrote out his resignation. *"I felt free, relieved, on a high. I didn't work for six months. It took me that long to get over the whole business. I heard later that the manager resigned because of stress. Quite a few other people have left as well. I've gone back to TV."*

Research assistant:

"My supervisor considered I was crap; that I knew nothing; that my opinion was worth nothing."

Margaret worked in a laboratory attached to a major public hospital. Her working week was split between laboratory work and seeing patients in the hospital. She began work as a research assistant on a part-time contract in the early part of the year. It was interesting work with new techniques to learn and research to keep up with. However, she quickly realised that the workload in the laboratory was heavy and needed someone working in it full-time rather than part-time. *"The people running the lab assumed that because I knew my other job so well, they could 'run into' my time allocation for the hospital job"*. Margaret discussed the situation with her boss at the hospital who indicated that as long as she got through her work with the patients, he wasn't too fussed about hours.

The laboratory supervisor started pushing Margaret into longer and longer hours, although paying her only for the three days she was employed to work. The work with patients was done after hours and squeezed around the lab timetable. The workload problems in the lab escalated when, after about six months, she was called into the Hospital Administrator's Officer's office and told she was owed ten and a half weeks annual leave which she had to take before December - seven months away.

When Margaret told him she was obliged to take annual leave before the end of the year, her laboratory supervisor became extremely angry. She had great difficulty getting him to speak to her.

In an effort to resolve matters she took him aside and suggested that they were having a bit of a communication problem. She asked him what she was doing wrong. Could he tell her how she could fix the problem? *"He immediately put the barrier up, he shut me out. Although he had always been really curt with me, he became much worse."*

Initially her supervisor was just moody and refused to respond to her questions or requests for advice. He would bark orders at her, but otherwise fail to acknowledge her presence. He sent her peremptory memos setting out her tasks. Their tone was rude and threatening. *"I thought it was my problem to start off with. I thought I didn't understand things properly because it was all so new to me, until someone else joined the laboratory."* This person had been Margaret's tutor at university. One morning he witnessed an episode in the lab where the supervisor tore into her. He was shocked and told Margaret that it wasn't her fault and that what was going on was 'rubbish.'

Margaret had been a good student and when he came into the lab her ex-tutor strongly encouraged her work. *"As he encouraged me, so my relationship with the other person in the lab deteriorated. I tried to understand why he was behaving in this way towards me. Perhaps, because my ex-tutor and I got on so well, my supervisor felt left out. But then he got on well with this other fellow too. If it hadn't been for my co-worker being so supportive, I probably wouldn't have lasted so long.*

The atmosphere in the lab was extremely tense and nerve racking. My supervisor had recently been awarded his PhD and he considered that I was crap, that I knew nothing; that my opinion was worth nothing. The other fellow had a PhD so he was on the same level and didn't get the same treatment. I couldn't even suggest anything. He was often unreasonable. He would tell me at 4 pm that this experiment had to be done today. He would never tell me the whole procedure. The protocol for an experiment would be given to me ten minutes at a time. I wouldn't be told that the protocol would actually go over three hours. To be told this at 4 o'clock! That was normal. I was doing twelve-hour days. Just absurd. When the holidays kicked in, I took it out of the two day a week job. The lab people then got very upset because I wasn't there five days a week. So I did it! I went into the lab in my holidays. I have done so many hours for them that it's disgusting, it's a joke."

Unbelievably, they were not satisfied. Margaret could never do enough. *"It became so upsetting that I sat down with the clinician, the fellow above the supervisor and in charge of the laboratory. It was the first of three meetings. I was crying because things were getting out of hand. 'What more do you want? I said to him. 'What more can I do?' He was absolutely adamant that my supervisor was behaving like this because I wasn't doing something right, that it was my problem that it was a 'personality clash.' I told him it was not a personality clash. He told me I must be in the wrong and that my supervisor, not me, had the PhD and the experience of working in US laboratories.*

The clinician was really patronising as well. He told me that the supervisor was there to stop me from 'goofing off.' It was clear from the way he brushed my complaints aside that I would get no support from him whatsoever. It was his job to deal with it but he always refused to do so. At our final meeting I took my counsellor along with me. In front of the counsellor he referred to me as 'a naughty girl needing spanking!' I look back now and think why did I put up with it? I suppose my reaction comes from my upbringing. You don't question authority. You don't question your teachers. At the same time I was so shocked that a person in authority could be so abusive or didn't even take my complaints seriously. I suppose I was a bit naïve."

"I found I couldn't talk any more, I got so upset. I couldn't talk to my parents about it. My husband is the only person I let know about it. He could see what was happening to me and wanted to come in and sort it out. I kept saying no, no, it's my problem; I've got to sort it out. So I wrote letters to the clinician setting out my problems and asking for his assistance. I sent copies to my supervisor and to the personnel department. The Personnel Manager at the hospital advised that I must work only the seven and half hours a day I was paid for and no more, as from that day. But how was I supposed to do that? I had six experiments going, all overlapping and I was responsible for them all. I don't think he understood my situation. At the same time he suggested I pull my head in because I was almost at the end of my contract and I risked not having it renewed if I made a fuss."

With great reluctance the Personnel Manager told Margaret there was a grievance procedure she could use if the other measures failed. Margaret eventually received a copy. *"The Personnel Manager insisted that I approach the Director of the Unit as he had a right to know what was going on in the lab, even through he was not immediately responsible for the work there. With some reluctance I made an appointment to see him. I also went to get counselling which was the best decision I ever made. By this time I was a snivelling heap and she was wonderfully supportive."*

The meeting with the Director of the Unit went much better than Margaret had expected. They knew each other through her work with patients. *"He told me he knew what had happened and asked what I wanted. I was really clear that there were only three things I wanted. They were for the bullying to stop; to work only the hours for which I was paid; and preservation of my work reputation which was being undermined by my supervisor. The Director agreed that this was reasonable. When I spoke to the clinician about the outcome of the meeting, he was wild. How dare I approach the Director! What business had I to do that! He said he could not agree with what I had done or my terms. At that point I told him I was taking leave."*

Margaret's contract ended the next year. She did not ask for it to be renewed. Nor was a renewal offered. In the following week she had three job interviews for lab work and was offered all three positions. She decided not to take them because she was mentally and physically exhausted. Several months later she went back to work in another lab.

Primary school teacher:

"There is supposed to be a degree of democratic decision-making in schools. All the staff are involved because the issues directly affect the way we work and our workloads. But this man constantly exercised his right of 'principal veto.' He took absolutely no notice of our views and opinions as professionals."

Jennifer was a primary school teacher for more than twenty years. She had been teaching in a rural school for three years when she took several months' long service leave. Returning to school, she found they had a new principal. The tension between some of the staff and the new principal was palpable.

"The problems were mostly around collaborative decision-making process at the school, things like developing curriculum, what sort of areas we would focus on, developing assessment procedures and so on. There is supposed to be a degree of democratic decision-making. All the staff are involved because the issues directly affect the way we work and our workloads. But this man constantly exercised his right of 'principal veto'. He took absolutely no notice of our views and opinions as professionals. The whole staff was bullied by this man."

Jennifer became a target. *"With absolutely no notice he would come into my classroom. He'd open the door, no greeting to myself or the children. He'd just walk down the side of the room and plonk himself in a chair at the back. And sit there, writing on a pad in a very obvious manner. It was very distracting and upsetting. The children would look around. They were wondering what was happening as well.*

It happened repeatedly. No reason was given by the principal for his behaviour. When Jennifer attempted to discuss the matter with him, he told her he was within his rights as a manager to do it. *"He said it was part of management assessment and he was merely doing his job."*

Jennifer's reaction was to blame herself. *"I'd get myself in a knot thinking what am I doing wrong?"* Other teachers were in the firing line as well. At a staff meeting when several complained to him of his behaviour he told them he had files on all of them. *"The implication was that he could make life very difficult for us. A principal has quite a lot of power over your career and can influence whether you get a promotion or a particular position."*

At a staff meeting several months later Jennifer expressed concern at the principal's constant exercise of the veto. She said his actions excluded staff from decision-making in any meaningful way. As the meeting closed, the principal told her that he wanted to see her in his office. *"When I went in, he was furious. He banged his fist down on the table and roared at me. 'Don't you ever contradict me again. What I'm doing is departmental policy.'"*

The principal's behaviour continued over the three years Jennifer remained at the school. Her own and other staff members' health was affected. *"During that time there were five or six stress cases among the staff. I was sick all the time as well. I seemed to get every stomach bug and flu going."* After one three day period on sick leave, she returned to school to find a note from the principal in her pigeonhole. It said that she had failed to meet an appointment and as a result he was behind in his framework preparation. It also said that she had not fulfilled her responsibilities to him and was to do so immediately. *"It made no mention of my sick leave. He was just so uncaring, going on about his administrative problems. I was in such a state that the note was enough to throw me. I started crying. I felt so upset that I could not go into the classroom. In the end I had to go home."*

Jennifer's school was one that had a reputation for innovation which was recognised by the Department. Yet feedback from the staff was ignored or not discussed by the new principal. *"If he decided that something was 'inappropriate,' a reader for example, the material would be put in an old shed. Our views were not sought. We lost some useful materials that way. On another occasion he was responsible for dismantling a resources room we had taken a great deal of time and energy to organise. We came to school to find the children packing it up. Again, no consultation."*

The principal's arbitrary decision-making caused friction in other areas. Experienced teachers who had for years supervised student teachers were told that that responsibility was to be taken away from them. The reason given was that their programs were not up-to-date. *"He did this when he had been at the school for only six months. He was not in a position to know if the programs were up to scratch or how well those teachers supervised."*

Concern among the staff was sufficient for them to contact the union. The union held a meeting away from the school to discuss the staff's problems with the principal. All but a few members of the staff attended. The union notified the principal of the staff's concerns. The principal subsequently called a meeting of all staff where he completely dismissed their concerns. *"He was extremely angry. He shouted that if we couldn't stand the heat we should get out of the kitchen. Then he threw a pile of transfer forms on the table."*

The atmosphere at the school grew even tenser. Morale was low. The staff contacted the CEO who acknowledged their concerns but did nothing. The union was unable to stop the principal's behaviour. One staff member was hospitalised with a stress ulcer.

The harassment continued unabated. Jennifer went out of her way to avoid the principal. *"I didn't even have to speak to him to feel agitated. I'd get panicky if I saw him in the corridor outside my classroom. It became so bad that for the last couple of months I had to have the union representative with me every time I met with the principal. At a 'clearing of the air' meeting, instead of being constructive, he decimated me. He told me that many people found me hard to work with. I knew this was completely untrue but I was devastated. The union rep was astonished at his behaviour.*

"He was relentless. At one time he rang me at home while I was off sick demanding that I come to school on an urgent matter. I got myself out of bed and drove to the school in a terribly worried state of mind. What could it be that was so urgent? Had some awful thing happened? When I got there he insisted I go over a document with him. But it was just an exercise in minor nit-picking grammar. That was all the emergency was. It could easily have waited."

138

Jennifer ended up leaving teaching. *"I finally got a 'C' placement out of there. It meant I was placed in a different school each term. At the end of the second placement I was exhausted. I went part-time for twelve months after that. But it all caught up with me. I don't think I can ever go back to teaching."* She is now studying for a master's degree and works part-time as a sales assistant.

Project officer:

A project officer was subjected to bullying by a colleague over a number of months. The behaviour directed at the project officer was hostile and harassing and included:

- Often finding fault with his work when it was inappropriate to do so (repeated unreasonable behaviour);
- Regularly subjecting him to offensive verbal abuse;
- Threatening to get him sacked and telling him that he and his family would end up in the gutter; and
- Publicly making disparaging comments about his relationship with his wife.

A number of incidents were witnessed by other employees. The colleague's bullying tactics had an adverse psychological effect on the project officer. Normally positive and outgoing, he became severely stressed and anxious. Eventually, he was unable to continue working for the organisation due to stress injury. (The behaviour created a risk to health and safety.)

"I don't think I can ever go back to teaching." She is now studying for a master's degree and works part-time as a sales assistant.

Apprentice panel beater:

In 1995, a 17 year-old apprentice panel beater in Melbourne was locked in his toilet cubicle as paint-stripping solvent was poured under the door and set alight by his 25 year-old supervisor. He suffered critical burns to 50 per cent of his body and was hospitalised for eight weeks. For almost two years after the incident, he was forced to wear a burns body suit. He suffered from depression and will probably never work again. His supervisor was fined $2,000 and the company that employed him another $5,000.

(Neales, When rites go wrong 6 September, 1997 Good Weekend P. 32)

Female apprentice diesel fitter mechanic:

In 1997, a 20 year-old female apprentice diesel fitter mechanic was subjected to workplace violence simply because she was the first female apprentice at the mine. She was bullied, called a slut, subjected to propositions and generally pushed around. She was subsequently awarded $48,000 in damages.

(Neales, When rites go wrong 6 September, 1997 Good Weekend P. 32)

Pizza delivery youth:

In August of 1997, a 27-year-old pizza store manager was found guilty of four counts of criminal assault against a 19-year-old delivery boy. The manager had tied the boy's feet with rope, placed him on the bonnet of a car and driven backwards and forwards with the boy sprawled across the front. He had also sprayed the boy with a fire extinguisher whilst he was in a toilet cubicle, jammed his leg in a door and cut the boy's face with his watch. The store manager was fined $650 and placed on a 12 month, $500 good behaviour bond.

(But boss guilty of attacking pizza boy' [14 August, 1998] Daily Telegraph. P9)

Case (a):

Workers at a medium-sized technical equipment rental firm have been having commercial difficulties, have reported health problems, including sleeplessness, lack of self-esteem, distress and increased consumption of alcohol, which they and/or their medical practitioners have associated with the work situation. The work situation includes, but is not limited to:

- Employees being yelled at;
- Use of personally abusive language by management to employees;
- Many staff feeling distressed at work;
- Work overload, due to staff doing the same work previously done by more people;
- Large amounts of unpaid overtime;
- No recognition of effort put in by staff.

Workers who have complained about the bullying and abusive behaviours have been sacked or isolated at work. Others are therefore afraid to speak up. Staff have asked the WorkCover Authority for assistance and although it has witnessed management shouting at and threatening staff - they have not intervened.

Case (b):

Another worker's professional credibility has been repeatedly attacked, including accusations of plagiarism by colleague, apparently triggered by rejection of sexual advances. A vicious verbal circle of abuse was not controlled, but supported by the HR manager. Health problems mean the worker is unable to return to work.

Case (c):

A caller to the ACTU helpline reported that unreasonable demands; threatening behaviour; shouting, swearing and insults; being told 'or else'; feeling unsafe; and being afraid to speak up, are all features of her former workplace - a large fruit processing/packing company. All the workers (who are mostly casuals with high job insecurity) are subjected to bullying behaviour by the management, except for a select few, who are 'in cahoots' with the management.

Case (d):

When witnesses are not present, a young female staff member is harassed by the senior manager of a major department store because of her physical appearance. Fear of losing employment has prevented her from lodging a formal complaint. Tactics used include: blaming her for errors that were not her fault; continually changing instructions and not being satisfied with her work which was previously considered more than acceptable; questioning interactions between people in the workplace which are an important part of the job; and micro-control over attendance, despite their willingness to work after hours. When bullying started, the young woman was not a union member, but she has since joined and sought assistance.

Case (e):

A young woman working full-time at a large café in metropolitan Melbourne discovered that all the employees were being underpaid. She raised this in an anonymous letter to her employer. However, she was pulled aside the following day by one of the owners of the business and asked if she had written the letter. She confirmed she had. From that day on she was bullied. Examples include:

- Only spoken to when she was needed to do something;
- Rostered to have lunch breaks on her own when formerly staff members were on lunch breaks together;
- Being made to wash dishes for three to four hours at a time, where previously she would wash dishes for a maximum of half hour;
- Not being provided with assistance when needed;
- Threatened with dismissal if she 'whinged,' or for 'spreading rumours';
- Had been promised 9 am to 5 pm Monday to Friday, when a position became available, but instead gave that roster to a new employee;
- Threatened by owner's family because they claimed she had called them 'a name' six months earlier.
- Finally she was sacked for apparently being "disruptive." An unfair dismissal application has been made.

Case (f):

A linen manufacturer who was found to have wrongfully dismissed a worker admitted that the threat of the sack was a motivational technique that had been used by the firm for ten years. In its decision, the Industrial Relations Commission found the worker was sacked because she failed to 'apologise' for her low productivity on a particular day. The IRC said this was not a valid reason for termination. The employer gave evidence that he had given notice of termination to the employee on twelve separate occasions for alleged 'bad performance,' but on each occasion before the notice expired her performance had improved and employment continued. The employer told the Commission he had given another employee notice of termination 27 times over a ten-year period, without actually sacking her. The following is taken from transcript:

Commissioner: *"[Your supervisor] says you used to give motivation speeches and part of that speech was 'if it's unsatisfactory you will be sacked, instant dismissal ...?"*

Employer: *"That was group therapy."*

Commissioner: *"Yes, it's strange group therapy. What I want to know is this, you said at one stage that you thought that terminating them was a bit of a prod to keep their production up. Is that correct?"*

Employer: *"Yes, I think that ... it's not probably appropriate by using the word 'prod.' It's a motivator."*

The Commission said in its decision that, if it were not for the statutory cap of 26 weeks, the employee would have been awarded even more compensation!

Case (g):

Where plagiarism of ideas and poaching of contacts by line managers blocked advancement, a major reduction in responsibilities destroyed this worker's self esteem. Constant and unwarranted questioning of his integrity - over business travel and use of credit card, made him lose face at work. As he had a high level of commitment to the organisation, these actions took a high toll on his mental and physical well-being. Now, he is unable to work in gainful employment anywhere.

Case (h):

In a relatively small public service workplace, the general manager continually verbally abuses staff. Those who have stood up to the manager have been retrenched or sacked. Many staff are on short-term contracts, so they are unwilling to support each other for fear of non-renewal of contracts. Work overload is common. An example of organisational bullying where the terms of employment - short fixed term contracts - compound the problems and the financial difficulties of the group are used as an excuse for poor treatment.

Case (i):

A grocery manager in a large retail chain has been harassing young men in the night-fill team and produce department over a period of years. There has been a history of similar behaviour in the manager's previous store. Some of his actions include:

- Failing to allow workers to take leave when owed;
- Isolating workers;

- Constantly criticising and calling workers belittling names, etc. 'peasant';
- Making offensive and disturbing comments about workers' private lives;
- Making threats to sexually assault the workers and members of their families.

These work conditions became unbearable and have severely affected the health of at least one of the young workers. The manager was finally demoted and transferred to the adjacent small town.

Case (j):

Daniel works a morning shift in the produce department. His elderly father suffered a stroke so Daniel needed to travel approximately seven hours by car to visit him each weekend to help with tasks and rehabilitation. He advised the company. Three weeks after this advice, he was handed a roster change, which involved working every night. He tried to negotiate to have at least the Friday night off and work Friday morning so he could visit his father, but the store manager refused.

This case ended up in the Industrial Commission with a workable resolution, but when Daniel returned to the store, fault was found with all of his work; he was constantly criticised for 'talking' on the job; unrealistic tasks were set by his manager; and he was watched all the time. In the end, he was forced to take sick leave and now has a workers compensation case under investigation for stress and bullying.

Conclusion

Workplace bullying occurs in all kinds of businesses, large and small. It occurs world-wide and seems to be escalating rather than slowing down. Unions, human resources and employee relations staff need to be diligent and stop workplace bullying in its tracks. Every company should have *enforceable* workplace bullying policies in place.

The only way this will happen if laws are put in place to protect innocent employees from workplace bullying, harassment and violence.

Chapter 11

HOW TO PREVENT AND STOP WORKPLACE BULLYING

AUSTRALIA

A few countries have taken the important step of implementing legislation that protects all employees against workplace bullying, harassment and violence. Australia is *not* one of those countries. It protects against only a small portion of bullying situations. There is no specific legal jurisdiction under which workplace bullying has been addressed, although it can breach numerous laws including unfair dismissal, sexual harassment and discrimination. Even in those cases, proving it can be a problem.

Only specific legislation can protect workers. It's been proven that no amount of *"Codes of Conduct"* or *"Guidance Notes"* will do this. Our legislation does *not* cover most situations where a bully makes another worker's life a living hell.

There have been many governmental and union-based studies into the incidence of workplace harassment. Millions of Australian taxpayer's dollars have been used to hire Task Forces to study bullying, harassment and violence. However most of their findings and recommendations have been ignored and government regulations have not been updated. So Australian companies still harbour and promote bullies and bullying behaviour.

What do some say about workplace bullying? They identify it as people being "too sensitive" or it's a "personality conflict" or "poor interpersonal relationships" - but bullying - they can't see it that way. *Well, it is bullying.*

In Australia, if an employee complains about bullying - s/he's labelled a "woos" or a "sissy." How dare these bullies try to make the victim feel guilty when they're the ones that are in the wrong! And how dare companies look the other way! This Cro-Magnon style of behaviour seems to be a way of life in Australia and it must stop.

It's the responsibility of every company to provide a workplace that's a safe and healthy place to work in. It has far too high an impact on the culture of the business, the way the business functions and the way it deals with its customers. There needs to be a corporate responsibility to deal with the bullying behaviour and recognise the signs of a toxic workplace. Employers need to set policies and procedures in place and take decisive action to deal with every bullying issue. Senior executives must not ignore bullying episodes. Unfortunately, many senior executives also bully their staff. They need to examine their company vision and see that *every* employee (including themselves) follows that vision.

Executives can show they care about employees by providing an environment free of harassment of any kind - not just lip service - but demonstrated by their own behaviour. It doesn't matter how good the technology is in a company - it's the employees that make things happen. Unhappy, harassed employees simply don't accomplish this. And it costs the company dearly.

A key impediment to reform is that many managers, supervisors and staff were trained in an environment where such behaviour was the *accepted* method of teaching, instructing or managing employees. It's this culture that needs to be changed through education and awareness and by taking practical steps in the workplace to minimise incidents of harassment.

However, self-regulation of bullying has not worked and existing laws don't provide adequate protection - because it is so ingrained in the company culture.

Workplace health and Safety acts in most States say employers have an obligation to ensure the health and safety of their workers, but have no specific wording that covers the majority of workplace bullying, harassment and violence situations. State *"Guidance notes"* and *"Codes of Conduct"* (not their laws) are making stabs at dealing with this behaviour, but they fall short of the mark by insisting that bullying must be ongoing. To the victim - one incident of bullying can be enough and should have all the protection of the law to deal with it.

Where it can be established that your stress is due to workplace bullying, you may be entitled to make a claim under Workers' Compensation, but unconfirmed reports state that routinely WorkCover reject 95% of stress leave claims related to workplace bullying. So, it's a good idea to approach your union as well.

Women can contact their state's *Working Women's Centre* www.wwc.org.au to help them prepare their claims. The Working

Women's Centres provide a free and confidential service that provides information and advice to women on any issue related to work. The Centres can also help in negotiations with employers on workplace issues or lodge complaints with the Human Rights and Equal Opportunity or Anti-Discrimination Commissions.

Workplace stress management

There are many areas where managers can work to reduce stress in order to create a workplace environment where there is higher productivity and fewer stress-related claims, sick days and accidents. To do this, managers should:

- Identify all the possible causes of stress;
- Eliminate harassment in the workplace. Conduct an assessment of all areas of workplace life that could contribute to stress.
- Determine the frequency and duration of stressors and the health impact on employees;
- Find ways of controlling stress levels by modifying the workplace, work systems or management style.

This process should be on-going. Frustration through lack of control can lead to a steady build-up of stress. Those who rate their jobs as demanding, but who have little control are more likely to suffer from workplace stress. A workers compensation claim for stress should be managed in the same way as all other occupational injury or illness. *Unfortunately most claims for occupational stress are initially disputed by the insurance company.* Those who have been subject to workplace harassment and have been forced to take stress leave will have to be diligent in their efforts to prove their case. And this is at a time when they are stressed to the limit to begin with.

Stressed employees worked to death

Changing work practices, the demise of job security, escalating demands, violence and bullying in the workplace are all leading to tired and stressed out employees prone to heart attacks, strokes, disease and depression and are more likely to take their own lives.

UK research shows that employees exposed to stress for at least half their working lives are 25 per cent more likely to die from a heart attack and have 50 per cent greater odds of suffering a fatal stroke. The research conducted by the UK's Trade Union Congress exposes stress as Britain's number one health hazard.

In Australia one of the leading causes of stress is overwork and incidences of the condition are on the rise. According to Australian research:

The ACTU says Australia has the second longest working hours in the OECD and on current trends, will soon have the longest. It says 31 per cent of Australian employees now work hours that would be illegal in Europe, adding that we now have one of the worst records in the world.

Teachers are one of the most overworked of all professions, with escalating demands now reaching titanic proportions. A new survey by the Australian Psychological Society says about 30 per cent of university academic staff responding to its survey said they were working more than 55 hours a week, more than eleven hours per day. Yet a study of work-related stress in Japan showed men working eleven hours were two and a half times more likely to suffer a heart attack than those working an eight-hour day.

NSW WorkCover says cases of occupational stress jumped 21 per cent between 1999/2000 and 2000/2001, with female incidences increasing at a faster rate than males.

Meanwhile, a national health survey from the Australian Bureau of Statistics says about 11.2 per cent of the workforce is taking an average of three days sick leave each fortnight in an attempt to cope with stress levels.

NSW Labor Council's occupational health and safety watchdog Mary Yaager says the research shows stress is a major problem. *"Australian employers are literally working their staff to death, with on-the-job stress, violence and fatigue edging their way up to become major causes of workplace fatalities. Stress and depression are caused by people not being able to balance their work and family lives, by workplace violence, long hours, a lack of fulfilment and fatigue.*

"Escalating demands as a result of downsizing without taking the well-being of employees into account mean they have been forced to take on more and more responsibilities with less and less support.

"This is just one way the changing labour market is favouring practices that contribute to rising employee stress levels.

"Employers in the short-term might be maximising profits, but this situation is not sustainable and unfortunately it is the workers that are paying the deadly price," Mrs Yaager says.

UNITED STATES

At the **Campaign Against Workplace Bullying** based in Bellingham, Washington, president Gary Namie talked about "bully-proofing" - recognising that the problem isn't you - it's the harasser - and about "bully-busting" or exposing the troublemaker. *"You need to divorce your identity from the job,"* says Namie, a psychologist. Sometimes, people need the support of a professional counsellor to do this. And it's psychologically healthier he says, for the victim to reveal the bully. *"You are not leaving with your tail between your legs."*

He advises appealing to the bottom line, how the bully is harming morale and productivity. *'If the victim speaks emotionally about being hurt, he's likely denigrated as thin-skinned - a loose cannon."* Many choose to stay and fight out of principle or practical need. Finding another job is rarely easy, especially in today's economy. Going to the boss's boss can be smart or suicidal. *"He might have hired the person and likes his style,"* warns Namie.

The backing of colleagues boosts a case. At a head office meeting, a sales representative for a retail chain was explaining how her manager bullied her, when four other staff members showed up on her behalf. They presented a letter detailing how the manager had singled her out for discipline and harassment. *"I was taken aback that they came,"* says the woman. *"A former manager told them I needed help and they showed up. I know it had a big impact on the meeting."* With the support of her union, she was eventually transferred to a different store. The manager later quit.

But don't count on support, say bullying experts. Many co-workers are afraid they'll be the next target if they speak up. To do nothing, though; can be dangerous. A person ends up taking all their depression and anger home.

CANADA

In Canada's Labour Code (which covers federally regulated employees) the definition of danger has been broadened. This could allow for protection against bullying say lawyers, although it has not yet been tested. In addition, a draft policy of the Workers' Safety Insurance Board includes stress-related illnesses, which if adopted, could allow bullied employees to claim any illness that resulted from bullying as a compensable injury, says labour lawyer Jeffrey Goodman of Heenan Blaikie.

July 30, 2003 - According to a survey from Environics for the **Women's Executive Network** (**WXN™**) most Canadians who report striking the right work-life balance are achieving this by taking charge of their life, through personal action or through their attitude. Far fewer credit employers or spouses or family for their success in this area.

"While conventional wisdom says that working for a flexible employer and having a reasonable amount of discretionary income are important factors in achieving the proper work-life balance, those Canadians who feel they have succeeded in achieving the proper balance have taken control of their own destiny," said Jane Armstrong, Senior Vice President of Environics. *"They are creating this balance for themselves and not depending on help from a spouse or from their employer."*

Among those who say they have struck the right balance, a total of 70 per cent of responses relate to factors about taking charge of their life through their attitude or action, including good time management, good planning, health or fitness, limiting their time at work, not worrying about insignificant things, will-power, making the time, hobbies, etc. A total of 16 per cent mention factors related to their spouse or family, such as a supportive spouse or partner, a stay-at-home spouse or partner or their family or household. A total of 15 per cent mention work-related factors, such as their work situation, flexible work arrangements or supportive workplace policies. A total of 21 per cent mention other factors.

SWEDEN

The movement against bullying in the workplace is gathering momentum. Sweden is one of the countries at the forefront. *It's had anti-bullying legislation since 1993.* The ordinance of the Swedish National Board of Occupational Safety and Health contains measures against Victimisation at Work. Studies estimate that 25 per cent of employees would be submitted to workplace harassment for at least a six month period at some point during their careers. 3.5 per cent of the

Swedish working population experienced workplace harassment at least weekly for a period of at least six months.

NORWAY

Data from a large Norwegian study showed no difference in the prevalence of workplace harassment between men and women. However, 49 per cent of the victims reported men as the perpetrators and 30 per cent reported women as the harassers. It found that 8.6 per cent of respondents had experienced workplace harassment behaviours during the past six months.

MALAYSIA

Malaysia does not have a formal method of dealing with sexual harassment in the workplace, but steps are being taken to alleviate that situation.

In April, 2002 a newspaper report states that the Human Resources Ministry may make it mandatory for companies to adopt the Code of Practice on sexual harassment. The ministry, through its Labour Department would promote it during its annual visits to workplaces. Many companies are aware of sexual harassment, but they do not know how to handle the cases. Many smaller companies did not adopt the code because they lacked staff with expertise. They receive fifty to sixty reports on sexual harassment every year, most involving sexual intimidation or annoyance.

The Minister, Datuk Fong Chan Onn said he was disappointed that only 241 large companies and a handful of others had adopted the code. In light of this, his ministry and the Attorney-General's Chambers were discussing the possibility of making it mandatory for all companies to adopt the code. He said, *"Sexual harassment at the workplace is a problem that has not been given sufficient attention and if left unchecked, it will create a hostile work environment."*

Chapter 12

WHAT ARE THE ANSWERS?

Lack of supervisory training

The vast majority of supervisors and managers in Australia simply don't know how to supervise. A supervisor is anyone who is responsible for getting work done through other people. This includes clerical supervisors, foremen/women, lead hands, managers, executives, vice presidents, general managers and even CEOs. Because most companies don't provide even basic supervisory training, these supervisors are forced to clone their role models - other supervisors - who don't know how to supervise either! Monkey see - monkey do! Most have been bullying their employees without realising that their behaviour is contrary to good business practice. It's a vicious circle with the employees in the middle. These difficult supervisors use bullying and harassing behaviour or do such things as:

- Use tantrums to control their employees;
- Embarrass their staff by disciplining them in front of workmates or clients;
- Label staff's behaviour (stupid, dumb) or make sarcastic remarks, instead of trying to correct the actual behaviour of the staff member;
- Harass staff (either through bullying or sexual harassment);
- Are perfectionists or control freaks and expect everything to be done perfectly. Just because they can do the job in ten minutes (they have fifteen years' experience) they expect the newcomer to do it in the same amount of time with the same amount of accuracy;
- Don't give recognition for a job well done. Instead, they concentrate on the two percent of the things their staff do incorrectly, instead of the ninety-eight percent they do properly;
- When dealing with customer complaints, they don't back up their staff and don't give employees a chance to tell their side of the story before acting. (They should say to the client, *"let me investigate this and I'll get back to you."*);

- Don't provide an up-to-date job description with key performance indicators and standards of performance for the tasks performed by their staff;
- Don't provide the necessary training to fill the gap between job requirements and employee's skills;
- Conduct performance appraisals on staff without a proper job description upon which to base their evaluation. (If the employee doesn't know what's expected of him/her and the supervisor doesn't know either - how can a fair evaluation of the performance be made?)
- Have one set of company rules for staff - another for themselves. Bend the rules when clients go over the head of front-line staff, causing embarrassment for staff members;
- No set policy and procedure manuals are available. Rules and regulations of the company are not clearly defined;
- Do nothing to improve the employee's interest in their jobs. Some are afraid their employees are now ready to compete for their job, so do as little as possible to develop their skills for their next step up. (It's a proven fact that more supervisors are *not* promoted because there is nobody prepared to take over their existing job);
- Are not available when their staff needs their help. They say they have an "open door policy" but are always "too busy" to deal with their staff's problems;
- Won't listen to their staff's suggestions about better ways to complete tasks. The person doing the job normally has the best ideas on how to do the job better, faster and more efficiently.
- Nepotism is rampant and friends and relative working in the same department.

Companies need to change their management approaches and corporate culture. They need to train anyone who supervises others - *before* putting them into the position or very shortly thereafter. These supervisors need to be aware of all the Acts and regulations relating to workplace bullying, harassment, abuse and violence and how to deal with it in the workplace.

Here is a summary of my findings and recommendations to overcome workplace bullying, harassment and violence in the workplace:

Finding: Most government departments responsible for the safety and well-being of employees fail to protect workers from workplace bullying, harassment and violence. Many governmental departments have spent a fortune on task forces to upgrade their regulations relating to workplace bullying, but have ignored the findings of these groups. Instead of changing the legislation to state in fact, "thou shalt not," and give the consequences should companies break those regulations, many have released *"Guidence Notes'* to businesses. Remember that: ***Regulations have the force of law, whereas "Codes of Conduct" and "Guidance Notes" contain only guidance material*** so they can be and are mainly ignored.

Recommendation: Review the findings of the taskforces and implement the changes they've recommended. Make them law - rather than leave it up to the discretion of individual companies to do the right thing. Have regular training sessions where government representatives make sure that supervisors and managers know their responsibilities relating to violence, bullying and harassment and back these up with the regulations in the acts that state these. I know training is done now, but most are not backed up by government regulations with "teeth."

Forget about sending *"Guidance Notes"* to businesses (unless they're just information on how to implement the government regulations shown in the different Acts). Send them copies of the legislated regulations and make sure they abide by them. Canberra should be setting an example and all laws related to Work-place Health & Safety, Occupational Health & Safety, Human Rights & Equal Opportunity, Anti-Discrimination and WorkCover should be the same across Australia. It shouldn't matter where an employee lives - the laws concerning violence, bullying and harassment should be the same. And the consequences to companies should be fast and effective.

Finding: Companies are not forced to post Zero-Tolerance Harassment and Bullying policies (should be made law) for their companies to see. Many companies see bullying as a way of doing business and they won't change unless forced to do so by government regulations. No amount of *"Guidance Notes"* will do this.

Recommendation: Companies must learn (through television if necessary) that workplace bullying is simply not acceptable. There have been a few stabs at doing this (which were well done) but it's simply not enough. Businesses need to be reminded that well-run companies always have clear policies and procedures (available to all employees) relating to human resource issues (such as bullying, discipline, written warnings, grievance procedures, sexual harassment, WorkCover, equal employment etc.) and that they are enforced.

Routinely, candidates that apply for positions should ask potential companies, *"Does your company have written policies and procedures relating to workplace bullying and harassment?"*

Only then, will some companies realise that they should have them in place. If they don't have them in place, the employee will know that his or her chances are slim that these companies will deal effectively with bullying episodes.

Finding: If companies don't deal effectively with bullying incidents, discipline the bullies and stop the unacceptable behaviour, employees will continue to have no other options but to quit their jobs or take their bullies (and the companies they work for) to court. This long and drawn-out process can take anywhere from two to five years to accomplish. Not only does it take a long time, but it can cost the employee tens of thousands of dollars in legal costs (often $50 - $100,000). In many cases, settlement does not even cover the legal expenses and *fines do not go to the victim*. Most come away feeling like they've been "had" and that the company (that defended the bully) appear to have condoned that despicable behaviour. In the interim, the victims may have to work side-by-side with their bully until their allegations are dealt with.

Recommendation: Bullying will continue, unless governments get off their duffs and legislate regulations that have some teeth in them relating to workplace bullying, harassment and violence. These government departments should be protecting the workers and supplying the legal assistance to the bullied employees. Employees should not have to bear the costs to legally stop their bully. Court fines of the companies should pay for the employees' legal fees.

Finding: If the employees are so stressed that they must go on stress leave while they wait for the bullying charges to be dealt with, they may or may not receive payment for that stress leave from their employer's WorkCover insurance company. Unfortunately victims often won't know that the payment will not be paid until three or four months into the stress leave - causing more financial grief to the victims. WorkCover insurance companies need to be monitored to ensure that this does not happen.

Recommendation: These WorkCover insurance companies must investigate every stress leave claim lodged by bullied employees with an open mind. They need to be able to see the issue from the employee's point of view and assume that the victim is indeed in dire need of their stress leave. I can only assume that because the company the employee is working for pays for the WorkCover, that the insurance company sees the issue only from the company's point of view.

Although WorkCover insurance companies state that they cover stress leave, I have unconfirmed reports that even with proper medical documentation, most of them automatically reject 95 per cent of all claims. Therefore employees are forced to fight WorkCover insurers to obtain the money they should so rightly receive. The last thing these stressed-out bullied people need is another battle to fight - but often that's exactly what happens! Many give up – they're too worn down to keep fighting.

Finding: The phenomenal cost of workplace bullying must stop. It's not only the employee who pays by going through the trauma, but companies pay dearly through loss of productivity of the victim and surrounding staff, payment for stress leave and having to replace either the bully or the victim (who often leaves in disgust). And how about the witnesses to the bullying? This results in lowered morale, they become less motivated to do a good job and become disgusted themselves when they observe that nothing is done to correct the bullying behaviour. They wonder *"Will I be next? What or who will protect me if the bully starts picking on me."*

Recommendation: Australian industry must be made aware of the horrific costs of workplace bullying. 1,100 Victorian claims for compensation as a result of workplace violence, harassment and bullying cost $26 million. Bullying costs the Australian economy up to $13 billion a year in absenteeism, compensation, management time and lost productivity - and these are not the most recent figures. With approximately 19.9 million population in Australia that means that companies stand to lose an average of $653.25 per person per year due to bullying and its after-effects. Not good for Australian business or the GNP!

Finding: Some bullied employees never recover from the trauma. Self-esteem plummets and stress levels rise. This can cripple the most assertive individual.

Recommendation: The only resolution to this is to stop bullying behaviour in its tracks. This can only occur with:

- The support of proper government legislation to deal with workplace bullying, harassment and violence;
- Monitoring to see that companies follow the regulations;
- Giving support to the "little guy" (the employee);
- A complete changeover from the macho, draconian way of supervision that's part of the Australian business culture.

Finding: If co-workers don't rally behind the victim, the target can suffer additional emotional trauma of having to go through the ordeal alone.

Recommendation: Many victims I spoke with were as traumatised by the lack of support they received from people who witnessed the bullying. Their faith in their fellow man was shattered (in some cases never to be restored) because their fellow workers refused to corroborate their information. *Witnesses to bullying behaviour must speak up - shame on them for not doing so.* I don't know how they can look themselves in the mirror every day - how they could even contemplate letting down a co-worker. The truth is the truth and witnesses should get some backbone and defend the victim - because who knows - they may be the bully's next target.

No longer should a person be ridiculed because s/he dobbed in a bully. Nor should it be acceptable for observers to stand by and not get involved in supporting the victim.

Finding: Families suffer due to the victim's agitation and stress. Spouses feel helpless as they watch their loved ones dwindle in stature before their eyes. The often carefree individual - suddenly can't function. The job they once loved, now involves a daily struggle to get up and go into work.

Recommendation: Until the victims receive the support they need from all avenues, these families will continue to suffer. Companies should be encouraged to have Employee Assistance Programs that provide free psychological treatment for employees facing trauma.

Finding: Although Australian corporations preach that they advocate that their employees should maintain a good work/life balance, many are literally working their employees to death. Stress levels are at all-time highs with no end in sight.

Recommendation: Laws must be enforced that protect workers from overwork with statutes such as:

- Hours of work must be confined within a period of 12 consecutive hours in any one day.
- If an employee works 44 hours or less in a one week period, but works more than 8 hours in any day, overtime shall be paid for each hour in excess of 8 hours per day.
- If an employee works more than 44 hours in a one-week period, the hours of work in excess of 8 hours in each day shall be totalled and the hours of work in excess of 44 hours in a week shall be calculated. The overtime rate shall be paid for whichever is greater. Employees must receive no less than one and one-half times their regular wage for overtime pay.
- If requested, instead of overtime pay, employees can receive time off with regular pay equal to the number of overtime hours worked.
- All employees who are not exempt are paid overtime pay. Exempt employees are supervisors or managerial staff - confidential in nature. If the person is a "working supervisor" or lead hand, who in addition to supervising staff, do essentially the same work as his/her staff; they are *not* exempt and should be paid overtime.

Finding: Many victims who leave the company without a proper resolution (and some even with one) are not able to obtain a proper reference from the bullying company. The target's faith in their ability to continue in their chosen field or to even do their job plummets and many spend months being unemployed. Often they must seek psychiatric help to get their feet back on the road to recovery.

Recommendation: In the ideal world, the regulatory bodies would be the ones taking the company to court and the employee would be supported both financially and emotionally through the process. Fines should be paid to the bully – not put back into a fund or the court's pockets.

After it's been proven that bullying took place and the employee has left the company - part of the settlement would be that the company must give a favourable reference. I know of one company that simply refused to give *any* kind of reference - leaving the receiver of the information wondering why the person left the company. No reference - is as damaging as a bad reference.

Conclusion

As I conducted research for this book I found myself becoming more and more depressed at the way the world deals with workplace bullying, harassment and violence. As an Australian, I became more and more disgusted with the lack of governmental action to stop it. We are not a third world country, yet we treat some of our people in the most appalling way! Australia should be ashamed of this governmental and corporate disgrace! Employees *must* be protected and unless governments become proactive - this will not happen.

The bottom line is that *"Codes of Practice"* and *"Guidance Notes"* are useless unless legislation (Acts relating to workplace bullying, harassment and violence) have regulations with some teeth. Occupational Health and Safety regulations appear to be the most logical Acts to include this coverage.

Australian society needs to look seriously at cleaning up the violence we now see in several of our sports. Sport used to be "sportsmanlike" but the violent actions we see in our football players can not be called sporting at all. The AFL and Aussie Rules administratiuon staff should look at the image they are giving to young Australian supporters. This is *not* sportsmanship – *it's bullying* and sets a terrible example for the impressionasble youngsters of Australia. They should be ashamed of themselves.

My next two books cover the lead-up to workplace bullying and talk about *Dealing with Domestic Violence and Child Abuse - Society's Judicial*

Disgrace! and *Dealing with School Bullying – Society's Edicational Disgrace!*.

If bullying does not stop in the home, it will be taken into our schools. If it isn't stopped there, it will then be taken into the workplace. Bullies must be stopped - and you can help make it happen!

Appendixes

Workplace bullying reports

There were many organisations and government departments that assisted me with my research. Their reports are found in the following Appendices to this chapter. Some of their information duplicates what I have said earlier in this book:

1. Australian Council of Trade Unions (ACTU Australia)

2. Australian Nurses Federation (ANF)

3. Australian Manufacturing Workers' Union (AMWU)

4. Cover to Cover - Magazine for CGU Workers insurance Clients

5. Independent Education Union (IEU)

6. Royal District Nursing Service (RDNS)

7. Australian Capital Territory

8. Victoria

9. New South Wales

10. Queensland

11. South Australia

12. Western Australia

13. Tasmania

14. Northern Territory

15. New law 1 July, 2015

Appendix 1

AUSTRALIAN COUNCIL OF TRADE UNIONS

"Being Bossed around is Bad for your Health" - ACTU Australia

www.actu.asn.au (A brochure distributed by the ACTU states:)

What is Bullying?

Many people think bullying is persecuting or 'ganging up' on individuals. But that's only part of the story. Most bullying is not so obvious. Bossing people around, intimidating, threatening or keeping them under pressure is also bullying. This is the most common form of bullying in Australian workplaces and is a risk to health and safety. Research by the ACTU and others reveals that this is the most common form of bullying in Australian workplaces.

Those seen to be most vulnerable include young workers, apprentices and trainees; women; older workers; and people of non-English speaking background, who may experience sexual and/or racist harassment. However bullying can happen to anyone. It occurs across all industries and in all professions.

Bullying is a growing problem:

Changes at work, brought about by deregulation, privatisation restructuring, downsizing and technological change, have contributed to an erosion of working conditions for many Australians. Casualisation and job insecurity create a climate where people are increasingly powerless and at risk of being bullied. The push for ever higher 'productivity' in an increasingly competitive environment can result in bullying tactics being used to drive workers to the limit.

Workers get the blame for poor performance or low productivity, no matter how well they do their jobs.

Health and safety effects:

Bullying can affect our health in many ways. Being bossed around is a major cause of stress at work. At worst, it can result in serious physical illness, alcohol and drug use, depression or suicidal thoughts. Other symptoms include headaches, sleep difficulties, high blood pressure, digestive problems, tearfulness, anxiety, nausea, anger, irritability and loss of motivation, concentration, self-confidence and morale. The effects of bullying also place pressure on family and friends.

The significant effects which working conditions have on the health of workers are largely underestimated or ignored in this country. If you and/or your colleagues are experiencing any of the signs and symptoms described here, then the cause may well be bullying. ***Bullying must not be tolerated.***

Who's doing the bullying?

Bullying can happen between co-workers and they may also be harassed by clients, customers, contractors or others from outside the workplace. However, research shows more workers are bullied by employers and managers than by fellow workers.

What can be done?

Everyone has the right to dignity and respect and to a safe and healthy environment at work. If bullying is happening in your workplace, there are ways to deal with it.

- Get the issues out in the open by talking with fellow workers.
- Hold a meeting away from the workplace if necessary.
- Get the workplace health and safety representative, OHS committee or other delegates to take up the issues.

Contact your union for assistance under these processes to:
- o   Identify the most important issues.
- o   Keep records of incidents, so they are not forgotten or misrepresented.
- o   Raise the issues with the employer through workplace representatives.
- o   Arrange counselling and/or other assistance for distressed workers if needed.

Under occupational health and safety legislation, employers have a legal duty to control all health and safety hazards in the workplace. This includes organisational structures and behaviours that may lead to bullying.

Employers have to consult with their employees about policies and procedures to eliminate all hazards and risks from the workplace. There is no excuse for causing or allowing bullying. If an employer will not act on these issues, health and safety representatives, in most states, can issue provisional improvement notices (PINS). These are official notices to an employer that a health and safety issue exists and needs to be fixed.

In all states, government health and safety inspectors can direct employers to fix problems in the workplace and may issue prohibition or improvement notices.

Some forms of bullying are outlawed by equal opportunity or anti-discrimination legislation. Your union can provide further information and advice. Call the ACTU Helpline 1 300 362 223.

Being Bossed around is Bad for your Health also includes the following information:

The workplace is no place for bullying. The ACTU aims to raise awareness amongst the community, workers, unions, employers, health professionals, OHS authorities and governments that:

Bullying is a serious health and safety hazard:

- Bullying is not just persecuting or ganging up on individuals - most bullying is not so obvious - bossing people around, intimidating or threatening them, or keeping them under constant work and time pressures is also bullying.
- Bullying is characterised by (usually a combination of) the following conditions at work:
  no say in how your job is done;
  interference with personal belongings or sabotage of work;
  shouting, or abusive language;
  open or implied threat of the sack or demotion;
  oppressive, unhappy work environment; and
  people afraid to speak up about conditions, behaviours or health and safety.
  unreasonable demands and impossible targets,
  restrictive and petty work rules;
  being required to perform tasks without adequate training,
  being forced to stay back to finish work or additional tasks;
  compulsory overtime, unfair rostering or allocation of work;\
  constant, intrusive surveillance or monitoring.

Workplace surveys:

As part of the ACTU National Health and Safety Campaign some unions surveyed workers about bullying. Results from over 3,000 responses received by the ACTU, from a range of unions representing the health, education, finance, manufacturing, clerical and administration, in the public and private sectors, are presented below:

- Over half the respondents (53 per cent) report an unhappy and oppressive workplace and 54 per cent say that that intimidating behaviour - shouting ordering and belittling people happens in their workplaces. Almost a third report abusive language.

- Forty-four per cent say that people are afraid to speak up about those behaviours in their workplaces or about working conditions and health and safety.
- Around a third report pressure of impossible targets and demands to perform tasks for which they have not been adequately trained.
- Twenty per cent have been threatened with the sack, 10 per cent have experienced physically threatening behaviour and 5 per cent report being assaulted at work.
- Almost 70 per cent report that either a manager or supervisor carries out the bullying behaviour and 14 per cent say it is the employer. Less than 30 per cent say that the bullying is carried out by fellow workers or by clients or customers.
- People are reporting a range of symptoms as a result of being bullied, including feeling stressed (73 per cent); feeling angry (67 per cent); feeling depressed (59 per cent); sleep difficulties (48 per cent); headaches and feeling helpless (45 per cent); feeling fearful (29 per cent); and stomach problems (24 per cent).
- Sixty per cent say that workplace bullying is affecting their home and social life and 44 per cent say that they have taken time off work due to the bullying. Most (39 per cent) have taken sick leave, 8 per cent have used recreation leave, 6 per cent have taken leave without pay, but only 4 per cent have received workers' compensation.
- Only 18 per cent say that anything is being done to stop the bullying behaviour.

Did you know?

According to the Tasmanian Anti Discrimination Commissioner, workplace bullying and harassment are significant by-products of privatisation, restructuring and downsising in government, business and industry.

A significant proportion of claims to the Tasmanian Anti Discrimination Commissioner involve bullying, harassment and employment discrimination generally.

The South Australian Working Women's Centre survey on bullying in 1997 found that over half the respondents had been bullied in the previous three months and almost all of those said it was still continuing.

Over 85 per cent of the SA Working Women's Centre survey respondents said that a person in authority - manager, employer or supervisor, carried out the bullying. Over 80 per cent added that others at work were also being bullied.

Griffith University's Dr. Paul McCarthy has estimated that 350,000 people are subjected to long term bullying in Australia, while 2.5 million experience some aspect of bullying over the course of their working lives. Workplace bullying may be costing Australian business up to $3 billion annually.

Although bullying affects employees at all levels, most perpetrators are managers. A study by the University of Manchester found that 94 per cent of people thought bullies can get away with it. 92 per cent say bullying is caused by work and one in six say that their employers 'encourage bullying management.'

The University of Manchester also found that bullying is associated with autocratic management styles, divisiveness and 'punishment for no obvious reason' and with a negative work climate, high workload and unsatisfactory relationships at work.

The World Health Organisation found that people experiencing anxiety or depression find it more difficult to manage usually daily tasks like work, shopping, exercise and hobbies than people suffering with physical conditions such as arthritis, diabetes and back pain.

What workers are saying about bullying:

The following is a selection of direct quotations from workers responding to union surveys on bullying:

"I take these problems home with me and of course it makes an impact on family relationships."

"If management would follow their own policies re consultative processes ... we wouldn't have half the problems."

"No sense of living or escapes from work - it goes home with you."

"More training. Less bully managers."

"I think everybody should be sat down and discuss why workplace is so unhappy and what we could do to please everybody."

"How to feel at work transfers to home, so I don't feel happy at home, so don't give my best to my family and friends."

"Staff turnover should be monitored to find out if something is wrong. This could be done through management and union."

"Stop protecting management. Affects around 90 per cent of staff."

"Stop restructure every 12 months."

"Should not be kept in position of authority. Should be given stern warning. Apology to staff."

"Compulsory overtime. Sometimes 10 - 12 hour days."

"Worried about being sacked if I don't do everything they ask."

"A lot of staff have become really quiet. No one is chirpy any more."

"Arguments with husband and children due to staying back to finish department manager's work. Hours being worked and they won't pay overtime."

"Lack of supervision, worker safety issues not addressed, insufficient staff resources - failure of professional duty of care."

"Most inappropriate behaviour of male staff towards female – rude, crude and revolting / workload unbelievable / unreasonable."

"Surveillance, constant questioning of one's tasks/work, no time for tea breaks, lack of promotion, sulking, changing duty statement."

"Rudeness, demands to perform menial, humiliating tasks, discrimination on the basis of nationality, forced to do work outside of personal expertise, frozen out of all work for months."

"Bullying has grown in a climate of unemployment and mass redundancies."

"Blaming employees for management mistakes."

"Harassment - being forced to work at level two - while only being paid at level one and threatened with removal if I don't."

"Fear of redundancy/intimidation by continuous hints at resource reduction ... that people over fifty are not really useful in the workplace."

Fear if one-year-old daughter gets sick and need time off, my hours will be cut or I'll be fired."

"Managers should be taught respect and mainly how to communicate with staff without bullying. To treat male and female staff the same. In my situation, the manager will shout and belittle me, but not my male offsider."

"Stomach ulcer, snappy and can't concentrate."

"Stress placed on family due to excessive overtime, anger."

"Large workload - stress - less time at home - arguments - eventual separation."

"Minor accident due to stress, strained atmosphere at home."

"Being afraid to come to work and fulfil duties."

"Being short-tempered with those close to me and always on edge."

"Depression and negativity obvious to family."

"You try to tell people why you are the way you are, but they don't understand."

"Someone in authority should address this with the manager in question - staff too afraid/intimidated to say anything for fear of retaliation."

"We are alone in the workplace, very difficult to say no - feel the whole situation is hopeless."

"Nothing will be done about it because how do you prove bullying when it is subtle and sly?"

"Management have reduced technicians from five to one. Increased responsibilities and new technology, but no training/remuneration."

"Should have a similar policy as sexual harassment - enforceable."

"Need minimum staff levels, reclassification and accountability from management for health and safety problems they cause."

"Felt suicidal."

"People shouldn't put up with it any more and should take a stand."

Who can help?

Everyone has the right to dignity and respect at work and to a safe and healthy working environment. If bullying is happening in your workplace, there are ways to deal with it.

If you are in a union:

The first step is talk about the issues amongst yourselves. Involve the elected health and safety representative, the health and safety committee and/or the union delegate or shop steward at your workplace. They should be trained to deal with health and safety and other work issues.

If there is no health and safety representative, union delegate or health and safety committee at your workplace, it might be a good time for the workers to elect one as your representatives. Australian state and territory laws vary in the legal support they give to workplace health and safety committees and to health and safety reps. Check with state branch of your union or the state trades and labour council for the legal position of health and safety representatives and/or committees in your state.

If the problems cannot be solved at the workplace, a union organiser or health and safety officer may be able to help. The health and safety representative or union delegate can contact the union on behalf of employees. This may include arranging for a union official to visit the workplace.

If you are not a union member:

Unions will usually require you to become a member before they can represent you or your fellow workers. However, if you and a number of your fellow workers have discussed the issues at your workplace, you could contact the union and arrange for a meeting with a union organiser. The meeting need not be at the workplace.

If you are unsure of the appropriate union to contact, call the ACTU Helpline 1300 362 223.

Occupational Health and Safety (OHS) Law:

Bullying at work is an occupational health and safety (OHS) issue.

Under OHS law, workers have the right to a safe and healthy working environment and employers have the legal duty to protect the health and safety of workers. This means that employers must not cause or allow bullying to happen at their workplaces.

[**Note:** I did a word check of all the Occupational Health &Safety Federal and State Laws but did not find the words workplace bullying, harassment or violence in *any* of them.]

Employers should ensure that they have policies and procedures in place to prevent bullying. These should be developed in consultation with workers and their representatives and unions. Policies should:

- Acknowledge that bullying is a health and safety issue which should be prevented
- Identify the key factors which contribute to bullying at work
- Outline simple, clear procedures for workers to raise concerns, without fear of intimidation or discrimination
- Include processes for ongoing review and evaluation

If the employer is unwilling to listen or to make improvements, it may be necessary to use other methods, for example:

Provisional Improvement Notices - In most states and in Commonwealth workplaces, elected health and safety representatives have the legal right to issue a Provisional Improvement Notice (PIN) to order an employer to fix a health and safety problem. PINs can be used for bullying as for any health and safety issue. Through issuing a PIN, the health and safety representative gives the employer time to fix the problems.

Cease work orders - If work is an immediate risk to health and safety, commonwealth and some state laws allow health and safety representatives to order that work stop immediately.

Government health and safety inspector - You may have the right to request assistance from a government health and safety inspector. This can include a request for a workplace inspection. Again, the law varies between states and territories, so check with your union or trades and labour council.

Most unions have workers' compensation officers and/or working relationships with specialist legal firms. An initial consultation may be free of charge. Contact the union or the ACTU Helpline 1300 362 223 for advice and assistance.

Anti-discrimination law:

Bullying can happen to anyone. However, those seen to be most vulnerable include young workers, apprentices and trainees; women, older workers; and people of non-English speaking background, who may also experience sexual and/or racially based harassment.

These forms of bullying are covered by equal opportunity and/or anti-discrimination legislation, which outlaw such behaviour at work. Your union can provide further information and advice or contact the Equal Opportunity Commission in your state or territory.

For health, advice and treatment:

People who are experiencing ill-health symptoms as a result of bullying should discuss the issues with their GP. Alternatively, some state Trades and Labour Councils operate alongside specialist workers' health centres, which can provide advice, assistance and recommend further actions. A list of Trades and Labour Councils can be found at the end of this document.

The Australian Psychological Society has a toll free, Australia wide counselling referral service - the telephone number is 1800 333 497. Calls to the APS referral service will put you in touch with a psychologist in your area, which will involve a professional fee.

The Mental Health Foundation has a national Telephone Interpreter Service on 131 450, which can link people of non-English speaking backgrounds with the local mental health service.

Trades and labour councils:

State trades and labour councils can provide occupational health and safety and related advice and assistance:

Victorian Trades Hall Council
54 Victoria Street
Carlton South VIC 3053 (03) 9662 3511

Labour Council of NSW

10th Floor, 377 - 383 Sussex Street
Sydney NSW 2000
(02) 9264 1691

Safework Queensland
16 Peel Street
South Brisbane Qld 4101
(07) 3846 2411

United Trades & Labour Council of South Australia
11 South Terrace
Adelaide South Australia 5000
(08) 8212 3155

Trades & Labour Council of Western Australia
Level 1, 79 Stirling Street
Perth WA 6000 (08) 9328 7877

Tasmanian Trades & Labour Council
379 Elizabeth Street
South Hobart Tasmania 7002
(03) 6234 9553

Northern Territory Trades and Labour Council
1st Floor, 38 Woods Street,
Darwin Northern Territory 0800
(08) 8941 0001

Trades and Labour Council of ACT Inc
17 Woolley Street
Dickson ACT 2602
(02) 6247 7844

Appendix 2

AUSTRALIAN NURSING FEDERATION

"ANF Policy to resist aggression" www.ohsrep.org.au

(Permission given by Victorian Trades Hall Council.)

The Australian Nursing Federation (Victorian Branch) launched its Zero Tolerance Policy in April with the aim of eliminating occupational violence and aggression against nurses in the workplace. The proactive approach of the ANF in dealing with this issue demonstrates the union's commitment to the health and safety of its members. In this interview ANF Violence and Aggression Policy Officer, Anne McFarlane, explains how the campaign came about, the factors that contribute to violence and aggression against nurses and how the new policy addresses this very serious workplace health and safety problem.

Serious concerns:

Nurses had been saying for a while that violence was increasing in the workplace and they wanted something done about it. The national branch of the ANF took the matter seriously and asked the state branches to look at the issues. We were very concerned in the Victorian branch so we dived into it.

Any area can be exposed to violence:

What I have noticed as the Violence and Aggression Project Officer is that there don't seem to be any areas that are immune to workplace violence. I really did think that there would be some areas that wouldn't be as likely to be exposed only to find out that I was completely wrong. Emergency, psychiatry and disability services are the noted 'high risk' areas. Rural and remote nursing is another one. Areas that are acknowledged on one level but not on another like aged care came up next. When I actually spoke to nurses they were telling me that violence was in intensive care, ordinary medical wards, anti-natal, post-natal and even renal dialysis. It just shows that any area can be exposed to violence.

A world-wide phenomenon:

We began the research by looking at the UK National Health Service Zero Tolerance policy that was adopted around 1998. In my research I have gone right back to the beginning of the 1990s and 1980s keeping track of everything available.

One of the main problems is that workplace violence is underreported. As a result there is very little statistical evidence to back up what you know is really happening out there. The International Nursing Council estimates that only 20 per cent of workplace violence is reported. That means 80 per cent is not reported so what we are looking at in the statistical evidence is only 20 per cent and that is worldwide. It is a worldwide phenomenon.

While violence has increased and I would say probably significantly, in the last ten years I think the main problem was the perception that it was part of the job and therefore not reported. It was around, perhaps not to the same extent as now, but it was there and it was traditionally one of those things that you took with the job.

Human cost most significant:

The human costs for the person experiencing the violence is the physical and psychological trauma. There is the loss of earnings and the increased financial strain that goes with medical costs. There are also implications for the family. If you have someone who has been traumatised it is going to have a big impact on family relationships. Employers tend to look more at the financial cost but in actual fact the human cost probably has just as much financial implication. Following a significant event there is usually quite a downturn in productivity related to low morale and also an increase in insurance premiums. Research by The International Council of Nurses found: *"Workplace violence and aggression interferes with the provision of quality of care and jeopardises the dignity and self-value of healthcare personnel."*

A practical policy:

There is a culture of silence that goes with the underreporting of violence against nurses. For a long time the few nurses who would stand up often felt they were invalidated. Nurses like to think that they can take care of any situation that comes up. They tend to see themselves as advocates for patients and often feel compromised if they experience violence. A nurse would often say nothing rather than complain about someone they have been trying to protect.

Management has at times decided not to take on something that might open a Pandora's Box. I think the beauty of the ANF Zero Tolerance policy is that it is based on the OHS framework. You don't have to interpret it; you just have to apply it. Other interventions often focus on things like the staff or client behaviour and that makes some people feel uncomfortable. They don't like to feel their behaviour is being judged and they don't like to judge others. The policy that we have doesn't rely on judgements. It is a practical policy.

Prevention is better than cure:

We are encouraging people to report more as the basis for future directions. As soon as you get into the first stage of acknowledging a problem then people will want something done. In every worksite where heath and safety issues are taken into account we have a policy that people can pick up and use.

Employers are misguided if they reject preventative practices. The compensation costs for nurses who experienced violence or aggression in the workplace last year were substantial. Those costs, the financial and the human, could have been avoided if attention was paid to the problem in a preventative way. The ANF is trying to push for a proactive approach to identify potential hazards and prevent people getting hurt.

Union members can access the policy on line at the ANF web site: www.ohsrep.org.au

Appendix 3

AUSTRALIAN MANUFACTURING WORKERS' UNION (AMWU)

Health and Safety Handbook 2003 Edition www.amwu.asn.au

Section 10: Workplace Bullying

The workplace is no place for bullying:

- Is this your Workplace?
- Unreasonable demands or impossible targets;
- Restrictive and petty work rules;
- Being required to perform tasks without adequate training;
- Being forced to stay back to finish work or additional tasks;
- Compulsory overtime, unfair rostering or allocation of work;
- Constant, intrusive surveillance or monitoring;
- No say in how your job is done;
- Interference with personal belongings or sabotage of work;
- Shouting or abusive language;
- Open or implied threat of the sack or demotion;
- Afraid to speak up about conditions, behaviours or health and safety.

What is bullying?

Many people think of bullying as persecuting or 'ganging up' on individuals. But that's only part of the story. Most bullying is not so obvious. Bossing people around, intimidating, threatening or keeping them under pressure is also bullying. This is the most common form of bullying.

Health and safety effects:

Being bossed around is a major cause of stress at work. At worst, it can result in serious physical illness, alcohol and drug use, depression or suicidal thoughts.

Other symptoms include headaches, sleep difficulties, high blood pressure, digestive problems, tearfulness, anxiety, nausea, anger, irritability and a loss of motivation, concentration, self-confidence and morale. The effects of bullying also place pressure on family and friends.

What can be done?

Most State and Territory governments have guidance information about preventing and dealing with workplace bullying. Make sure you get a copy. Ways of dealing with bullying include:

- Get the issues out in the open by talking with fellow workers;
- Hold a meeting, away from the workplace if necessary;
- Get the workplace H&S Rep. H&S committee or other delegates to take up the issues;
- Contact the union/union organiser for assistance;

Use these processes to;

- Identify the most important issues.
- Keep records of incidents, so they are not forgotten or misrepresented;
- Raise the issues with the employer through delegates and/or H&S Reps.;
- Arrange counselling and/or other assistance for distressed workers if needed.

Employers have to consult with their employees about policies and procedures to eliminate all hazards and risks from the workplace. There is no excuse for causing or allowing bullying.

In all States, government health and safety inspectors can direct employers to fix problems in the workplace and may issue prohibition or improvement notices.

Sexual Harassment is illegal and is another form of bullying. The AMWU has specific leaflets for members about this form of bullying.

Appendix 4
CGU - COVER TO COVER

Quotes from "Cover to Cover - September 2001 Edition No. 5"

(**Note:** This magazine is sent to GGU's WorkCover Clients and was referred to in Chapter 9 - Case Study]

A 1998 Morgan Poll found that nearly 50 per cent of Australian workers had been verbally and/or physically assaulted by a co-worker and nationally, several landmark cases have awarded substantial compensation to victims of serious bullying incidents.

Preliminary results from the ACTU (Australian Council of Trade Unions) anti-bullying OH&S campaign (involving more than 3,000 surveys) reveal that nearly 70 per cent of respondents were bullied by a manager or supervisor. Only 18 per cent of respondents said something was being done to stop the bullying behaviour.

[**Note:** Australia should be ashamed of these figures. Most victims can't afford to take their cases to court - and the bullies know this! Australian law needs to be changed so victims are protected without having to spend large amounts to take their cases to court.]

It has been suggested that the increase in bullying reports could be attributable to an increase in bullying behaviour and/or a greater willingness among victims to report and/or take legal action against offensive behaviour.

Sole workers and night workers, such as service station attendants and milk bar owners are particularly vulnerable to workplace violence perpetrated by people from outside the workplace. However, according to 'Violence in the Workplace, Australian Institute of Criminology 1999' there is a greater risk of encountering violence from someone *inside* the workplace.

What types of behaviour constitute bullying / violence in the workplace?

Any form of physical, verbal or psychological intimidation is classified as violence, according to 'Violence at Work, Queensland Workplace Health and Safety guide 1999.' The Guide says that the experience of violence is subjective, so that what is perceived to be violence for one person may not be for another and people who witness acts of violence can also be affected.

WorkCover Corporation SA defines violence at work as any incident where an employer or employee is abused, threatened or assaulted in situations relating to their work. Within this definition:

- 'Abuse' is any unreasonable behaviour that involves the misuse of physical or psychological strength or power.'
- 'Threat' is a statement of the intent to harm a person or damage their property.
- 'Assault' is any attempt to cause injury to a person and includes actual physical harm.

Managers may victimise employees through inappropriate methods of supervision, employees may be violent towards their managers and workplace pranks may go horribly wrong and cause untold damage to the victim. In 1995, a 17 year-old apprentice panel beater in Melbourne was locked in a toilet cubicle. His 25-year-old supervisor poured paint stripper solvent under the door and set it alight. The apprentice suffered burns to 50 per cent of his body and was hospitalised for eight weeks. He had to wear a burn suit for almost two years after the accident, suffered from depression may never work again. The supervisor was fined $2,000 and the company $5,000.

[**Note:** How could this paultry figure be chosen to make up for all the pain and suffering that young man went through? Shame on Victoria WorkCover! And why did he not get the police involved and charge the man with assault causing bodily harm?]

Employees should not have to adjust to hurtful behaviour. The person telling the joke, performing the prank or issuing the threat is the one who has to modify their or her behaviour and to be responsible for it. Their employer is even more accountable.

What steps can an employer take to assist in the prevention of these incidents?

Mounting acknowledgment that workplace violence is placing health, safety and productivity in jeopardy is indicative that preventive measures are necessary.

It's an implied part of the employer's duty of care under each State and Territory OH&S Act to prevent workplace violence. Legislation requires employers to ensure, so far as is reasonably practicable, the health, safety and welfare to employees and to consult with employees and their representatives in the management of risks.

Employers should adopt a zero tolerance attitude to any form of violence. Some control measures recommended in 'Violence in the Workplace' include, but are not limited to:

- Pre-employment screening to weed out potentially violent employees.
- Termination guidelines for employees who display potentially violent behaviour.
- Formal violence reporting procedures.
- Confidentiality of all reports of violence.
- Non-violent conflict resolution strategies.
- Crisis management systems.
- Supportive environment.
- Grievance procedures for employees and customers.
- Clear manager, supervisor and worker accountabilities.
- Appropriate surveillance systems.
- Workers to be trained in workplace specific violence prevention and life-preserving strategies.
- Establish clear behavioural standards for your workplace.

How do victims report an incident?

A reporting system should be in place, which enables employees to report incidents of violence to management.

Some employees may not report acts of insidious violence perpetrated against them. They may feel intimidated or embarrassed, powerless due to their position in the organisation, bound by cultural constraints, not aware of their rights and prone to peer pressure. The employer needs to make efforts to prevent this scenario from arising.

Queensland Workplace Health and Safety suggests strategies including monitoring sick leave patterns and workers' compensation date and collecting feedback from worker attitude surveys, exit interviews, union representatives, mentors and consultative committees.

When the employer is the perpetrator of workplace violence it can make the situation even more difficult for the victim. In these situations, employees must go straight to the local OH&S Authority, union representative or if serious enough, the police.

What actions need to be taken post incident?

In the case of serious incidents, first aid may need to be applied and police and ambulance services called to the scene.

The location of the incident needs to remain undisturbed and witnesses are to remain at the scene or at least their telephone numbers sought, until the police arrive. The family of employees and clients are to be contacted prior to the media being informed of the incident. Affected employees should be given relief from their duties and critical incident stress debriefing.

According to WorkCover NSW it is vitally important that employees are in no way made to feel responsible for violent incidents until the facts of the incident are known by police and management and they have been debriefed and counselled. If the burden of guilt is wrongly attributed to a staff member or client, it may contribute to the development of post-traumatic stress.

Management needs to investigate less serious allegations. It is the responsibility of the employer to determine how the violence occurred and in all cases of violence to implement prevention strategies to avoid it happening again.

Fear of returning to work, anxiety, stress, depression, grief and guilt may all be part of the reaction to a violent event. A post-incident management plan needs to be implemented, involving the use of trained counsellors to assist employees through the initial post-incident period and beyond if necessary. If symptoms are not treated, they can worsen and leave the victim feeling threatened, vulnerable and worthless.

Are employers liable for these incidents?

In some circumstances, employers may be vicariously liable for the conduct of the perpetrators and, along with the alleged perpetrators, may also be charged for breaching OH&S laws. Alleged perpetrators may have charges laid against them under the criminal law as well as OH&S law. Employees can also sue their employers, claim workers' compensation and make complaints to the Anti-Discrimination Board or the Federal Human Rights and Equal Opportunities commission. Similar avenues apply in all states and territories.

In South Australia, the WorkCover Corporation has produced *'Guidelines for reducing the risk of violence at work'* to help employers, employees and their representatives identify the potential for violence at work and to provide practical guidance for the development of risk reduction strategies. To obtain a copy of that booklet, contact the WorkCover Corporation Bookshop.

[**Note:** *Keep in mind that only government regulations and Acts are enforceable - not* **"Codes of Conduct"** *or* **"Guidelines."**]

Appendix 5

INDEPENDENT EDUCATION UNION - IEU

"Preventing Workplace Bullying" - Workshop Overheads for IEU Women's Conference, August, 2001.

www.ieu.asn.au/issues/general/18.html

(Permission given by Workers Health Centre to use excerpts from Peggy Trompf's article).

Stressors at work - Job related:

- Work overload or boring and menial work;
- Lack of control over work, lack of decision-making, poor working conditions or environment;
- Physically demanding work, excessive work rates, unrealistic deadlines;
- Poorly organised shift patterns;
- Hours of work and travelling time/distance to work;
- Ambiguous job responsibilities and reporting structures;
- Job insecurity;
- Threat of physical violence or other job hazards;
- Isolation;
- Dirty or potentially unhealthy work;
- Organisation related;
- Working conditions (heat, cold, noise and vibration, light, poor ergonomics, poor amenities, lack of privacy, physical security, overcrowding);
- Unsafe or hazardous systems of work and work practices;
- Poorly designed or performing plant / equipment;
- Poor communication between management, supervisors and the workforce;
- Lack of positive workplace OH&S culture;
- Insufficient or ineffective training and job induction;
- Poor staffing levels;
- Poorly resourced management;
- Lack of peer group or work group support;
- Conflict or competition between work groups;
- Poor performance management system, management feedback and support;
- Harassment, abuse, victimisation or discrimination condoned or practised by management, supervisors or elements of the workforce;

- Poor H.R. policies on recruitment, promotion, redundancis, retrenchment and termination of employment;
- No formal grievance or complaint handling;
- Poor compliance and management of existing grievance procedures, involving an absence of objectivity and equity by supervisors and management in grievance handling and resolution.

Change related:

- Poor planning of restructuring and reorganisation;
- Changes in plans, procedures, work layout and technology without consultation
- Involuntary transfer;
- Voluntary and involuntary redundancies, retirement, retrenchment;
- New job and responsibilities;
- New supervisor or co-workers;
- Inadequate planning and management of technological change.

Risk identification - conflict at work:

- High absenteeism/sick leave;
- Low morale;
- Complaints about environment or behaviours;
- Workers compensation claims;
- Staff turnover;
- High risk work;
- Poor grievance procedures;
- Poor management;
- Poor staff training;
- Unclear policies or none;
- No consultation.

Controlling workplace conflict:

- Organisational policy to control workplace conflict where it poses an OH&S threat;
- Contains procedures to identify, control and monitor conflict hazards and risks;
- Must be developed in consultation with workers;
- Should contain procedures about awareness raising on unacceptable behaviours at all levels of organisation;

- Should contain guidelines for intervention for those exposed to; stressful/conflictual/bullying situations;
- Should have workable, effective grievance procedures in place;
- Should have checks and balances to ensure fair hearing;
- Should include training options;
- Should provide for regular monitoring and review of policy.

Finally, we have found the following description by Wilkie (1996) to be useful in identifying stress breakdown.

Stage One:

You suddenly experience free floating anxiety if the level of stimulation or the processing task required of the brain exceeds the brain's processing capacity at that time or the brain's capacity has been diminished by lack of sleep, low blood glucose, nutritional deficiencies, effects of drugs or their withdrawals.

Can be experienced if you are trying to do too many things at once, trying to do something difficult e.g. waiting for an unknown time; working with people who frequently change their mind; being in a no-win situation.

You may be able to keep going by drawing on will power and extra reserves, but you are likely to suffer from another two symptoms.

Stage Two:

Failure to get motivated. Can't get started on jobs, though can if someone helps out. Self-starter has run down. This condition is caused by depletion of neurotransmitters. which are replenished by sleep.

Failure of emotional control/bursting into tears, laughter, irritability.

Aggression and violence in stage two occurs when emotional control is low or lost. Can occur particularly when defending territory and more likely when stressed worker is using legal or illegal drugs.

Stage Three:

Major behavioural changes, relative intolerance of sensory stimulation … suddenly the cat's walking too heavily!

Loss of ability to ignore things previously tolerated, overreaction and road rage.

Change response patterns that superficially resemble a change of personality. *"I don't know what's come over her."*

185

In summary, the first symptoms are warning signs, the second caused by fatigue and the third by impaired circuit breakers.

The point is to listen to yourself and take early steps to intervene.

You can see our doctor or take whatever steps you think is right to help out ... but don't ignore these important signs.

The Workers Health Website: www.workershealth.com.au

Appendix 6

ROYAL DISTRICT NURSING SERVICES (RDNS) RESEARCH UNIT

Preventing Workplace Violence: Toward a best practice model for work in the community

by Tina Koch and Sally Hudson (For nursing staff - excerpts only).

A flyer seeking expressions of interest was distributed throughout the organisation and community nurses were asked to volunteer. Nine community nurses joined the PAR group. Reviewing the 'violence' literature confirmed that a model for violence prevention applicable to community practice did not exist. The community setting was defined as the client's home, the clinic, the office, the road and pathways between these venues. All members of the PAR group collected stories from colleagues. Staff were informally asked: *"Tell me a community story or incident you experienced as 'violent.'"* In this way, sixty-eight (68) stories of violent behaviours directed at staff were generated, all anonymously given.

We were able to reach consensus that violence was whatever the nurse telling the story felt it was and we would accept their construction. In this way, the PAR group used these stories to gain a better picture of violence in the community. The group used a slightly modified WorkCover SA definition of violence to guide their discussions that is: 'workplace violence is defined as ... any incident where an employer or employee is abused, threatened or assaulted in situations relating to their work.'

In a preliminary analysis of the 68 stories, the PAR group noted that abuse/aggression accounted for 43 per cent, threats 25 per cent and assault/physical violence 32 per cent. We noted that many incidents had not been officially reported, reinforcing the view that underreporting is a common phenomenon, particularly when violence is experienced as abuse or threat. Abuse and threats in the community workplace are common and the stories confirmed that staff often deal with these as an everyday episode not seen as worthy of reporting. On the contrary, all episodes of physical violence were reported, except where the event took place many years ago when reporting processes were not available.

An education package has been prepared for all nursing staff, designed to 'walk' staff through the model. Precisely because staff work in a variety of shifts it was considered important to develop an educational tool that could be accessed easily (a video was prepared).

The organisation's senior management group ratified the model for use throughout the service. The education package now forms part of the orientation program.

Workplace violence, in any form, as 'part of the job' is unacceptable. This project challenges social attitudes to the tolerance of workplace violence. The general perception of this problem is usually restricted to physical assault. Verbal harassment, intimidation, expression of uncontrolled irritation, displaced anger applied unreasonably and abuse are not always considered violent acts. Like the term sexual harassment, which has not been brought into the public consciousness, what constitutes workplace violence is still not well understood and is seen as inevitable in particular jobs. Redefinition of the concept of workplace violence is necessary for employment in the community. Lack of definition in the literature between the concepts of workplace violence and bullying has also added to the general confusion.

The UK Health and Safety Authority has been reported as saying that nurses are five times more likely to be attacked than other workers. The same Authority said that other categories of employees at risk were social and care workers (BBC Online, 1997). A survey in Canada described findings where 80 per cent of nurse participants had experienced some form of violence in their career. Almost 6,000 violent incidents were reported in the 12 months leading up to the survey (Cruikshank, 1995). Another survey in the Accident and Emergency (A&E) department of a major Irish public hospital found that:

- 60 per cent of nurses and attendants had been physically assaulted at least once while working in the A&E department and that;
- 40 per cent had been assaulted within the past 12 months (Rose 1997.216)

These results are similar to other research in the UK, US, New Zealand and Canada. Rees & Lehane (1996) did a study of 5 nurses who had witnessed a total of 23 incidents. His findings indicated that most participants had changed their work practices, they were more aware of the feelings of their colleagues involved in incidents. He writes: *This study has demonstrated that those witnessing violence can experience similar emotional difficulties as the victims of violence. Male staff appear to have difficulty in accepting emotional support in the form of counselling (Rees & Lehane, 1996.47).*

Some practical strategies:

- Carry out continuous actual or mental safety audits. Look for hazards (and help) on the way to and from home, work and client locations. Check each street, road lane or car park you use. Audit the immediate surroundings each time you stop the car at lights, client's house or at office car parks.

- Audit each work area for entrances, exits and other people, animals or things that may injure you or that you can call on for your own defence.
- Stand back from and to one side of the door after knocking at the client's house, while remaining visible to anyone looking through the peephole.
- Ask permission to enter the house.
- When going in the door of the house try to let the client in before you if they are outside.
- Check the locks on the door as you walk in. Secured deadlocks or chains will make any escape impossible should a difficult situation arise.
- Assert your rights and insist that doors behind you remain unlocked while you are visiting.
- Make a mental note of the exits as you walk into the house.
- Be aware of specific protocols that may exist for a specific client, e.g. exact appointment times or a joint visit.
- Carry your mobile phone, with the battery charged, into the house with you. Even if you have to lock yourself in the toilet for safety, you are still able to call for help
- If you become concerned about your safety while visiting a client at home, leave as quickly as possible.
- **Keep your car keys with you in the client's house. A key ring that attaches to your belt is a good investment in your own safety. It also ensures that you never have to go searching for your keys.**
- If there are people hanging around your car, stay away from the vehicle. Move to a safe place and summon police.
- Check the spaces you must walk through to get to your car, workplace or house.

Organisational:

- Implement a referral system that identifies potentially violent situations associated with a client or a residence.
- Make other service providers aware that you expect to be advised of known (or likely) potential or actual violent situations associated with a client.
- If hazards are associated with other people or animals in the client's environment, the exclusion of these from your workplace should be a condition of service.
- Issue each field staff member with a duress alarm or an equally effective means of summoning immediate help. This may mean that day staff are also monitored by the security firm, in addition to evening and night staff.

In the clinics:

- Ensure that clinic premises have at least two doors to allow escape if the need arises.
- Install duress alarms to the nearest police station or security firm.
- Ensure a second person is available as necessary (buddy system).
- Monitor the use of clinics as a 'dumping ground' for clients who have a history of violence.
- Develop contingency plans for clients with a history of violence e.g. clear appointment times and/or the presence of two people.

Know your options in a situation of violence:

This section is an acknowledgment that despite the best efforts, violent episodes may still occur. This is not an endorsement of the popular view that many acts of violence are spontaneous, random and unpredictable. It is, however, recognition that cues have been missed.

The negotiated option:

Bowie suggests that negotiation approaches should be done in a calm, easy style, speaking as to a friend or equal, not expressing or showing, fear, anger or contempt. Ideally, try to negotiate a win-win outcome with the client.

Another option used is to leave the situation. This is certainly one advocated by RDNS ESR Committee, only 31 per cent of staff responded in this way.

The leaving option:

When in a situation of violence or threat of violence, RDNS prefers its staff to use the leaving option. Before leaving, consider what must be done to escape and how to reach the nearest place of safety. Try to leave as a positive action rather than a panic reaction. Leave when in a situation that seems unsafe.

The no action option is used frequently, again, this relates to the interpretation of the professional role of the nurse. Here duty of care is interpreted as seeing the home visit through to the end despite feeling unsafe and uncomfortable.

The no-action option:

This is a deliberate choice of action in order to achieve a later, more favourable situation. The time to use the no-action option is when you need to wait until the situation becomes clearer, to see if it will improve. Alternatively, use no-action when confronted with weapons or by an assailant on drugs or who is mentally disturbed and realising that your actions might jeopardise others' lives (e.g. displacement of violence onto others).

The seeking backup option:

This is an option for you to seek help in dealing with an aggressive client. It is used to provide help and expertise. It may also be used to provide better protection or 'strength in numbers' when you feel vulnerable. Calling for backup may involve the use of concealed alarms, coded messages or other means of getting appropriate backup. In some situations you may have to physically call out for support.

The surprise or diversion option:

Surprise or diversion is a sudden change of mood, focus or direction. The objective of surprise or diversion is to interrupt the attacker's train of thought or action, confusing them and/or re-focusing their attention on something else. This may create an opportunity for you to take control of the situation and/or escape. Using humour can sometimes also be a useful distraction as long is it is not used in a sarcastic or demeaning manner. You may be able to initiate a surprise or diversion by feigning a collapse, unconsciousness, a fit or a heart attack.

The blending option:

The aim of blending is to re-direct your energy so that you have joined forces with the other person and you are able then to move in the same direction. It can be used effectively for both verbal and physical attacks, with the type of blending required defined by the situation. The worker ends up physically or emotionally alongside the assailant rather than in opposition. This unexpected blending of forces may surprise or unbalance the attacker, this gives the worker the opportunity to take control or flee immediately. Blending is an active alternative to no action when more time to plan is needed or the time to act has not yet come.

The evasive self-defence option:

Bowie suggests that Evasive Self Defence (ESD) is only used in order to enable a worker to avoid personal injury or to escape from a dangerous situation. It should be used in the least intrusive way possible and not drawing undue attention to the incident. Negotiation should be used whenever possible alongside ESD. We generated many stories but not one that exactly fits this option. However you may like to consider this story.

The restraint option:

The Restraint option is complex and controversial. Ineffectual or inappropriate attempts at restraint may cause more damage to the worker and client than the initial aggressive behaviour. It is used only when all other methods are inappropriate or have been tried and failed.

The fight option:

Fighting is a last resort, in order to save life or avoid injury. Difficult personal judgements need to be made about the level of force to be used in order to save self and others from attack that is perceived to be life threatening. Complex judgements about duty of care and the legal requirements of "reasonable force" to defend against attack, vary from service to service and state to state.

Appendix 7

AUSTRALIAN CAPITAL TERRITORY

I wrote an e-mail to ACT stating, *"I've searched every web site I can relating to workplace safety in the ACT, but can't find any legislation that protects employees against workplace bullying or harassment. Can you let me know what protection employees have against this?"*

I received the following reply from Copyright and Information, Library and Information Services, NOHSC:

"*Occupational health and safety legislation in Australia is state-based. The only Commonwealth legislation for OHS is the National Occupational Health and Safety Act which affects Australian Government employees only.*

The National Occupational Health and Safety Commission (NOHSC) develops national standards, including codes of practice and guidance notes, which allow for a common approach to occupational health and safety legislation. National standards are documents declared by NOHSC which prescribe preventative action to avert occupational deaths, injuries and diseases. In appropriate circumstances, national standards may take the form of national model regulations.

NOHSC documents are instruments of an advisory and guidance nature only, except where a law, other than the National Occupational Health and Safety Act or an instrument made under such a law, makes them mandatory. The application of any NOHSC documents in a particular State or Territory is the prerogative of that State or Territory and they take on the regulatory responsibilities of any such application. In other words, NOHSC does not implement legislation for the Commonwealth, State and Territories and each jurisdiction can take up and amend NOHSC documents to suit their own regulatory process. Therefore, there could be differences between individual States and Territories in implementing model regulations (as well as standards, codes of practice, etc) and subsequently the way legislation is implemented."

About occupational health and safety regulation in Australia (www.ohs.anu.edu.au/ohs)

(Permission given by the National Research Centre for Occupational Health & Safety Regulations. Since written, there have been a couple of changes to the Tasmanian and Queensland legislation.)

Federal structure:

Australia is a federation, with six states and two internal territories and a federal government. The legislative powers of the Federal Parliament are set out in the Commonwealth Constitution. The Commonwealth Constitution does not give the Commonwealth a general power to legislate for OHS, hence there are ten OHS statutes (six state Acts, two territory Acts, a Commonwealth Act covering Commonwealth employees and a Commonwealth Act covering the maritime industry).

There are also specialist OHS statutes covering the mining industry in some states. Finally, in 1985 the federal government legislated for the formation of the National Occupational Health and Safety Commission (NOHSC). NOHSC is a tripartite body, with members appointed by federal, state and territory governments and members appointed by the Australian Chamber of Commerce and Industry and the Australian Council of Trade Unions. Amongst its functions, NOHSC can initiate research, collect statistics and develop national standards. Because of the Federal Parliament's constitutional limitations, NOHSC standards need to be adopted by state and territory governments before they have any legal force.

Historical development:

Historically each Australian state adopted most of the provisions of the 19th century British health and safety legislation (particularly the 1878 Factories Act and later 1901 Act), so that by 1970 each of the six states had an OHS statute implementing the traditional British model of OHS regulation. This traditional model relied upon detailed, highly technical specification standards. It was enforced by an independent state inspectorate vested with broad inspection powers and relying on negotiated compliance utilising informal enforcement methods (advice, education and persuasion) coupled with formal prosecution using the criminal law in the last resort. The great advantage of this traditional specification standard approach was that duty holders knew exactly what to do and OHS inspectorates found the legislation relatively easy to enforce.

The weaknesses of this traditional approach are well known. It frequently resulted in a mass of detailed and technical rules, often difficult to understand and difficult to keep up to date. Standards were developed ad hoc to resolve problems as they arose and concentrated mainly on factory-based physical hazards, resulting in uneven coverage across workplaces. Specification standards did not encourage or even enable employers to be innovative and to look for cheaper or more cost-efficient solutions. They also ignored the now well-accepted view that many hazards do not arise from the static features of the workplace, but from the way work is organised. The traditional factory legislation created a climate of dependence on state regulation, with little involvement in OHS by workers and unions.

The Reform of Australian OHS law: 1972-2000

By the late 1960s, the weaknesses in this traditional model, based as it was on the British model, coupled with political and economic develop-ments, created a policy environment in which the recommendations of the 1972 British Robens Report appeared attractive. The report proposed a modification of the regulatory model, based on two principal objectives, each of which responded to the criticisms of the traditional model.

The first was the streamlining of the state's role in the traditional regulatory system, through the "creation of a more unified and integrated system" (Robens Report, para 41). This involved bringing together all of the OHS legislation into one umbrella statute, containing broad "general duties" covering a range of parties affecting workplace health and safety, including employers, the self-employed, occupiers, manufacturers, suppliers and designers of plant and substances and employees. The skeleton statutory general duties are to be "fleshed out" with standards in regulations and codes of practice.

A unified OHS inspectorate was to have new administrative sanctions (improvement and prohibition notices) to supplement prosecution. Prosecutions were to be brought against corporate officers, as well as against the corporate employer.

The second objective, recognising the practical limitations of external state regulation, was the creation of "a more effectively self-regulating system" (Robens Report, para 41). "Self-regulation" *is a much misunderstood notion* and is often wrongly confused with "deregulation." To some, self-regulation describes the move away from prescriptive standards and allows duty holders to choose the means by which they will comply with general duties and process - and performance-based standards (see below). In the Robens vision, self-regulation involves workers and management, at workplace level, working together to achieve and improve upon, the OHS standards specified by the state.

The most important element in the Robens' model of self-regulation was that, *"There should be a statutory duty on every employer to consult with ... employees or their representatives at the workplace on measures for promoting safety and health at work and to provide for the participation of employees in the development of such measures."* (Robens Report, para 70)

The principal vehicle for employee representation was to be the health and safety representative, who was, in the pure Robens model, to be consulted by employers. Employees were also to be represented on health and safety committees. The Robens model also envisaged greater co-operation between the OHS inspectorate and employee representatives, an obligation upon employers to develop OHS policies and rules and a requirement for Boards of Directors to lodge prescribed OHS information with corporate regulators.

Beginning with South Australia in 1972, Tasmania in 1977, Victoria 1981 and New South Wales 1983, each of the Australian jurisdictions has enacted new OHS statutes. The statutes currently in force in each jurisdiction were enacted in

- 1985 (Victoria),
- 1986 (South Australia and Northern Territory),
- 1984-1987 (Western Australia),
- 1989 (Australian Capital Territory),
- 1991 (Commonwealth Employees),
- 1993 (Maritime industry),
- 1995 (Queensland and Tasmania) and
- 2000 (New South Wales).

All of the statutes are based on the UK Robens model, although some go beyond the Robens model in some respects.

Standard setting:

Each of the Australian OHS statutes adopts the well-known three tiered approach recommended by the Robens Report - broad, overarching general duties and more detailed provisions in regulations and codes of practice (called advisory standards in Queensland). Provisions in *regulations have force of law, whereas codes contain guidance material,* breach of which is evidence of contravention of an applicable regulation or general duty provision.

The general duties generally cover employers, the self-employed, occupiers, manufacturers, suppliers and designers of plant and substances, employees and in Queensland, principal contractors in the construction industry. They require the duty holder to provide and maintain, as far as is reasonably practicable, a working environment that is safe and without risks to health - although the wording of these provisions differs markedly from jurisdiction to jurisdiction. The big sleeper in the general duty provisions is the duty imposed upon employers and self-employed persons to "others" or non-employees. Initially envisaged by the Robens Report as covering the "public," recent case law in both Great Britain and Australia makes it clear that the duty covers newly emerging forms of work relationships, from contractors and sub-contractors, to labour hire arrangements, home-based work and even franchising.

Before the 1990s, most of the OHS regulations in the Australian jurisdictions were contained in separate instruments and it was not uncommon for a jurisdiction to have over a dozen sets of regulations, each covering a specific hazard. Since the mid-1990s many of the Australian OHS regulators have brought all supporting OHS regulations together in one general regulation. Beginning in the late 1980s Australian regulations and codes of practice have tended to steer clear of specification standards and instead rely on general duty requirements, performance standards, process requirements and documentation requirements. Instead of telling duty holders exactly how they are to achieve compliance, performance standards define the duty holder's duty in terms of goals they must achieve or problems they must solve and leaves it to the initiative of the duty holder to work out the best and most efficient method for achieving the specified standard.

Process requirements prescribe a process or series of steps, that must be followed by a duty holder in managing specific hazards or OHS generally. They are often used when the regulator has difficulty specifying a goal or outcome, but has confidence that the risk of illness or injury will be significantly reduced if the specified process is followed. Most regulations now require the duty holder to identify hazards and assess and control identified risks. Process-based standards have spawned greater reliance on documentation requirements. Increasingly OHS statutes are requiring duty holders to document measures they have taken to comply with process-based standards, performance standards and general duty standards. Probably the best example of an Australian documentation requirement is the requirement in the Queensland Workplace Health and Safety Regulations for principal contractors, demolishers, contractors and subcontractors to prepare workplace health and safety work plans prior to commencing certain kinds of construction work. Principal contractors, subcontract-tors and contractors are required to exchange copies of their own work plans before starting work and are required to discuss with each other the relevant OHS issues, based on their work plans. The regulation envisages that the work plan requirement operates as a risk assessment tool and as a mechanism to co-ordinate the OHS measures taken by principal contractors, contractors and subcontractors. Failure to comply with the requirement is an offence. Codes of practice (advisory standards in Queensland) increasingly provide guidance on hazard identification, risk assessment processes and contact.

A notable development in standard setting in Australia during the 1990s was the movement towards national uniformity in standards in regulations and codes of practice. The process was overseen by NOHSC, which in 1991 established a tripartite National Uniformity Taskforce, which identified several key first order priorities for achieving national uniformity: plant, certification of users and operators of industrial equipment; workplace hazardous substances; occupational noise; manual handling; major hazardous facilities; and storage and handling of dangerous goods.

NOHSC developed standards in the first six of these areas and the jurisdictions were well on the way towards adopting these standards by the end of 1996, although it should be noted that jurisdictions were quite inconsistent in their methods of adoption, particular in choosing whether to implement the standards in regulations or codes of practice and in their drafting styles. The national uniformity process was not complete when the Howard government came to power in 1996 and that government has significantly down-sized NOHSC, with the result that the move towards national uniformity has slowed dramatically since mid-1996. Lack of uniformity in Australian standards remains a significant problem.

State enforcement:

Most of the Australian OHS inspectorates are now unified, with multi-skilled generalist OHS inspectors, although some jurisdictions have retained some specialists in some areas, such as construction and dangerous goods. Some jurisdictions have specialist investigators, whose energies are devoted entirely to the investigation of incidents for the purposes of prosecution.

The trend since the 1980s has been for the inspectorates to move away from a central control model, to a regionalised model, with regional managers as the key decision-makers and broad policy frameworks being produced by the central offices. In the past year or so, many inspectorates have changed their organisational structures and have divided their field inspectorates into industry-based teams.

Most jurisdictions now have a balance of proactive and reactive inspections (i.e. responses to injuries or complaints). Proactive inspections are increasingly centred less on random inspections and more on targeted programs.

Some inspectorates have trialled the inspection of OHS management systems rather than workplace hardware and there is more attention being paid to systems of work in inspections than there were in the past. However, a challenge still facing OHS inspectorates is to adopt the more rigorous inspection strategies championed by the US OSHA and some of the European OHS, which tend to emphasise management systems as the focal point of an inspection.

All of the Australian OHS statutes give inspectors broad inspection powers and empower inspectors to issue improvement and prohibition notices and to prosecute duty holders found to be in breach of the legislation. In New South Wales, Queensland, Tasmania and Northern Territory (and in the near future, Victoria) inspectorates can also issue infringement notices, although the circumstances under which infringement notices may be issued vary quite markedly, particularly as between New South Wales and Queensland. All of the OHS statutes provide that the principal penalty for OHS offences is the fine. The maximum fines in the jurisdictions also vary considerably: from $125,000 in the Northern Territory, to $550,000 in New South Wales (or $825,000 for repeat offences). In New South Wales, sanctions also include adverse publicity court orders and a court order that requires the offender to participate in an OHS-related project.

Until recently, most of the OHS inspectorates did not have publicly available enforcement policies. In the past few years, this has changed and now most of the agencies have enforcement strategies and policies. There is, however, little consistency as between jurisdictions in relation to enforcement policies and practices.

Although most of the Australian OHS statutes make provision for the prosecution of culpable managers and directors of corporations in breach of the OHS statutes, most prosecutions are conducted against corporate employers and there is still a strong leaning towards prosecuting employers responsible for injuries or fatalities involving machinery. Enforcement action against manufacturers, designers and supplier of plant, equipment and substances is rarely initiated. In relation to prosecution, it should also be noted that increasingly the Australian public prosecutors are considering bringing manslaughter prosecutions under the general criminal law where gross negligence causes workplace deaths. There have been a few successful manslaughter prosecutions, one involving a small company in Victoria in 1994 and a couple in Queensland. In Victoria, Queensland and Western Australia there have been proposals afoot to ensure that the legal rules attributing liability to corporations for manslaughter are reformed to make it less difficult to pin liability for manslaughter onto corporations.

While the general duty owed by employers and self-employed persons to persons other than employees has the potential to cover work relationships outside the employment relationship, the Australian OHS inspectorates have been slow to enforce these obligations outside the area of the traditional employment relationship. Nevertheless, in the past few years inspectors are beginning to investigate and prosecute offences involving sub-contracting and labour hire relationships. The challenge for OHS regulators is to develop regulations, codes of practice and guidance material to cover non-employment work relationships and to begin to examine hazards arising from these relationships and to take enforcement action where appropriate.

Worker involvement in OHS:

All of the Australian OHS statutes make provision for worker representation in OHS matters, principally through the institutions of health and safety representatives and committees. But once again, the provisions vary markedly between the jurisdictions.

In all jurisdictions but the Northern Territory, the OHS statutes make provision for worker elected health and safety representatives. In Victoria, South Australia, the Commonwealth and the ACT, the powers given to representatives are quite broad and include rights to training inspection, consultation information and similar issues. They include the power to issue a provisional improvement notice (a default notice in South Australia) and the right to order that direct work cease (though the provisions vary between the jurisdictions). Western Australia, Queensland and Tasmania give much weaker consultative powers to representatives. The Tasmanian and Northern Territory codify the common law right of a worker to refuse to perform dangerous work. Each of the statutes provides for health and safety committees, comprised of employer and employee representatives.

In the Northern Territory, all consultation takes place through health and safety committees. Until it passed new legislation in 2000, in New South Wales worker participation was solely through health and safety committees, although members were given some rights (for example to inspection and information) resembling those given to health and safety representatives. The OHS Act 2000 imposed upon employers a duty to consult with its employees to enable employees to contribute to the making of decisions affecting their OHS. Consultation can take place through health and safety representatives or committees or through any other arrangement agreed to by employers and employees. If one of the employer's employees requests, at least one health and safety representative must be elected by employees. The provisions appear to be much weaker than the provisions for health and safety representatives in Victoria.

There has been very little empirical research done into the operation of the health and safety representative provisions. What data there is suggests that the introduction of representatives has caused major changes in OHS attitudes and practices. They worked best when the OHS legislation gives them a significant role and when management adopted a positive attitude to OHS and gave representatives enough time to perform their duties. A further factor in the success of the representative provisions is union support.

Conclusion

The most notable conclusion that emerges from an overview of the Australian OHS legislation is its lack of uniformity. Even if the analysis is limited to the statute book, the differences in wording of the statutory standards, the differences in sanctions (particularly levels of fines and use of infringement notices) *and the variation in health and safety representative provisions is a matter of great concern.* The lack of uniformity is even greater if the analysis extends, as it should, to inspection and enforcement practices. *There is an urgent need for OHS regulators in the various jurisdictions to develop uniform enforcement policies and strategies.*

A second noteworthy point is the need for OHS regulators to pay greater attention to work relationships outside the traditional employment relationship. With the dramatic changes that are taking place in the Australian labour market, mirroring changes taking place elsewhere in the world, regulators need to develop standards, guidance material, inspection programs and enforcement strategies that accommodate subcontracting, labour hire, home-based work and franchise arrangements. Particularly important is the need to think more flexibly about health and safety representatives. Currently the provisions are limited to employees and exclude sub-contractors and the like. European developments in relation to regional health and safety representatives should be examined.

Third, one notable omission from most of the Australian OHS statutes when compared with their European counterparts is the absence of requirements to promote the use of multi-disciplinary health services by employers. Some of the Australian statutes have mild provisions obliging employers to employ or engage the services of OHS experts in order to discharge their obligations, but there is no systematic attempt to require employers to engage OHS experts. The most successful pro-vision appears to be the Queensland provision requiring an employer to appoint a workplace health and safety officer when there are 30 or more workers normally employed at a prescribed workplace; or, if there are fewer than 30 workers, the employer thinks that it is necessary.

[**Note:** You will notice that not once in this long definition were my questions relating to workplace bullying, harassment and violence discussed or answered.]

Appendix 8
VICTORIA

Employees in Victoria are protected from workplace bullying - but only if the bullying relates to discrimination (that also covers sexual harass-ment) or an employee my charge a company with unfair dismissal if they can prove that they were forced to quit their job because of bullying or because of their membership in a trade union. The bullying itself in the latter case is not covered unless they feel they have been forced to quit their job. All other forms of bullying (and this is the vast majority of cases) are not covered by government regulations.

WorkSafe:

WorkSafe Victoria chief, John Merritt, said the code would help employers who needed to tackle bullies head-on. He also stated, *"Unfortunately, bullies often get away with it because their victims don't have the support in the workplace to deal with the problem. The draft code aims to help victims of bullying to understand their rights and give guidance to employers to stop bullies in their tracks. Bullies need to be stopped and they can be, if employers and workers join forces. The code is not meant to threaten traditional management practices. The code defines bullying as repeated unreasonable behaviour that has the effect of victimising, humiliating or threatening another person."*

Workcover Minister Bob Cameron has approved release of the draft code. As part of the code, employers were encouraged to develop a "no bullying policy" provide training information and instruction, look for warning signs, encourage reporting of incidents, investigate them and take any necessary action. Action could range from mediation to informing Workcover and the police in some cases where there has been violence.

Business groups are expected to oppose the code because of a fear that it will damage profits and undermine established management practices. Under the new arrangements, WorkSafe Victoria would investigate reports of bullying and, if the boss or business was considered to have breached obligations set out by the code, charges could be laid.

Victorian Employers Chamber of Commerce and Industry chief Neil Coulson said the code could undermine businesses. He stated, *"We surveyed our members in the lead-up to the election and the issue of most concern was the level and complexity of regulation being imposed on businesses. **A lack of clarity of definitions of bullying could open up a Pandora's Box in terms of*** *asserting blame. We are more than prepared to work with the authority on appropriate measures to deal with occupational violence, but we are concerned about a code. The majority of employers try to do the right thing. Workplaces are dynamic. There are disagreements. If we have an authority hell-bent on regulating behaviour in the workplace, which is clearly subject to interpretation, it creates a level of uncertainty."*

In a VTHC Health and Safety Unit website survey which attracted over 5,000 respondents, the overwhelming majority wanted the government to formally act on this serious health and safety issue and introduce a Code or Practice for bullying and violence in the workplace. A task force was set up and many meetings were held and a proposed Code of Practice was recommended.

In the proposed Code of Practice, bosses who bullied employees would face fines of up to $250,000 and possibly $600,000 in fines. The Code of Practice was intended to prevent corporate bullying and encourage employers to develop anti-bullying policies, to be alert for warning signs and conduct investigations. *It would give WorkSafe officers the right to investigate reports of bullying and lay charges if the code was breached.* The new code aimed to stamp out repeated verbal and physical abuse, including isolating or excluding workers or assigning them meaningless tasks unrelated to their jobs.

In February 2003, the results of that investigation were published, not in a new Code of Practice, but in a document entitled: *WorkSafe Victoria - Prevention of Bullying and Violence at Work - Guidance Note.*

My findings

Since writing the above information, I've learned that the State of Victoria has *not* changed their laws relating to bullying. Instead they've released a *"Guidance Note"* for employers. I personally, was very disappointed to see that it was called a *Guidance Note* - that did not add more laws to protect bullied employees. I'm convinced that bullied workers are not adequately protected and doubt that bullied employees will have the governmental protection required to stop workplace bullies in their tracks. The WorkSafe officers will not be laying charges if the code is breached - that will still be up to the victim.

The Guidance Notes encourage companies to have anti-bullying policies and procedures, but if the company does not comply, it doesn't appear that any punishment is given unless the victim takes the company to court. And if a company does not enforce existing anti-bullying policies, those who are bullied will still need to be very wealthy to be able to afford to take the bullies and their companies to court. There is no indication that WorkSafe will pay the employee's portion of legal fees should the company not deal properly with their bullying charges.

These court cases can take up to five years to settle and can cost the victim anywhere from $50,000 to $100,000 or more in legal fees. Many do not recoup their court costs, let alone obtain a proper settlement for the pain and suffering they go through. And this doesn't count for the emotional and psychological trials the victim will continue to face daily if they stay at their place of employment with their bully. Most victims just want to get on with their lives. Many throw their hands in the air and either leave their job or continue to put up with the bullying.

The "Guidance Note" also stipulates that the bullying must be repetitive and on-going. I believe that one traumatic psychological bullying episode is enough and should be dealt with immediately to stop a recurrence and have protection under the Occupational Health and Safety regulations. According to the "Guidance Note" only those involving single incidences of *physical* violence are covered but don't mention psychological abuse.

I was pleased to see that it states "Bullying has been linked to situations of role conflict and uncertainty. Employers should make sure that employees understand their role and have appropriate skills to do their job." *I have found that the vast majority of supervisors and managers in Australia have had little or no basic supervisory training.* They therefore follow the lead of other supervisors and managers who unfortunately do not know any more about supervision than they do. Unless TAFE and other higher learning institutes start really pushing for this training to be done, this need will not be met. I have people coming to my "Survival Skills for Supervisors and Managers" seminars with BA and MBA degrees - and they admit that they weren't taught even the basics of supervision. We need to fill that gap and our learning institutes are the ones can do it.

I was also pleased to see that it states *"Employees who have a designated role in handling reports of bullying will need specific training to assist them to carry out this task."*

WorkSafe Victoria Prevention of Bullying and Violence at Work - Guidance Note

[**Note**: This is *not* a law or regulation].

This *"Guidance Note"* is divided into two sections - Part one - Preventing workplace bullying and - Part two - Preventing occupational violence. (I will concentrate only on the workplace bullying section.) The following are headings (and some information) from that document:

What is bullying?

1.1 Defining workplace bullying:

Workplace bullying is repeated, unreasonable behaviour directed toward an employee or group of employees, that creates a risk to health and safety. Within this definition:

"unreasonable behaviour" means behaviour that a reasonable person, having regard to all the circumstances, would expect to victimise, humiliate, undermine or threaten.

[**Note:** This explanation is so vague you could drive a truck through it!]

"behaviour" includes actions of individuals or a group and may involve using a system of work as a means of victimising, humiliating, undermining or threatening.

"risk to health and safety" includes risk to the mental or physical health of the employee.

The following types of behaviour *where repeated or occurring as part of a pattern of behaviour* could be considered bullying:

- Verbal abuse;
- Excluding or isolating employees;
- Psychological harassment;
- Intimidation;
- Assigning meaningless tasks unrelated to the job;
- Giving employees impossible assignments;
- Deliberately changing work rosters to inconvenience particular employees;
- Deliberately withholding information that is vital for effective work performance.

This list is not exhaustive. Other types of behaviour may also constitute bullying.

What about a single incident?

According to the definition, a single incident of bullying-style behaviour does not constitute workplace bullying. However, since an employer has a general duty to provide his or her employees with a safe workplace and safe system of work, single incidents of bullying-style behaviour should not be ignored or condoned.

If the behaviour displayed during a single incident of bullying behaviour involves a physical attack or threat of physical attack, it may be dealt with under the guidance note as an instance of occupational violence.

2. Preventing workplace bullying;

3. **Consultation:**

4. **Create awareness:**

5. **Develop a policy:**

5.1 "No bullying" policy
5.2 Building commitment to the policy

6. **Inform, instruct and train:**

7. **Identify risk factors:**

7.1 Indirect signs of bullying:

In a workplace, bullying can sometimes be signalled indirectly. Because these signs may not always be connected with bullying, they need to be examined within the overall context of the organisation. Indirect signs of bullying may include: employees leaving the organisation reporting dissatisfaction with working relationships (i.e. at exit interviews);

- High levels of absenteeism associated with particular shifts;
- An increase in workplace grievances or complaints;
- Negative results from employee surveys;
- High levels of staff turnover;
- Issues raised at staff meetings;
- Deterioration of relationships between colleagues, customers or management;
- Regularly torn clothing/uniforms;
- Regularly damaged personal affects or work tools;
- An employee experiencing a number of minor workplace injuries;
- Employees becoming withdrawn and isolated.

8. **Control risks:**

9. **Encourage reporting:**

10. **Responding to incidents/reports:**

Appendix A - Duties under the Occupational Health and Safety Act, 1985

The *Occupational Health and Safety Act, 1985 (OHS Act)* imposes legal responsibilities on both employers and employees. These duties extend to the risks to health and safety from workplace bullying and occupational violence. (There is other legislation that also may impact on a workplace when a situation of either bullying or violence occurs - see Appendix C). The following outlines some of the duties under the OHS Act. Employers and employees should make themselves aware of all laws that apply to them in the workplace.

[**Note:** This Act has **not** been changed since 1985 and copies of it still do not mention workplace bullying, harassment or abuse.]

Employer duties:

Employers have a general duty under section 21 of the OHS Act to provide and maintain so far as is practicable a working environment for employees that is safe and without risks to health. (Employers owe the same duty to independent contractors and their employees who are working at the workplace. The employer's duty to these employees extends only to matters over which the employer has or should have control.)

Workplace bullying and occupational violence create an unsafe working environment and risks to the health of employees. Therefore, employers have a duty under section 21 to ensure, *so far as is practicable,* risks to health and safety from bullying and violence in the workplace are eliminated or reduced. (According to the OHS Act, "what is practicable" can vary depending on a range of circumstances. These are explained in section 17.1 of this guidance note). *The employer's duty to control risk only applies to situations of workplace bullying and occupational violence that are reasonably foreseeable.*

[**Note:** How can someone possibly foresee bullying behaviour?]

Employee duties:

Employees have duties under section 25 of the OHS Act to take reasonable care of their own health and safety and the health and safety of others. They must cooperate in any action taken by their employer to comply with the OHS Act.

Section 25 also prohibits employees from wilfully or recklessly interfering with or misusing, anything provided in the interests of health and safety. In addition, they must not wilfully place at risk the health and safety of any person in the workplace. If an employee bullies or attacks another employee, it is *likely* to amount to a breach of section 25.

Appendix b "No Bullying" Policy examples (2)

Appendix c - Other legislation

(Other legislation may apply whether or not the bullying or violence falls within the definitions used in this guidance note.)

Occupational violence or bullying *may* also come within the scope of certain state and federal legislation. Obligations under such legislation are additional to any obligations under the *Occupational Health and Safety Act 1985* and *WorkCover is not responsible for the administration of any of this other legislation.*

Anti-discrimination legislation:

State and federal anti-discrimination legislation prohibits behaviour that amounts to discrimination or sexual harassment. The relevant legislation includes:

- Equal Opportunity Act 1995 (Victoria)
- Racial and Religious Intolerance Act 2000 (Victoria)
- Human Rights and Equal Opportunity Act 1986 (Commonwealth)
- Racial Discrimination Act 1975 (Commonwealth)
- Sex Discrimination Act 1984 (Commonwealth).
- Disability Discrimination Act 1992 (Commonwealth).

Bullying and violence that occur within the workplace will be covered by the legislation if the bullying or violence:

- Amounts to discrimination on the basis of a prescribed attribute;
- Meets the legislation's definition of unlawful harassment.

Criminal law:

The criminal law in Victoria is a combination of common law and legislation. The key piece of legislation is the **Crimes Act 1958 (Victoria)** which aims to punish all forms of criminal behaviour. Most forms of occupational violence will be criminal offences and as such, subject to investigation by the police. Relevant offences include: assault, threats to kill and threats to cause physical injury.

However, there are some examples of occupational violence that will not be offences under criminal law e.g. Where an employee is physically attacked by a person, such as a psychiatric patient, who is incapable of forming the necessary intent.

Industrial legislation:

Industrial law in Victoria is primarily governed by the **Workplace Relations Act 1996 (Commonwealth)** which includes provisions relating to unfair dismissal and freedom of association. This Act can apply to bullying or violence in situations where:

- The bullying involves an employee or employees, being unfairly dismissed.
- Employees are bullied, attacked or threatened, because of their trade union membership or industry activity.

Workplace Violence - Your Rights, what to do and where to go for help

(*Job Watch* - the employment rights watchdog written by Oonagh Barron). www.job-watch.org.au

Their guide was a joint publication by Job Watch and the Victorian Workcover Authority. It covers:

1. Workplace Violence

- What is workplace violence?
- Who can intervene in situations of workplace violence?
- What sorts of things could be workplace violence?
- Employers and workplace violence.
- WorkCover and workplace violence.
- If you are put at risk.
- Apprentices and workplace violence.

2. Forms of Workplace Violence

- Criminal acts: Police and workplace violence.
- What to do.
- Checklist for criminal workplace violence.
- Definitions from the Crimes Act 1958 (Vic).
- Sexual harassment - what is sexual harassment - What to do.
- Racial abuse - remedy - what to do.
- Verbal abuse - what to do.

3. Legal Options

- Intervention orders.
- Police involvement.
- Unfair or unlawful dismissals.
- Constructive dismissal.
- Equal opportunity laws.

- Assistance for victims of crime.
- WorkCover.

4. Where to go for help

- ACTU Workers' Line 1 300 362 223
- Centre Against Sexual Assault (CASA)(03) 9344-2210
- Equal Opportunity Commission of Victoria (03) 9281-7100
- Federation of Community Legal Centres (03) 9602-4949
- Human Rights and Equal Opportunity Commission 1 300 369 711
- Job Watch (03) 9662-1933
- Police 000
- Office of Post-Compulsory Education, Training and Employment (03) 9412 6600
- Victims Referral and Assistance Service (03) 9603 9797
- WorkCover Advisory Service 1 800 136 089

From January to June in 2001, the Victorian WorkCover Authority received 1,100 claims for compensation as a result of workplace violence, harassment and bullying. Compensation payments are predicted to be $26 billion.

WorkSafe said the Code of Practice for the Prevention of Bullying and Violence was intended to prevent corporate bullying and encourage employers to develop anti-bullying policies, to be alert for warning signs and to conduct immediate and effective investigations. *However, enforcing this code is the problem.* A proper regulation or Act would give WorkSafe officers the right to investigate reports of bullying and lay charges if the regulation was breached. The final code was set to be approved by Workcover minister Bob Cameron by mid 2002.

[**Note**: Legislation and Acts have *not* been changed. Most recent Occupational Health & Safety Act was enacted in 2004 – still no mention of bullying, harassment or violence in the Act.].

Appendix 9

NEW SOUTH WALES

[**Note:** Occupational Health and Safety Regulation 2001 does *not* mention workplace bullying, harassment or violence. Although WorkCover New South Wales updated their Workers Compensation Legislation in 2002, I was unable to find any reference to workplace bullying, harassment or violence.]

Workplace Violence Awareness - A secure workplace for young Australians

(Part of the project - A Secure Workplace for Young Australians - run in conjunction by WorkCover NSW and the National Children's and Youth Law Centre. Copyright resides with WorkCover New South Wales). (www.workcover.nsw.gov.au) This project covered the following topics:

- Workplace Violence Includes
- Triggers for Intervention
- Dealing with a potentially violent incident
- Dealing with a violent incident
- Dealing with a complaint of violence, bullying or harassment
- Investigating a complaint
- If you see a violent incident
- When you receive a complaint of bullying and harassment
- Investigation
- A model protocol for starting the investigation of a complaint of (non-criminal) bullying or harassment
- Model grievance procedure
- Model conduct of interview protocol
- A model record of interview
- Legal Consequences

Criminal Laws

[**Note:** Occupational Health and Safety Laws newest 2001 - does *not* include workplace bullying, harassment and violence]

- Breach of contract
- Personal injury liability
- Workers Compensation
- Anti-Discrimination Law
- Prevention
- Prevention strategies for your business
- Model Code of Conduct [These do not change legislation.]

A Model Protocol for starting the investigation of a complaint of (non-criminal) bullying or harassment

[**Note** - this is **not** an Act, law or regulation - just a guideline.]

This Model Protocol does *not* apply to the investigation of a charge of misconduct that would be, if true, a breach of discipline or would, if true, amount to a criminal offence.

1. Meet the person named in a private place.
2. Tell them they have been the subject of a complaint or accused of violence, bullying or harassment.
3. Give the respondent a copy of any written complaint. If it has not been written down, write down and read the details of the allegations to the respondent.
4. Tell the respondent that this will be investigated according to the principles of natural justice and that these include:
    o Knowing the details of the allegations and who made them.
    o Having the opportunity to respond to the allegations as outlined.
    o An impartial, independent and confidential process; and
    o A fair hearing and a decision-maker who has not prejudged the issue.
5. Reassure the respondent that natural justice principles also mean that they are presumed 'innocent' unless and until the facts show otherwise and that the investigation will be proceeding on this basis. Caution the respondent about the need to maintain confidentiality. He or she is not to speak to others, in particular to any other person who might be named in the complaint or other people in the workplace who would be influenced in their behaviour if they knew of it, about either the fact or the substance of the allegations made. This is in the respondent's interests as well as the organisations and the complainant's.
6. Caution the respondent that a breach of confidentiality carries serious personal consequences. They could be sued for defamation. There could be a further complaint of victimisation. Such a breach would be serious misconduct and might result in disciplinary action up to and including dismissal.
7. Tell the respondent that the complainant has the right to progress their complaint through an external body, such as the various State, Territory and Commonwealth Commissions that receive complaints of breaches of human rights or equal opportunity laws and the Industrial Relations Commission.

    [**Note**: These cover only a small portion of bullying situations.]

8. Tell the respondent that in addition to {name of employer's} legal obligation under occupational health and safety laws, WorkCover and

anti-discrimination law, {name of employer} has legal and personal responsibility for maintaining a work environment free from violence, bullying and harassment. The respondent must understand the seriousness of the allegations and the need for the investigation.

9. Tell the respondent who is to carry out the investigation and that they will be interviewed, in order to respond to the allegations outlined in the statement of complaint.

10. The respondent must be told that he or she is entitled to have a support person present at that interview and they will have the same range of support and resources made available to them by {name of employer} as to the complainant during the investigation process.

11. Give the respondent a written notice that details the date, time and venue of the proposed interview, the name of the persons who will interview him or her.

12. The respondent should be told that, normally, further interviews of witnesses who can either substantiate or refute the allegations outlined in the complaint will be interviewed by the same person, immediately following the respondent's response.

13. A respondent should be invited to nominate such persons to be interviewed. He or she must not contact these persons him or herself about the matter or discuss any part of the process with them.

14. The respondent should be told that any concerns or issues that arise out of this process can be raised confidentially with either the manager conducting this interview (yourself) or by another named independent person.

15. All those interviewed will be asked to sign a protocol to confirm that they have read and understood the outline of the investigation interview process. You should give a copy of it to the respondent. All matters relating to requests for documentation and administration of the interviews are to be handled by (name a person with central administrative responsibility in the client's office or in the investigation team). The respondent should be reminded of this avenue.

16. You should stress that the organisation takes the allegations seriously and expects that the respondent and witnesses will co-operate fully and truthfully with the investigation process.

17. The respondent should be told that they are expected to conduct themselves in a manner that will not bring disrepute to either themselves or their employer, by engaging in behaviour that cause complaint of victimisation by the complainant or witnesses or potential witnesses. If they do, this might result in a disciplinary charge against them.

This legislation commenced on September 1, 2001 and affects work-places with 20 or more employees. The act sets out the requirements for putting systems in place to identify, access, control and/or eliminate health and safety risks. Employers must ensure that their communi-cations mechanisms relating to OH&S meet the stringent requirements of the act.

[**Note**: The Act had been updated in 2011, but I could *not* find any legislation relating to workplace bullying, harassment or violence in this Act.]

Employer's Responsibilities:

Employers bear the vicarious liability caused by the bully's behaviour. Employers owe each employee a duty of care. Employment law is framed around the employee holding the employer responsible. No one signs a contract agreeing to work in a war zone. Employers who ignore the bullying will have to be accountable and pay damages. Human Resources departments frequently write off bullying as "personality clashes" much to the delight of the bully who is always trying to heap all the blame onto the target.

Some employers are more scared of serial bullies than they are of their targets, therefore it's easier and cheaper and less risky to get rid of the target. By the time the bullying case against them occurs, the target is probably traumatised, suffering a psychiatric injury, facing loss of job and income and may not have union or legal support. Therefore, the employer is much more likely to win their case against a target than against a resentful and vindictive serial bully.

Legal action:

In many cases the bully places the target in the position of having no option but to take the employer to tribunal or court. In the majority of cases, this is the first time the target has ever been involved in legal action and their unfamiliarity with the legal system is a vulnerability that bullies and abusive employers exploit.

Gaining compensation for psychiatric injury is a long and arduous process that's very expensive both financially and emotionally. The areas most commonly quoted are breach of duty of care under the Health and Safety laws. *Some can take as long as ten years of the person's life* and the victim may have a much harder time finding employment or end up working at a lower salary and/or position. *Should they win in court, their settlement is usually based on slightly less than what the person would have earned had they quit their job under normal circumstances. If they lose, they face hefty legal bills and the bully gets away with it again.*

NSW Labour Council's union safety website "UnionSafe"

UnionSafe has published a number of Workplace Bullying Fact Sheets that can be downloaded by visiting the Safety Reps section of this website or clicking: unionsafe.labor.net.au/safety_reps/index_10.html.

Here are some that relate to workplace bullying:

- Can you spot a bully?
- Factsheet 1: Defining Workplace Violence
- Factsheet 2: What is Workplace Bullying?
- Factsheet 3: The Effects of Bullying/Types of Bullying Behaviour
- Factsheet 4: What workers Can Do
- Factsheet 5: What the Union Can Do
- Factsheet 6: How OHS Reps and Committees can Help Prevent Bullying
- Factsheet 7: Cultural Diversity/What we can do
- Factsheet 8: Model Policy
- Factsheet 9: Checklist
- Factsheet 10: Is Bullying Illegal?
- Factsheet 11: Resources
- Stressed Employees Worked to Death
- Bullies On The Rise

Bullies on the rise:

Bully-free workplaces are part of a shrinking minority, according to a new survey of Australian employees in which just 12 per cent stated there was no bullying in their current workplace.

Meanwhile a whopping 85 per cent of employees say they have either been personally attacked or seen others bullied at work, according to the Health Works survey of more than 325 human resource and occupational health and safety professionals.

It says bullying in the workplace is on the increase yet preventative and practical measures for dealing with the problem are not keeping up, with only 47 per cent of businesses saying they have a written policy for bullying in the workplace.

"Workplace bullying is becoming more and more prevalent. In fact, we've found that up to half of all employees will experience some type of bullying during their working lives," says Ken Buckley, CEO of Health Works.

Fifty-six percent of employees have or know of a colleague who has taken sick leave as a result of bullying in the workplace, with intimidation the most common type of bullying (66 per cent) followed by humiliation (48 per cent) ridicule (42 per cent) insults (39 per cent) offensive language and degrading (24 per cent).

Other forms of bullying reported included stand over tactics, gossiping, being left out of events or excluded from luncheons and not approving leave.

"Bullying occurs at all levels of the organisation and can directly have an effect on the victim's health and wellbeing such as severe stress, anxiety, panic attacks, sleep disturbance, depression, concentration difficulties and raised blood pressure," Buckley says.

But he has a number of tips for dealing with bullying when the issue arises, including: contacting your union; keeping a detailed diary of incidents (including witnesses who will back you up); approaching the bully directly; telling them you dislike their behaviour and ask them to stop; and informing your supervisor and/or the next in line.

Health Works has published a *'Communication at Work'* booklet addressing on the job bullying, which is available from its website at www.healthworks.com.au

Appendix 10
QUEENSLAND

Report of the Queensland Government Workplace Bullying Taskforce

(Division of Workplace Health and Safety, Department of Industrial Relations)

The Queensland Taskforce proposed that workplace bullying be treated as workplace harassment. The following definition was recommended for inclusion in legislation (Recommendation 5 of the Taskforce Report):

Workplace harassment is repeated behaviour that:

1. Is directed at an individual worker or group of workers; and
2. Is offensive, intimidating, humiliating or threatening; and
3. Is unwelcome and unsolicited; and
4. A reasonable person would consider to be offensive, intimidating humiliating or threatening for the individual worker or group of workers.

Recommendation 8:

That:

8.1 'SafeWork SA Authority' establish a Code of Practice with the following provisions:

- A definition of inappropriate behaviour in the workplace;
- A definition of workplace violence;
- An explanation of responsibilities of employers and employees in regard to inappropriate behaviour in the workplace;
- A preventions model; and
- Reporting systems.

8.2 OHSW Act be amended to provide for Workplace Services Inspectors to refer workplace bullying matters to the Industrial Commission for mediation or conciliation.

The Queensland Government, Division of Workplace Health and Safety, Department of Industrial Relations has redefined bullying as 'workplace harassment' in its report published in March 2002. Their report was divided into five chapters. Here are the highlights of the chapters:

Chapter One: Introduction

Recommendations: Prevention and Management Framework

1. That the Government adopt a prevention and management framework to address workplace harassment that includes:

    a.   a comprehensive policy statement

    b.   the proposed statutory definition of workplace harassment

    c.   the proposed prevention and management framework

    d.   the participation of the Department of Industrial Relations, the Queensland Industrial Relations Commission, the Anti-Discrimination Commission and WorkCover.

2. That the Department of Industrial Relations develop and make an advisory standard on the prevention and management of workplace harassment under the *Workplace Health and Safety Act 1995* in consultation with relevant stakeholders, including members of the Workplace Bullying Taskforce.

3. That the advisory standard include the following elements:

    a.   proposed statutory definition

    b.   guidance on identifying workplace harassment

    c.   legal obligations and rights - references to the full suite of legislation

    d.   model policy, procedures and training, including alternative resolution/mediation processes

    e.   claims management

    f.   services/avenues of assistance

    g.   flexibility for small workplaces.

4. That the *Industrial Relations Act 1999* be amended to:

    1. List workplace harassment as an industrial matter in Schedule 1 of the Act [**Note:** Not done as of September, 2013]

    2. Include a definition of workplace harassment in Schedule 5 of the Act

    3. Add a subsection to section 231 of the Act to enable mediation to be used to assist the Commission in handling disputes specifically about workplace harassment.

5. That the following definition be considered as the basis for the definitions in the *Industrial Relations Act 1999,* the Workplace Health and Safety advisory standard and in the Public Service Codes of Conduct, as required: Workplace harassment is repeated behaviour, other than behaviour that is sexual harassment, that:

    1. Is directed at an individual worker or group of workers; and

    2. Is offensive, intimidating, humiliating or threatening; and

    3. Is unwelcome and unsolicited; and

    4. A reasonable person would consider to be offensive, intimidating, humiliating or threatening for the individual worker or group of workers.

    5. To give effect to section 231 of the *Industrial Relations Act 1999*, the Taskforce notes that further legislative or regulatory changes may be

required. Such amendments should be considered by the Department of Industrial Relations in consultation with Taskforce members and other relevant stakeholders.

6. That the workers' compensation arrangements and claims management procedures for injuries resulting from workplace harassment be examined and reviewed in terms of:
   a. Timeliness
   b. Rehabilitation
   c. Meaning of 'reasonable management action'
   d. Evidentiary and process requirements.

7. That an advisory service be established that:
   a. Provides information
   b. Assists employers and employees to identify cases of workplace harassment
   c. Encourages management of the issue at the workplace level
   d. Refers complainants to the relevant agency for assistance.

Implementing the prevention and management framework:

8. That the regulatory agencies responsible for implementing and enforcing government policy on workplace harassment develop policies and procedures on enforcement for workplace harassment, in consultation with Taskforce members and other relevant stakeholders.

9. That training programs for staff in government agencies responsible for implementing and enforcing government policy on workplace harassment be developed to deal with workplace harassment complaints, in consultation with Taskforce members and other relevant stakeholders.

10. That the Government establish a network of non-government agencies and government agencies responsible for implementing and enforcing government policy on workplace harassment to ensure ongoing coordination between agencies is effectively maintained, in consultation with Taskforce members and other relevant stakeholders.

11. That the Government review the implementation of legislation and standards recommended in this Report after a period of two years from when the legislation/standards commence.

Public sector recommendations:

12. That the Public Service Commissioner amend Directive 32/99 (Grievance Resolution) and Directive 9/96 (Code of Conduct) to require the mandatory inclusion of the definition of workplace harassment and to promote the principles which underpin public service employment.

13. That Directive 32/99 (Grievance Resolution) be amended to improve the management of timeframes of grievance investigations and to incorporate

mediation as the first stage in workplace grievance investigations related to workplace harassment.

14. That all public service agencies be required to classify and record the number of workplace grievances. That the OPSME monitor and analyse workplace harassment grievance data and work with individual agencies to stem the incidence of workplace harassment grievances across the public service.

15. That the OPMSE together with the DIR establish a 'Workforce Management Network' to coordinate whole-of-government education and prevention strategies in relation to workplace harassment and other workforce management issues.

Awareness information and education strategy:

a. That a comprehensive education and awareness strategy be developed by Government in consultation with industry and implemented by peak employer and employee bodies and community organisations as appropriate. The education and awareness strategy should:

   o include accessible information and education products for workers and managers/supervisors and others in control of workplaces

   o cemphasise the critical role of workplaces in preventing and managing workplace harassment.

16. That the Government support research into the extent, incidence, costs and causes of workplace harassment and groups of workers at risk.

17. That the Government establish data collection systems across relevant agencies to monitor the incidence of workplace harassment and workers' compensation costs associated with these.

Chapter Two: Characteristics and Extent o f Workplace

Harassment: Recommendations

1. That the Government support research into the extent, incidence, costs and causes of workplace harassment and groups of workers at risk.

2. That the Government establish data collection systems across relevant agencies to monitor the incidence of workplace harassment and workers' compensation costs associated with these.

Chapter Three: Definition: Recommendations

That the following definition be considered as the basis for the definitions in the *Industrial Relations Act 1999,* the Workplace Health and Safety advisory standard and in the Public Service Codes of Conduct, as required: Workplace harassment is repeated behaviour, other than behaviour that is sexual harassment, that:

a. is directed at an individual worker or group of workers; and
b. is offensive, intimidating, humiliating or threatening; and
c. is unwelcome and unsolicited; and
d. a reasonable person would consider to be offensive, intimidating, humiliating or threatening for the individual worker or group of workers.

Chapter Four: Prevention Management & Education:

Recommendations:

1. That a comprehensive education and awareness strategy be developed by Government in consultation with industry and implemented by peak employer and employee bodies and community Organisations as appropriate. The education and awareness strategy should:

    o include accessible information and education products for workers and managers/supervisors and others in control of workplaces
    o emphasise the critical role of workplaces in preventing and managing workplace harassment.

Chapter Five: Regulatory Strategies: Recommendations

1. That the Department of Industrial Relations develop and make an advisory standard on the prevention and management of workplace harassment under the *Workplace Health and Safety Act 1995* in consultation with relevant stakeholders, including members of the Workplace Bullying Taskforce.

   [**Note:** I checked their website www.whs.qld.gov.au ***Workplace Health & Safety & Other Acts Amendment Act, 2003*** that was released in June, 2003 and there is still nothing that discusses workplace bullying, harassment or violence.]

2. That the advisory standard include the following elements:
   a. proposed statutory definition
   b. guidance on identifying workplace harassment
   c. legal obligations and rights - references to the full suite of legislation
   d. model policy, procedures and training, including alternative resolution/mediation processes
   e. claims management
   f. services/avenues of assistance
   g. flexibility for small workplaces.

3. That the *Industrial Relations Act 1999* be amended to:
   1. list workplace harassment as an industrial matter in Schedule 1 of the Act. [Not done as of September, 2003].

   2. include a definition of workplace harassment in Schedule 5 of the Act. [Not done as of September, 2003].

4. Add a subsection to section 231 of the Act to enable mediation to be used to assist the Commission in handling disputes specifically about workplace harassment. [**Note**: I could not find this section.]

5. To give effect to section 231 of the *Industrial Relations Act 1999*, the Taskforce notes that further legislative or regulatory changes may be required. Such amendments should be considered by the Department of Industrial Relations in consultation with Taskforce members and other relevant stakeholders.

[**Note**: I checked their website www.qirc.qld.gov.au and this act has **not** been updated.]

6. That the workers' compensation arrangements and claims management procedures for injuries resulting from workplace harassment be examined and reviewed in terms of:
   a. Timeliness
   b. Rehabilitation
   c. Meaning of 'reasonable management action'
   d. Evidentiary and process requirements.

7. That the Public Service Commissioner amend Directive 32/99 (Grievance Resolution) and Directive 9/96 (Code of Conduct) to require the mandatory inclusion of the definition of workplace harassment and to promote the principles which underpin public service employment.

8. That Directive 32/99 (Grievance Resolution) be amended to improve the management of timeframes of grievance investigations and to incorporate mediation as the first stage in workplace grievance investigations related to workplace harassment.
   a. That all public service agencies be required to classify and record the number of workplace grievances.
   b. That the OPSME monitor and analyse workplace harassment grievance data and work with individual agencies to stem the incidence of workplace harassment grievances across the public service.

Chapter Six: Proposed Prevention and Management Framework:

Recommendations:

That the OPMSE together with the DIR establish a 'Workforce Management Network' to coordinate whole-of-government education and prevention strategies in relation to workplace harassment and other workforce management issues.

A Workplace Harassment Implementation Group comprised of high-level public service officials has considered the Taskforce's recommendations. The

Implementation Group's response to these recommendations is currently with the Queensland Government and the Minister of Industrial Relations.

[**Note**: I checked *Workplace Health & Safety & Other Acts Amendment Act, 2003* that was released in June, 2003 and there is still nothing that talks about workplace bullying, harassment or violence.]

I followed up on this taskforce report in September, 2003 asking the following questions:

- After the report was submitted - what happened? What changes came about as a result of this extensive study?
- Did Queensland follow the recommendations of the Taskforce that the *Workplace Health and Safety regulation, 1997* be amended to prohibit exposure to workplace harassment with a statutory definition of workplace harassment incorporated into the regulation?
- Were comprehensive administration guidelines developed and made mandatory by WorkCover?

I received the following reply from one of the policy officers of Workplace Health and Safety Policy Department of Industrial Relations, Queensland:

"In response to your questions, a Workplace Harassment Implementation Group comprised of high-level public service officials has considered the Taskforce's recommendations. The Implementation Group's response to these recommendations is currently with the Queensland Government and the Minister of Industrial Relations.

I am not aware of the Taskforce report making recommendations to amend the Workplace Health and Safety Regulation 1997 or WorkCover developing mandatory administrative guidelines for workplace harassment."

When I contacted Workplace Health and Safety Queensland to answer the following questions, they replied:

Question: Specific steps an employee would take if they're faced with workplace bullying.

Answer: Workplace Health and Safety Queensland (WHSQ) have developed a guide for workers on workplace harassment which addresses the options available to workers to manage workplace harassment. This can be obtained at the following address: www.whs.qld.gov.au/guide/gde32v1.pdf

The Draft Advisory Standard for Preventing Workplace Harassment also provides workers with some guidance regarding how workplace harassment should be prevented or managed. This document is currently out for public comment until 31 October [2003] and can be obtained from the following website:

www.whs.qld.gov.au/ris/index.htm

Question: The cost in time and money (to the employee) of lodging such a complaint.

Answer: WHSQ has only addressed the human costs to workers affected by workplace harassment, not the costs resulting from lodging a workplace harassment complaint.

Question: Does Occupational Health and Safety investigate complaints or does the employee have to resort to taking his/her employer to court?

Answer: There are a number of options currently available to workers who are seeking to resolve a workplace harassment complaint using a formal procedure. Workers may choose to lodge their complaint:

- internally with their employer, provided the employer has a system in place to manage formal workplace harassment complaints;

- externally with the: Trade Union; Fair Treatment Appeal (available only to public sector employees); Queensland Industrial Relations Commission; Anti-Discrimination Commission Queensland; Queensland Police; Workplace Health and Safety Queensland. The role of WHSQ is to ensure that policies and procedures to deal with workplace harassment have been developed and are effectively implemented within the workplace. *Workplace Health and Safety Inspectors will not investigate the details of the complaint, adjudicate or mediate between the respondent and the complainant.*

The nature of the workplace harassment would dictate which of the above-mentioned agencies the worker could lodge their complaint with. For example, a worker may lodge a complaint with ADCQ or Queensland Police if the harassment constituted or had elements of, discrimination or assault.

[**Note:** There needs to be one specific law or Act that covers *all* types of workplace bullying, harassment and violence. //The Workplace Health & Safety Regulations were replace in 2011 – there was no mention of bullying, harassment or violence in the new Act.]

Appendix 11

SOUTH AUSTRALIA

South Australia - Public Sector

(Information relating to the Public Sector can be obtained on: www.ocpe.sa.gov.au/publications)

(Permission given by Gary Collis [South Australian Employer Ombudsman] to include the following information.)

I was very impressed with how quickly and thoroughly he dealt with my enquiries. It appears as if he is doing his best to help employees deal with workplace bullying.

"Bullies Not Wanted - Recognising and Eliminating Bullying in the Worlplace" www.employeeombudsman.sa.gov.au

The South Australian Office of the Employee Ombudsman receives over 500 complaints each year on workplace bullying issues and the figure is increasing. For many years Gary Collis has provided support to those targeted by workplace bullies and worked with unions and employers who are committed to providing bully-free work environments. Their report includes the following chapters:

Chapter 1: What is Workplace Bullying?
Chapter 2: Who are the Bullies and who are their Victims?
Chapter 3: How Widespread is Workplace Bullying?
Chapter 4: Reporting Workplace Bullying
Chapter 5: What Causes Workplace Bullying?
Chapter 6: Consequences of Workplace Bullying
Chapter 7: Legislation that may be used to curb Workplace Bullying
Chapter 8: Dealing with a Workplace Bully - A Guide for Victims
Chapter 9: Dealing with Workplace Bullying - Guidelines for Managers
Chapter 10: Eliminating Workplace Bullying at its Source
Chapter 11: Using the Occupational Health, Safety and Welfare
       Legislation to Prevent Workplace Bullying
Chapter 12: Rights of Any Person Accused of Workplace Bullying
Chapter 13: Sources of Advice, Information and Assistance in The
       Workplace

In his web page he states:

Q. *"Are there any laws against workplace bullying?"*

A. *"Yes, there are several different laws that can be used, depending upon the form that the bullying takes. These include: 'normal legislation covering assault and threatening behaviour where the bullying involves causing (or threatening to cause) physical harm to a person. Such bullying should be reported to the police. South Australian and Commonwealth anti-discrimination laws where the bullying is based on a person's ethnic background, sex, age, disability, sexual preference, etc. The South Australian Occupational Health, Safety and Welfare Act requires employers to protect their employees against threats to their health and safety while at work. This includes threats to their well being caused through intimidation, humiliation, embarrassment, etc. If you believe that you are being bullied at work you should seek advice as to the form of action that is most appropriate for your circumstances. Sources of help are described later in this brochure. "*

[**Note:** Although Gary Collis mentions that intimidation, humiliation, embarrassment. etc. are covered in the regulations - I examined the existing South Australia's Occupational Health, Safety and Welfare Regulations, 1995 (with amendments until September 1, 2002 - all 357 pages of it!) and not once did it use the words intimidation, humiliation or embarrassment or address the problems of abuse, bullying or harassment. Since that time a review has been done to upgrade the system, but so far I still haven't found any laws or regulations that actually protect workers against workplace bullying and harassment in Southern Australia unless they are discrimination, sexual harassment or violence situations.]

The following covers that review:

Reviews of the Occupational Health, Safety and Welfare System in South Australia (December, 2002) (Just excerpts relating to bullying).

In announcing the Review, the Minister for Industrial Relations, the Hon. Michael Wright, MP stated: *"It is approaching twenty years since the present systems of workers compensation and occupational health, safety and welfare in South Australia were conceived. South Australia has been a leader before. This review will put us back at the front of the field"*

"This is all about delivering world's best practice for South Australians. The review process aims to engage stakeholders and the community and to develop recommendations through a consultative, participative process."

A prime feature of the Review is the belief that workers should go home from work in relatively the same condition they arrived at work.

Academics, OHSW specialists and key stakeholders all stated that guidance material, COPs42 and ACOPs43 or new Regulations and education were the way to deal with the issues of workplace bullying and violence in the workplace. Improved definitions and descriptions of acceptable and nonacceptable behaviours should be included in COPs [Codes of Practice]. Conciliation and mediation processes, which allowed resolution of the matter between parties, should also be incorporated.

An industry association stated that including workplace bullying in occupational health, safety and welfare legislation could only be justified on the assumption that the workplace contributed to the offence. This group stated that the issue is best dealt with under 'human resource management and industrial legislation.'

Discussion of Issues:

Workplace bullying is notable for having no statutory definition in South Australian legislation. The absence of specific legislative recognition of workplace bullying is commonplace around Australia. In recent years most Australian jurisdictions have developed voluntary guidance material that addresses either workplace bullying or occupational violence.

The creation of a definition in South Australian legislation may help facilitate the effective handling of workplace bullying complaints and such a definition should also be consistently applied in all relevant legislation.

Through submissions and consultation, it is evident that there may be sizeable under-reporting of workplace bullying. As social attitudes towards the issue change and as more options for addressing complaints become available it is possible a significant increase in numbers of complaints may flow through workplaces and the agencies that address workplace bullying. The resource implications of this should be considered.

The Proposal:

It is proposed a COP [Code of Practice] be developed which includes:

- A definition of inappropriate behaviour in the workplace;
- A definition of workplace violence;
- An explanation of responsibilities of employers and employees;
- A preventions model; and
- Reporting systems.

The Review supports Recommendation 168 of the Review of the Industrial Relations System that Inspectors be able to refer workplace bullying matters to the Industrial Commission for mediation or conciliation. Subsequently - a draft bill was placed in parliament.

Draft bill - The Occupational Health Safety and Welfare (SafeWork SA Amendment Bill, 2003)

It recommends:

Insert of section 55A

32. After section 55 insert:

Inappropriate behaviour towards an employee

55A. (1) If -

(a) an inspector receives a complaint from an employee that he or she is being bullied or abused at work; and

(b) the inspector has reason to believe that the matter is capable of resolution by conciliation or mediation under this section, the inspector may, after consultation with the relevant parties, refer the matter to the Industrial Commission for conciliation or mediation.

(2) A reference under subsection (1) will be made by written instrument that complies with any prescribed requirements.

(3) The inspector must ensure that the parties are furnished with a copy of any reference under subsection (1).

(4) If a matter is referred to the Industrial Commission under subsection

(1) the Industrial Commission must attempt to resolve the matter by-

(a) conciliation; or

(b) mediation, as the Industrial Commission thinks fit.

(5) For the purposes of any conciliation or mediation, the Industrial Commission may -

(a) call a conference of the parties to the matter and at that conference seek to resolve the matter by agreement or in any other way; and
(b) interview the parties separately or together; and
(c) inform itself in any other way as it thinks fit; and
(d) endeavour to resolve the matter amicably; and
(e) in the case of a mediation, give directions with a view to resolving the matter.

(6) The Industrial Commission may at any time bring conciliation or mediation proceedings to an end if the Industrial Commission considers that the proceedings will not result in the resolution of the matter.

(7) Nothing said or done in any proceedings under this section can subsequently be given in evidence, nor is a member of the Industrial Commission involved in any conciliation or mediation disqualified from sitting with respect to the matter in other proceedings under this Act.

(8) The Industrial Commission must inform the Department when any proceedings before the Industrial Commission under this section are concluded or brought to an end.

(9) The Industrial Commission and the Department must consult from time to time in relation to the operation of this section and the Industrial Commission may, after consultation with the Department, prepare and publish guidelines to assist parties involved in proceedings under this section.

It's not clear what will happen with these recommendations. Hopefully they will soon be included in legislation so that all employees are protected against workplace bullying, violence and harassment.

When I contacted Gary Collis South Australian Employer Ombudsman of South Australia, to answer the following questions, he replied:

Question: Specific steps an employee would take if they're faced with workplace bullying.

Answer: Formally I would advise the employee to inform the employer in writing, of a workplace hazard, who the hazard is, dot point the examples of behaviour that is having a detrimental effect on the health of the employee and finish off with the statement that the employee is now asking the employer to comply with their duty of care.

Question: The cost in time and money (to the employee) of lodging such a complaint.

Answer: As to time and money, well the time is as long as it takes to write the incident report and there is no cost, if the employer does not comply with his/her duty of care then I would advise the employee to make a formal complaint to Workplace Services OHSW Inspector and again there is no cost to doing this. Having investigated the matter, the inspector can then pursue a prosecution if the employer is found to have knowingly breached the OHS/W Act.

Question: Does Occupational Health and Safety investigate complaints or does the employee have to resort to taking his/her employer to court?

Answer: Workplace Services investigate, so the employee does not have to pursue the matter

He added another note: *"Of course all of the above sounds quite simple but as we know, all the rules, policies and procedures are useless if there is no confidence by the employees that the employer will not take the easy way out and simply move the victim. Effective management of the first incident will reduce the incidents of bullying, because as we know, there is only bullying when behaviour has been allowed to continue."*

"Workplace Bullying Project" Working Women's Centre SA Inc.
www.wwc.org.au

The Workplace Bullying Project was conducted by the South Australian Working Women's Centre in 1997 and was **substantially funded by WorkCover.** The purpose of the project was to document the nature and experience of workplace bullying; identify the health, safety and welfare effects on individuals; broadly calculate the cost of bullying to organisations and to develop strategies to combat it.

Data was collected from 342 questionnaires, seven case studies and three focus groups. These sources provided detail on bullying behaviour and situations, their effects on individuals' health and working life and action taken by respondents and their managers to deal with the bullying.

Analysis of the questionnaire data shows that workplace bullying either by managers and employers or by co-workers is largely unacknowledged or misunderstood. Bullying has a destructive and debilitating effect on its targets and few effective mechanisms or procedures exist, either at the workplace or more widely, to deal with it. Consequent high rates of sick leave, absenteeism, reduced productivity and resignation mean significant costs for organisations.

The report calls for greater use of current occupational health and safety legislation to combat bullying at work, for a community and workplace education program on the unacceptability of workplace bullying. As well, it calls for the training of key workplace personnel to recognise and understand the signs and effects of workplace bullying. Collaboration between occupational health and safety personnel, management, employees and unions to develop anti-bullying programs within work-places is recommended. An outline for a model anti-bullying program is included.

[Here are excerpts from that report]

While all workplaces have the potential to produce bullies, some researchers believe that certain managerialist values may foster and encourage bullying behaviour at all levels in an organisation. 'Strong' or 'kick arse' management may disguise an atmosphere of intolerance and intimidation, encouraging a reign of terror in the name of getting the job done.

Crawford, a UK psychotherapist, describes the bully as someone who has failed to resolve childhood conflicts effectively and is unable to manage anger and frustration. While he maintains that individuals are and should be given authority by organisations to act and to wield power, Crawford sees bullying as, *"a symptom of organisational dysfunction"* (Crawford, 1997, p.221).

Robyn Mann in Australia likens the effects of psychological abuse in the workplace to those suffered by victims of mental and physical torture. Her definition stresses the sustained, psychological nature of the abuse and the

232

deliberate, destructive intent of the abuser. The abuse she describes includes that which falls within the range of behaviours considered in the project. Mann maintains that, *"The form of abuse systematically undermines self-esteem and self-confidence over a period of time. The abuser is not always in a position of legitimate power, but has power over resources and 'in-house' knowledge and particularly, power by association due to alliances with people in positions of legitimate power."* (Mann, 1996, p.84)

Mann writes that elements of psychological abuse in the workplace correspond with elements of torture and the results of having undergone torture. Abusers, she says, *"Work their way into situations where they will have influence over the vulnerable - new appointees, newly promoted staff and those in highly stressful working situations where deadlines and client satisfaction are crucial."* (Mann, 1996, p.85)

4.3.5 Bullying by a person in a position of authority

In all, 293 respondents (85.7 per cent of the total group) reported being bullied by a person in a position of authority i.e. manager, employer or supervisor. To ascertain the nature of the bullying, respondents were given a list of behaviours and situations and asked to indicate whether or not they had experienced them.

[Following this information they show several graphs entitled:]

- Frequency of bullying actions and behaviours by a person in a position of authority
- Frequency of bullying actions by co-workers
- Comparison of bullying behaviours by managers and co-workers
- Action by respondents to deal with bullying
- Perceptions of management effectiveness
- Percentage of respondents noting degree of effect of bullying on well-being
- Percentage of respondents indicating degree of support
- Categories of leave taken as a result of bullying
- Time away from work as a result of bullying

4.9 Advice on how to deal with bullying

Most respondents had spent considerable time thinking over their bullying experience, their own reactions, what they might have done or not done, how their managers might have reacted and how the situation might be improved. The advice which respondents had to give to a person being bullied is summarised below. In general the comments have more positive tone and reflect a pro-active way of dealing with the bullying than appears in the responses to other sections of the questionnaire. This phenomenon may be explained by the nature of the bullying experience. The sapping of self-confidence which victims of bullying frequently experience does not allow them to advocate strongly on their own behalf. While victims of bullying may be aware of what they should do in terms of procedure to combat the bullying, they may be unable to initiate the process without support.

Advice to a person being bullied

Don't put up with it!

- Don't put up with it because help is out there.
- Don't take it - complain loudly. Whatever you do, don't shut up and take it like I did.
- No matter how hard it is, take action.
- I would go straight to the top to make my complaints to management and/or union, although this doesn't guarantee results.

Keep up your confidence

- Keep believing in yourself.
- Concentrate on the positive things in your life.
- Believe in yourself.
- The problems you are experiencing are brought about by mean-spirited individuals.
- They have the problem - not you.
- Nurture yourself. Read and understand about bullying issues.

Resign

- Don't continue to search for a solution.
- Recognise when the problem is irresolvable and get out early.
- There is no help available. Trying to get support only escalates the problem. Look after your own health and find another job.
- If a manager allows bullying at work, it would be best to look for another job where people appreciate your work.

Seek advice and support

- Recognise it as bullying and find reliable support people.
- Join a union and go to a doctor for help.
- Seek help early, if not from your superiors then from an outside professional.
- Seek support and talk to your manager. If your boss is the bully then you have a BIG problem.

SAEBOW - South Australian Employees Bullied Out of Work

This help/information line was founded by Catherine Crout-Habel in March 1999, following her own workplace bullying experience. It is a self-funded service with callers paying for postage and printing of material. Her website, *"Bullies Down Under"* was launched on Australia day, 26th January, 2000 and can be accessed on www.catrin.mtx.net. The aims of SAEBOW and the *"Bullies Down Under"* website are to:

- Break the silence on workplace bullying.
- Provide information to challenge workplace bullies.
- Validate the experiences of those targeted by a bully.
- Establish links with other websites tackling bullying.
- Suggest resources and support organisations for the targets of bullies.
- Provide information for employers to assist in the creation of a bully-free work environment.

SAEBOW is strongly involved in lobbying politicians to introduce effective legislation to stop workplace bullying before people are injured and forced onto the WorkCover scheme.

Appendix 12

WESTERN AUSTRALIA

[**Note:** WorkSafe Division of the Department of Consumer and Employment Protection in Western Australia's report entitled *"Safety and Health in the Workplace depends on you" (2002)* www.safetyline.wa.gov.au does *not* cover workplace bullying or violence in the workplace (just workplace safety). However, they do have the following information booklets:]

- Workplace Violence Code of Practice
- Dealing with Workplace Bullying - a Guide for Employers (Guidance Note)
- Dealing with Workplace Bullying - a Guide for Employees (Guidance Note)
- Dealing with Workplace Bullying – New Guidance Notes
- Excerpts from their *"Guide for Employees"*

[**Note:** Keep in mind that *regulations have force of law, whereas codes contain guidance material only*.]

Resolving issues:

The *Occupational Safety and Health Act 1984* requires employers to attempt to resolve occupational safety and health issues with safety and health representatives, safety and health committees or employees, according to the relevant procedures for the workplace. If these procedures do not succeed, the *Act* sets out to resolve the issue.

If an issue remains unresolved and there is a risk of serious and imminent injury or harm to someone, either the employer or a safety and health representative may ask for a WorkSafe inspector to attend the workplace. If there is no safety and health representative, an employee may ask an inspector to come to a workplace. An inspector so notified will attend the workplace and take whatever action under the *Act* he or she considers appropriate.

The inspector's role is not to mediate between the bullied person and the alleged bully, but to ensure the employer and employees meet their obligations under the Act.

[**Note:** Because the *Act* does *not* discuss regulations relating to workplace bullying, harassment or violence I can't see that they would be able to stop workplace bullying.]

Other legal considerations

Where bullying involves sexual harassment or discrimination, the employee may involve WorkSafe and additionally may lodge a claim under the *Equal Opportunity Act, 1984.*

Should an employee consider he or she has been dismissed as a result of making a complaint in relation to bullying or is forced to resign due to the affects of bullying, the employee may be entitled to lodge a claim under the unfair dismissal provisions in the *Industrial Relations Act 1979.*

The *Public Sector Management Act 1994* governs the behaviour of public sector employees and bullying can be a breach of the *Western Australian Public Sector Code of Ethics.* Physical assault and sexual assault are criminal matters and should be referred to the police.

Appendix One: Overview Relevant Legislation

Legislation: Occupational Safety and Health Act 1984

Situation: The Act includes general duties for employers and employees, requirements for the resolution of issues and the functions of safety and health representatives and committees.

Legislation: Occupational Safety and Health Regulations 1996

Situation: Regulation 3.1

A person who, at a workplace, is an employer, the main contractor, a self-employed person, a person having control of the workplace or a person having control of access to the workplace must, as far as practicable-

(a) Identify each hazard to which a person at the workplace is likely to be exposed.
(b) Assess the risk of injury or harm to a person resulting from each hazard, if any, identified; and
(c) Consider the means by which the risk may be reduced.

[No mention of workplace bullying, harassment or violence.]

Legislation: Equal Opportunity Amendment Act 1992 and Commonwealth Disability and Discrimination Act 1992

Situation: Where bullying involves acts of discrimination or sexual harassment a complaint may be lodged under this legislation. Discrimination occurs when someone is treated less favourably due to parental status, religion, political belief, marital status, sex, race, age, impairment, pregnancy or sexual orientation.

[Except for this specific area, workplace bullying, harassment and violence are not covered.]

Legislation: *Workplace Agreements Act 1993*

Industrial Relations Act 1979 and Minimum Conditions of Employment Act 1993

Situation: Where a worker is dismissed or forced to resign as a result of workplace bullying, the worker may be entitled to make a claim under the unfair dismissal provisions.

[It sounds to me like their recommendations encourage bullied workers to quit their jobs, if their company doesn't stop the bullying.]

Legislation: *Workers' Compensation and Rehabilitation Act 1981*

Situation: A worker who suffers an injury or disease as a result of workplace bullying may submit a claim for workers' compensation. However, they have to demonstrate that it was caused by the employment, that the employment was the major significant factor causing injury/disease and circumstances do not meet the exclusions documented in the *Act.*

[**Note:** Workplace bullying *not* covered.]

Legislation: *Public Sector Management Act 1994 (State Government Departments)*

Situation: The public sector employee can lodge a complaint to the Office of the Public Sector Standards Commissioner (OPPSSC) when not satisfied with the outcome of an investigation. The *Western Australian Public Sector Code of Ethics* governs the behaviour of Public Sector Employees.

[More information later.]

Legislation: *Criminal Code*

Situation: When workplace bullying involves physical assault or threat of assault, the incident becomes a police matter and is dealt with under the *Criminal Code.*

Legislation: *Common Law*

Situation: An employer has a duty to protect workers from workplace bullying. This duty exists in tort and as an implied term in the employment contract. Under common law, the employer who does not make suitable precautions may be liable for any physical or psychological injury suffered by the victim.

[It sounds as if the employee must take the employer to court that could take several years to do and cost them dearly.]

Legislation: Industrial Relations Commission (IRC)

Situation: When a dispute exists between an employer and a worker, a notice of industrial dispute can be lodged with the IRC.

[Again with high court costs.]

Legislation: Industrial Award

Situation: Usually contain grievance procedures that can be used in disputes involving bullying.

[In a telephone conversation I had with one of the inspectors from the Service Industries Team, Manufacturing, Transport & Service Industries Branch, I was informed that *any fines that were obtained from companies contravening the Acts do not go to the victim of the bullying.]*

When I asked the inspector to answer the following questions:

1. Specific steps an employee would take if they're faced with workplace bullying.
2. The cost in time and money (to the employee) of lodging such a complaint.
3. Does Occupational Health and Safety investigate complaints or does the employee have to resort to taking his/her employer to court?

She replied that all those questions were answered in the Dealing with Workplace Bullying - a Guide for Employees.

Question one was clearly answered. Question two was not. Question three reinforced that "The inspector's role is not to mediate between the bullied person and the alleged bully, but to ensure the employer and employees meet their obligations under the Act." Because workplace bullying, harassment and violence are not specifically covered in the Occupational Safety and Health Act 1984 it's not clear what the next step would be for the bully except to take the employer to court.

Western Australian Public Sector Code of Ethics

Here are some excerpts from the *Code of Ethics*: (You can find the complete Code of Ethics on their web page:)
www.wa.gov.au/opssc/documents

Under *Justice* it states: "*Justice* means being impartial and using power fairly for the common good. It means not abusing, discriminating against or exploiting people."

Under *Respect for Persons* it states: "*Respect for persons* means being honest and treating people courteously, so that they maintain their dignity and their rights are upheld. It means not harassing, intimidating or abusing people."

Scope and Coverage

The Code of Ethics applies equally to all: *public sector employees,* including chief executive officers and chief employees; public sector bodies established or continued for a public purpose under written law, including boards, committees and trusts.

[**Note:** It's interesting to note the next paragraph:]

The Code of Ethics does *not* apply to: elected officials including Members of Parliament and local government representatives; Parliament's employees; local government employees; sworn members of the Western Australia Police Force {i.e.: police officers}; universities; any court or tribunal established under a written law; the Governor's establishment electorate offices of Members of Parliament.

[**Note:** One can only surmise that it doesn't matter whether these people are impartial or abuse, discriminate against or exploit people. It could also be taken to mean that they are allowed to harass, intimidate or abuse people. It makes one wonder doesn't it?]

Appendix 13

TASMANIA

(From *Anti-Discrimination Commission Tasmania* web page that discusses bullying) www.justice.tas.gov.au

The Anti-Discrimination Commission Tasmania was established by Tasmanian Parliament on 10 December 1999. The Commission administers the *Tasmanian Anti-Discrimination Act* **1998.**

The Commissioner has the following functions:

- To advise and make recommendations to the Minister of Justice on matters relating to discrimination and prohibited conduct;
- To promote the recognition and approval of acceptable attitudes, acts and practices relating to discrimination and prohibited conduct;
- To consult and inquire into discrimination and prohibited conduct and the effects of discrimination and prohibited conduct;
- To disseminate information about discrimination and prohibited conduct and the effects of discrimination and prohibited conduct;
- To undertake research and educational programs to promote attitudes, acts and practices against discrimination and prohibited conduct;
- To prepare and publish guidelines for the avoidance of attitudes, acts and practices relating to discrimination and prohibited conduct;
- To examine any legislation and report to the minister as to whether it is discriminatory or not; and
- To investigate and seek to conciliate claims;

The Anti-Discrimination Act 1998 outlaws discrimination on any of the following attributes or identities:

Age, Breastfeeding, Disability, Family responsibilities, Gender/sex, Industrial activity, Irrelevant criminal record, Irrelevant medical record, Lawful sexual activity, Marital Status, Parental Status, Political activity, Political belief or affiliation, Pregnancy, Race, Religious activity, Religious belief or affiliation, Sexual orientation, Association with a person who has or is believed to have, any of these attributes or identities.

The Act also covers the following prohibited conduct:

- Any conduct which offends, humiliates, intimidates, insults or ridicules another person on the basis of *gender, marital status, pregnancy, breastfeeding, parental status, family responsibilities;*
- Sexual and sexist harassment;

- Victimisation (in relation to claims);
- Inciting hatred (by public act) - on the grounds of *race, disability, sexual orientation, lawful sexual activity, religious belief or affiliation or religious activity;*
- Publishing, displaying or advertising matter that promotes, expresses or depicts discrimination or prohibited conduct.

Areas covered by the Act:

- Employment (including paid and unpaid);
- Education and training;
- Provision of facilities, goods and services;
- Accommodation (including residential and business);
- Membership and activities of clubs.

Administration of any law of state and any state program on any ground specified in *attributes/identities* - gender/sex, marital status, pregnancy, breastfeeding, parental status or family responsibilities.

Please note - if you have an interest in specific issues relating to sports and recreation, please follow the link to sport and recreation Tasmania. www.development.tas.gov.au/sportrec There you will find information on play by the rules - a training and information web site to promote "sporting behaviour' in sport and recreation clubs and associations plus information on how to prevent and deal with inappropriate behaviour including discrimination, harassment and favouritism, bias and various forms of abuse.

What is bullying?

Bullying must be addressed and effectively dealt with. The costs are more far-reaching than organisations recognise and higher than any 'dollar' amount acknowledged by business.

Bullying is:

"... long-standing violence, physical or psychological conducted by an individual or a group and directed against an individual who is not able to defend (her/himself) in the actual situation." [Roland 1988]

"... 'one off' abuses, 'small' acts of violence, shouted orders, unreasonable demands, niggling words repeated daily, pleasant words one minute, demeaning the next, acting 'well' 'in public' and abusively in private, isolation, 'pushing', pressure, being spoken to roughly or as if one doesn't count ... " [Scutt 2000]

"... endemic in Australia and ... many of our institutions and professional groups are willing to use bully tactics to maintain positions of power and privilege ... Bullying is the same, whether the victim is a school child, a battered wife, a middle management executive or a whistleblower." [McCarthy, Sheehan, Wilkie 1996]

What are the costs of bullying?

Workplace bullying may result in:

- Long periods of sick leave or 'stress leave;'
- A catastrophic drop in production by the whole unit, division or group;
- A person being paid without having any 'real' work to do;
- Intervention by personnel officers, consultants, managers, occupational health staff, the company's healthcare nurses, union advocates and psychologists.

Economic costs are often quoted. A Tasmanian Government Agency assessing average costs of internally investigating one sexual harassment complaint found it cost $36,500 to investigate a bullying claim. This included interviewing the claimant, alleged harasser, other witnesses etc. It *excludes* health and production costs of bullying.

The reduction or complete loss of productive work and 'lesser' consequences can amount to between $US30,000 and $US100,000 for each employee exposed to bullying conduct. [Dr Heinz Leymann 1990]

The costs of internal investigation of complaints through grievance procedures and of external claims through Anti-Discrimination, Workers Compensation, Industrial Relations and courts can be high.

Is bullying worth it?

The psychological and emotional consequences of bullying impact on victims/survivors and others in the workplace.

The state of mind of people bullied at work, at school, in sporting organisations, clubs and other bodies can be fraught. Bullying can cause deep emotional scars not easily recognised or remedied. Sufferers, targets or victims/survivors of bullying often find it difficult to reveal their painful experiences, even to people close to them. Despair and isolation can result in workers and students attempting suicide and even succeeding.

Health effects include headaches, sleep difficulties, bedwetting, high blood pressure, anxiety, nausea, anger, loss of motivation and concentration, destruction of self-confidence and low morale. This impacts on work and family life and outside work and home. Bullying places significant pressure on people at work, family and friends.

What to do about bullying: Get Help and now!!

If you are a bully - stop it. Learn to control your own behaviour or employers, courts and tribunals will do it for you. Bullying is an employer organisation, business, government and corporate responsibility. All organisations and individuals must act to stop bullying.

Act to look at the contributing factors. Act to make people aware of their rights and responsibilities:

If needed, remove the bully from the workplace or organisation;

- Support the victim/survivor;
- Don't take the side of the bully, against the bullied - this makes *you* a bully-by-proxy;
- Work to end intimidation in all environments by getting the issue out in the open;
- Talk with colleagues, workers, fellow students etc. or a supervisor, manager, counsellor, teacher etc;
- Organise with like minded people to support one another and gain a feeling of solidarity against bullies and bullying;
- Find out about your legal position;
- Empower yourself through reading about what to do about bullying and talking with others;
- Talk to your health and safety representative, union delegate or teacher so that they take up the issue;
- Contact your union for assistance or call – Anti-Discrimination Commission: 1 800 632 716
  Workplace Standards: 1 300 366 322
  Office of the Employment Advocate: 1 300 366 632
  Working Women's Centre:1 800 644 589
  ACTU Helpline:1 300 362 223
- Claim and claimant under Commission documentation refer to complaint and complainant under the *Anti-Discrimination Act* **1998.**

What legislative safeguards are there?

Occupational Health & Safety

Occupational health and safety legislation says that employers have a legal duty to control all health and safety hazards in the workplace by eliminating them or otherwise safeguarding workers' health. Bullying is a workplace safety hazard. Internal organisational structures, practices or behaviour that involve bullying are the employer's responsibility. It is the employer's responsibility to eliminate them.

Anti-discrimination law

Some forms of bullying are outlawed by equal opportunity or anti-discrimination legislation. In some cases bullying is covered under laws dealing with discrimination based on race/ethnicity, age, sexual orientation, lawful sexual activity, sex/gender, marital status, pregnancy, breastfeeding, parental status, family responsibilities, disability, industrial activity, political belief or affiliation, political activity, religious belief or affiliation, religious activity, irrelevant criminal record, irrelevant medical record or association with a person who has or is believed to have, any of these attributes or identities.

Section 17 (1) of the Tasmanian *Anti-Discrimination Act 1998* says that a person must not engage in any conduct which offends, humiliates, intimidates, insults or ridicules another person on the basis of sex/gender, marital status, pregnancy, breastfeeding, parental status or family responsibilities in circumstances in which a reasonable person, having regard to all the circumstances, would have anticipated that the other person would be offended, humiliated, intimidated, insulted or ridiculed. *This includes bullying.*

[Note: I have *not* been unable to find this reference in their Act.]

There is no excuse for causing, allowing or tolerating bullying

At all times:

- Keep records of issues, incidents, problems or occurrences and do this as accurately as you can and as close as possible to when these issues have happened;
- Raise issues with employer, school, club, institution or organisation through appropriate representatives;
- Arrange counselling or other assistance immediately if needed;
- The Anti-Discrimination Commission (ADC) Tasmania deals with claims of discrimination, harassment and bullying within Tasmania.;
- The ADC's community education arm is a free service to community groups for information about the Tasmanian *Anti-Discrimination Act* (ADA) 1998. Anti-Discrimination Australia (Tasmania) designs and delivers 'fee for service' training courses tailored for the needs of all organisations that wish to familiarise themselves with the new ADA 1998.

For further information: **Anti-Discrimination Commission Tasmania** Email: AntiDiscrimination@justice.tas.gov.au

Workplace Standards Tasmania

When I contacted Workplace Standards Tasmania to answer the following questions, they replied:

Question: Specific steps an employee would take if they're faced with workplace bullying.

Answer: None.

Question: The cost in time and money (to the employee) of lodging such a complaint.

Answer: None.

Question: Does Occupational Health and Safety investigate complaints or does the employee have to resort to taking his/her employer to court?

Answer: None.

I did receive a note sent by the Chief Inspector of Workplace Standards Tasmania as follows:

"As you are aware, the issue of workplace bullying can be complex and is reliant on knowing the circumstances of each situation before providing advice. The Inspectorate is currently looking more closely at how we can better advise industry on this matter. The risk assessment process is the basis on which we will advise employers of their duty of care obligations. A new publication is currently in draft form. It is anticipated this will provide some assistance to the Inspectorate on these issues once complete. You will no doubt be aware of the WA publications on this subject."

Workplace Standards Tasmania helpline replied:

"Workplace Standards Tasmania is currently editing and preparing information on workplace bullying. This will be part of a large kit for employers and workers, with other information on workplace stress and alcohol and other drug misuse. When we release new publications, they are posted on our website at:

www.workcover.tas.gov.au/node/PubsGeneral.htm

One can only hope that these recommendations will result in the update of their Acts and regulations to include workplace bullying, harassment and violence - and soon. Until that is done, how many more employees will suffer while they drag their feet?

Appendix 14

NORTHERN TERRITORY

Work Environment - Violence in the workplace - Bulletin WH 01 07

NT WorkSafe - Northern Territory Department of Employment, Education and Training who administer the Work Health Act (NT) www.nt.gov.au/deet/worksafe/corporate/bulletins/pdf/15.01.pdf

[**Note:** They advise that they were not the original authors of the document, but concur with the contents therein. The information contained in this document originated from one of their interstate counterparts some years ago on a mutual agreement basis.]

"Employers are under obligation to provide safe and healthy workplaces and employees are also obliged to take reasonable care at work. Violence in the workplace is not acceptable. This information bulletin provides practical steps for addressing violence in the workplace."

What is violence at work?

The expression of violence takes many forms, ranging from physical assault and verbal abuse to intimidation and low level threatening behaviour.

The term "violence at work' applies to 'any incident in which employees and others are abused, threatened or assaulted in circumstances arising out of or in the course of work undertaken. This also includes employers, self-employed people and any other person who may be affected by a violent incident in the workplace.

It is important to recognise that violence is a workplace hazard and reasonably practicable steps should be taken to protect employees and others in the workplace from violent incidents.

Violence at work can happen in a variety of workplaces. It may cause mental and physical pain and suffering and may result in permanent disability or even death.

Employees may be exposed to various forms of violence and threatening behaviour. The violence may come from members of the public, students, patients or clients or from supervisors, managers or other workers.

Working alone or at night may increase risk

Recent workers' compensation figures indicate that 74 per cent of workplace assaults in Western Australia occurred in the community services industry.

More than half of the assaults were to nurses, social workers, guards, security officers and prison officers.

Forms of violence such as verbal abuse, intimidation and threatening behaviour not resulting in physical injury are difficult to quantify, but may have significant effects upon the psychological well being of employees. Employees who deal with members of the public in service industries and government agencies are likely to be exposed to these forms of violence. The threat of robbery or attack is a significant factor for employees who handle such items as cash or drugs.

(See full web page for this information. Other headings in their bulletin include:)

- Why reduce the risk of violence and aggression at work?
- What causes violence at work?
- Management Plans to reduce the risk of violence at work
- Steps to developing a Management Plan to reduce violence at work
- Back-up
- Monitor
- Review

[**Note**: I learned that Northern Territory WorkSafe uses the ***Work Health Act of November, 2002*** for OH&S protection. I searched the entire document (166 pages) but could find no reference to "abuse," "bullying," "harassment," "intimidation," or "violence" so wonder which Act the above refers to.]

The Northern Territory Government did not reply to my enquiry asking the following questions:

1. Specific steps an employee would take if they're faced with workplace bullying.
2. The cost in time and money (to the employee) of lodging such a complaint.
3. Does Occupational Health and Safety investigate complaints or does the employee have to resort to taking his/her employer to court?
4. The reply I received from Northern Territory WorkSafe states,

"Yes, we do investigate bullying cases on an as-need basis although to date we have had very few reported cases. We use the Queensland bulletin as a guide. It is in two parts one for workers and one for employers."

Appendix 15

NEW LAW JULY 1, 2014

FairWork Commission Australia

On July 1st, 2014 the FairWork Commission Australia put forward the following guidlines that have very little effect on workplace bullying. For instance the Commission can make an order to prevent a worker being bullied at work, but that the Commission cannot issue fines or penalties and cannot forward financial compensation. They also state that a worker must still be exposed to bullying by the same individual or group at work – the Commission can only make an order if there is a risk that the worker will continue to be bullied. What about the workers who have been bullied so severely that they've been forced to leave their jobs? How do they receive compensation for their victimisation?

Most victims just want the bullying to stop without fanfare, however the following makes that impossible: The Commission is required by law to publish its decisions. Decisions are published on the website www.fwc.gov.au and generally include the names of parties to the matter.

So this new Guide has very few teeth that will help employees stop bullying at work. The guide reads as follows:

Guide Published **8 July 2014** www.fwc.gov.au 1/9

Anti-bullying

1. About bullying at work

A worker may apply to the Fair Work Commission (the Commission) for an order to stop bullying at work from continuing. This right comes from the *Fair Work Act 2009*.

What is bullying at work?

Bullying occurs when:

- a person or a group of people **repeatedly** behaves unreasonably towards a worker or a group of workers at work

  [Author's note: To the victim - one incident of bullying can be enough and should have all the protection of the law to deal with it.]

AND

- the behaviour creates **a risk to health and safety**.

Bullying does not include reasonable management action carried out in a reasonable manner.

Bullying behaviour may involve any of the following types of behaviour:

- aggressive or intimidating conduct
- belittling or humiliating comments
- spreading malicious rumours
- teasing, practical jokes or 'initiation ceremonies'
- exclusion from work-related events
- unreasonable work expectations, including too much or too little work, or work below or beyond a worker's skill level
- displaying offensive material
- pressure to behave in an inappropriate manner.

However, this behaviour must be repeated and unreasonable and must create a risk to health and safety in order for it to be bullying.

What is 'reasonable management action'?

Reasonable management action carried out in a reasonable manner does **not** constitute bullying.

Reasonable management action may include for example:

- performance management processes
- disciplinary action for misconduct
- informing a worker about unsatisfactory work performance or inappropriate work behaviour
- directing a worker to perform duties in keeping with their job
- maintaining reasonable workplace goals and standards.

However, any reasonable management actions must be conducted in a reasonable manner. If not, they could still be bullying.

For more information on the ways to manage workers who are not performing their job as required, download the Fair Work Ombudsman's **Best Practice Guide - Managing underperformance** from: www.fairwork.gov.au

2. What to do if there is bullying, or reports of bullying at work?

Try to resolve the issues at the workplace

Where possible and safe, workers should try to address issues of bullying at work within the workplace. There may be processes already in place in the workplace to deal with issues of bullying.

Workers are encouraged to raise the issues with their:

- supervisor and/or manager
- health and safety representative
- human resources department

Workers can also speak to their union for information and advice on how to raise and deal with the issues in the workplace.

Federal, state or territory work health and safety (WHS) regulators may be able to provide information on how to raise issues of bullying at work. Contact details for your local regulator can be found in **_Where to get help_** at section 10 of this guide.

Employers and principals are encouraged to respond quickly and appropriately to the issues being raised. They have a duty of care to provide a safe workplace under WHS laws.

[Author's note: I rechecked the Queensland WHS laws (2011) and no where in their document did they discuss bullying, harrassment or violence.]

An **employer or principal** is:

- the person or business that employs or engages the worker who is alleging they are being bullied at work, and/or
- the person or business that employs or engages a person against whom bullying has been alleged.

Employer organisations, industry or trade groups registered with the Commission, chambers of commerce and peak industry bodies may be able to provide informtion on how to resolve issues of bullying at work.

The Department of Business (or equivalent) in most States and Terrirories often has information to assist small businesses manage their staff, resolve disputes and develop HR policies (including policies that deal with bullying). Contact details for the relevant Department in your state or territory can be found on the Commission's website www.fwc.gov.au

[Author's note: This is a clear case of pass-the-buckitis.]

Many of the state and territory WHS regulators have guides for employers/principals on how to deal with bullying at work, which can be found on their websites. Details of these websites can be found in **_Where to get help_** at section 10 of this guide.

Take care of your health and wellbeing

Bullying at work is a serious issue that can affect people in a number of ways. If you have been assaulted or fear that you may be assaulted you may wish to consider contacting the police.

- If you are feeling anxious or depressed it is important to speak to someone. Many workplaces have an employee assistance program

(EAP that can offer confidential support and assistnace. Otherwise you can:

- make an appointment to visit your doctor, or
- call **Lifeline** on **13 11 14**. Lifeline is a 24 hour service.

3. What can the Commission do to stop bullying?

The Commission can make an order to prevent a worker being bullied at work if satisfied that:

- the worker has been bullied at work by an individual or group of individuals, and
- there is a risk that the worker will continue to be bullied at work by that same individual or group.

The Commission is a tribunal, and is required to hear from all relevant parties before making orders. It does not conduct investigations into allegations of bullying at work.

What is an order?

An **order** is a ruling made by a Commission Member after he or she has heard and determined a matter. Once an order has been made, anyone bound by the order must comply with it. Courts can impose substantial penalties on parties who fail to comply with orders.

In anti-bullying matters, a Commission Member can make any order the Member considers appropriate to prevent the worker being bullied.

The Commission **cannot issue fines or penalties** and **cannot award financial compensation**. The focus of any orders the Commission may make must be to prevent further bullying. Actions that the Commission might consider could include:

- requiring the individual or group of individuals to stop the specified behaviour
- regular monitoring of behaviours by an employer or principal
- compliance with an employer or principal's bullying policy
- the provision of information and additional support and training to workers
- review of the employer's or principal's bullying policy.

[Author's note: So do the victims still have to take the bullies and their companies to another court to receive financial compensation for the bullying?]

However each case will be considered on its merits and parties should consider the specific circumstances of the workplace when seeking orders or responding to proposals for orders.

Before making an order, the Commission must take into account:

- any outcomes arising out of an investigation into the alleged bullying conducted by another person or body
- any procedures available to the worker to resolve the alleged bullying and any outcomes arising from those procedures.

What other agencies deal with bullying at work?

Information on the other agencies that deal with bullying at work can be found in *Where to get help* at section 10 of this guide.

4. Who can apply to the Fair Work Commission?

The national anti-bullying laws only apply to certain workers in Australia. To make an application for an order to stop bullying, a person must:

- be covered by the national anti-bullying laws, and
- meet the definition of a 'worker.'

A **worker** includes:
- an employee
- a contractor or subcontractor
- an employee of a contractor or subcontractor
- an employee of a labour hire company who has been assigned to work in a particular business or organisation
- an outworker
- an apprentice or trainee
- a student gaining work experience
- a volunteer.

Workers are only covered by the national anti-bullying laws if they are at work in a 'constitutionally-covered business.' This includes a business or undertaking conducted:

- by a constitutional corporation - for example, a proprietary limited company or an incorporated association conducting trading or financial operations
- by the Commonwealth or a Commonwealth authority
- by a body corporate incorporated in a Territory
- principally in a Territory or Commonwealth place.

Who is not covered by these anti-bullying laws?

Workers are only covered by the national anti-bullying laws if the bullying occurs while they are at work in a constitutionally-covered business.

Businesses that are not constitutionally-covered may include businesses or undertakings conducted by:

- sole traders or partnerships
- state government departments and some state public sector agencies
- some local government organisations
- corporations whose main activity is not trading or financial.

[Author's note: I'm a sole trader but sometimes employ others to do work for me – does this mean they are not protected if I bully them? And why are bank employees, investment brokers and government employees not covered?]

Members of the Defence Force are not covered by these laws.

The Commission may dismiss an application if it considers that the application might involve matters that relate to Australia's defence or national security.

The Commission can only make an order if there is a risk that the worker will **continue** to be bullied at work by a particular individual or group. Accdordingly, orders cannot be made where a worker is no longer engaged in connection with the workplace where they alleged the bullying conduct occurred, or if a worker is no longer exposed to bullying by an idividual or group at work.

If a worker is not covered by the national anti-bullying laws, refer to section 10 of this guide. *Where to get help.*

5. How to apply for an order to stop bullying

A worker who reasonably believes he or she has been bullied at work may make an application to the Commission for an order to stop bullying

If there is more than one worker who believes they are being bullied, each worker will need to make a separate application. Related applications may however be heard together where appropriate.

The application form

The form used to make an application for an order is Form F72 – Application for an order to stop bullying. This form can be completed using the form which is available on the Commission's website www.fwc.gov.au

The application form is also available:

- by calling the Commission on 1300 799 675
- from the Commission's public counters in each capital city.

The Commission will inform those people who might be affected by an application that made by a worker for an order to stop bullying, by providing them with a copy of the application. This is called 'serving' an application.

This will include providing a copy of the application to:

- the employer or principal
- the person or people named in the application as allegedly engaged in bullying behaviour
- the employer or principal of this person or people (if different from the worker's employer/principal).

The Commission will only serve the Form F72 – Application for an order to stop bullying and may not serve additional documents unless they directly respond to a question in the application.

The application fee

Applicants are required to pay an application fee. The current application fee is available on the Commission's website (www.fwc.gov.au/resolving-issues-disputes-and-dismissals/lodge-application. [This fee is currently $67.20.]

Time Limits

There is no time limit on making an application. However, **a worker must still be exposed to bullying by the same individual or group at work** – the Commission can only make an order if there is a risk that the worker will **continue** to be bullied.

[Author's note: What about the workers who have been bullied so severely that they've been forced to leave their jobs?]

6. How to respond to an application for an order to stop bullying

After a worker has made an application for an order to stop bullying, the Commission will ask for a response from:

- the employer or principal who employs or engages the worker, and
- the person or people the worker has named in their application as having allegedly engaged in bullying behariour.

The response should be made by completing the relevant response form. This is the first opportunity the parties will have to respond to the allegations outlined in the worker's application. It is not necessary to provide evidence or supporting material. There will be an opportunity to make further responses and provide additional material as the matter progresses.

Response from an employer or principal

Once an application has been received, the Commission will send the employer/principal a Form F73 – Response from an employer/principal to an application for an order to stop bullying.

The Commission will also serve them with a copy of the worker's application form, so that the worker's allegations can be addressed. The Comission will only serve the Form F72 – Application for an order to stop bullying and may not serve other attachments unless they directly respond to a question in the application.

The employer/principal must complete its response and send it to the Commission **within 7 days.** The employer/principal must also serve a copy on all of the other parties to the matter. The other parties are:

- the worker who has made the application
- the person or people the worker has alleged is bullying them; and
- any other employers/principals involved.

The response should also be served on any representatives for these parties. Further information may be provided by the Commission about which parties should be served with the employer/principle's response.

Response from a person named in an application for an order to stop bullying

The Commission will also send a copy of the worker's application to the person(s) they've named in their application as having allegedly engaged in bullying behaviour. A person named by the worker as having allegedly engaged in bullying behaviour can respond to the application, but is not required to do so. If the person wants to respond, they must complete the form F74 - Response from a person against whom bullying has been alleged and send it to the Commission **within 7 days.** The person must also send a copy to all of the other parties to the matter. The other parties are:

- the worker who has made the application
- the person or business who employs or engages the worker
- the person or business who employs or engages the person (if different); and
- any other person who is alleged to have bullied the worker.

The response should also be served on any representatives for these parties. Further information may be provided by the Commission about which parties should be served.

Objecting to an application

When responding to a worker's application for an order to stop bullying, objections to the application can be made on a number of different jurisdictional grounds. A party can make this kind of objection if they think that the Commission, for a technical or legal reason, cannot hear the matter.

These objections include that:

- The Applicant does not meet the definition of a 'worker'
- The Applicant is not working in a 'constitutionally-covered business'
- The Applicant was not 'at work' when the alleged bullying behaviour occurred
  [Author's note: What if the bullying occurs after hours – it still constitutes workplace bullying and should be covered.]
- The Applicant is a member of the Defence Force
- The application relates to matters involving Australia's defence or national security, or an existing or future covert or international operation of the Australian Federal Police
- The alleged bullying behaviour was reasonable management action, carried out in a reasonable manner.

Objections should be recorded on the response forms. It is still necessary to also complete all other sections of the response form.

7. What happens at the Commission?

Once the Commission has received the application form, a staff member will call the worker to confirm the details of the application.

The Commission will then serve a copy of the application form on:

- the employer(s) / principal(s), and
- in most cases, the person or people against whom the bullying has been alleged.

and will ask them to respond in writing. (See section 6 of this guide: *How to respond to an application for an order to stop bullying* for more information.)

The Commission will then decide how best to deal with the matter.

Mediation

If appropriate, the Commission will schedule a mediation session to try to help the parties resolve the dispute themselves.

Mediation is an informal, voluntary, private and generally confidential process facilitated by a Commission Member or by one of the Commission's anti-bullying mediators. The Members and mediators are independent and do not take sides.

The style of each Member and mediator may vary but, in general, mediation will include the following steps:

- the Member or mediator explains his or her role and the manner in which mediation is to be run
- each side briefly outlines their story, including what happened, any relevant facts, and what they want

- the Member or mediator may ask questions and may speak with the parties separately
- the Member or mediator will try to help the parties reach an agreement by identifying common ground and suggesting possible options for resolution, and
- if an agreement is reached, the Member or mediator can assist the parties to record their agreement in writing.

The mediation may take place in person, by telephone or by video conference.

Given the nature of the jurisdiction and the orders available, the Commission will not be promoting or recommending the resolution of these applications on the basis of monetary payments.

Conferences & hearings

If the Commission thinks that the matter is not suitable for mediation, or if the matter can't be resolved by the parties at mediation, the Commission may hold a conference or hearing.

The purpose of a conference or hearing is to enable the Commission to determine whether an order to stop bullying should be made. A conference is generally conducted in private, while a hearing is generally open to the public.

The Commission may also hold a preliminary conference so as to better inform the Member about the parties and issues involved.

The Commission will write to the parties with the details of any conference or hearing. This is called a Notice of Listing. The Notice of Listing will include the time, date and location of the conference or hearing. It may also include instructions (also known as 'directions') for the lodgment of written material with the Commission.

Adjournments

If a party can't attend on the date of the mediation, conference or hearing, or there is any other reason why the matter should be delayed, parties can apply for an adjournment.

An application for an adjournment must be made in writing, and you must provide full reasons as to why the adjournment should be granted. Adjournments will only be granted where there are substantial grounds.

Any request for an adjournment should be made as soon as the parties become aware that the date is unsuitable.

If a party does not attend a hearing when required, orders may be made in their absence.

For more information on hearings and confenences, including information on what will happen on the day, read the fact sheet *About hearings &*

Conferences which can be found on the Commission's website www.fwc.gov.au

8. Costs

In general, parties to an application for an order to stop bullying will bear their own costs.

However, the Commission may order a party to pay some or all of the costs incurred by another party if the Commission is satisfied that:

- the application or response to the application was made vexatiously, or without reasonable cause, or
- it should have been reasonably apparent that the application or response to the application had no reasonable prospects of success.

9. Privacy

In general, applications for orders to stop bullying and discussions in private conferences are confidential between the parties. Where formal hearings are conducted, these are open to the public unless the Commission orders otherwise.

The Commission is required by law to publish its decisions. Decisions are published on the website www.fwc.gov.au and generally include the names of parties to the matter.

If parties do not want their matters heard in public or their names and other details published in Court Lists or decisions, they will need to make an application to the Commission for an order to that effect. This application can be made in writing to the Member of the Commission for an order to that effect. This application can be made in writing to the Member of the Commission dealing with the matter.

For further details of the Commission's practices in collecting, using and disclosing personal information, you can access the Privacy Notice for anti-bullying matters at www.fwc.gov.au , or ask for a hard copy to be provided to you.

10. Where to get help

Interpreters

The Commission can arrange for an interpreter to be present at your mediation session, conference and/or hearing at no cost to you. However, you must notify the Commission as early as possible of your need for an interpreter, and provide details of the required language.

Legal or other representation

Representation is where another person (such as a lawyer, union official or family member) speaks or acts on your behalf.

There is no requirement for you to be represented when you appear at the Commission. In any conferences or hearings, you will need the permission of the Commission Member dealing with your case if you wish to be represented by a lawyer or paid agent unless that person is:

- one of your employees or officers (if you are an employer/principal) or
- employed by a union or employer organisation, a peak union or peak employer body.

If you decide to represent yourself in proceedings you will need to make sure you are well prepared. You are welcome to bring one or more individuals with you for support. There are generally no objections to this, although in a private conference you should be prepared to tell the Commission why you would like the person to be present.

Different arrangements apply when voluntary mediations are conducted by staff of the Commission and you will be advised of these in advance of any such process.

Commission staff & resources

Commission staff cannot provide legal advice or advice on how best to run a case. Commission staff can, however, can give you information on:

- processes in the Commission
- how to make an application to the Commission and how to respond to an application that affects you
- how to fill out forms
- where to find documents such as legislation and decisions
- other organisations that may be able to assist you.

The Commission's website www.fwc.gov.au also contains a range of information on workplace bullying that may be of assistance.

Where else can I go to have my bullying at work issues dealt with?

Bullying at work can be a breach of health and safety laws, which are administered by regulators federally and in each state and territory. Regulators may decide to respond to complaints of bullying at work and can prosecute for breaches of health and safety laws. Like the Commission, the regulators cannot award financial compensation. Contact details for the state and territory regulators can be found on the Commission's website www.fwc.gov.au.

If you think you are being bullied for a discriminatory reason, this may be a breach of equal opportunity laws. Contact details for anti-discrimination and equal opportunity bodies in each state and territory can be found on the Commission's website www.fwc.gov.au.

Other specific laws also apply to some workers, such as public servants and defence personnel.

BIBLIOGRAPHY

Blase, Joseph & Blase, Jo, *Breaking the silence – Overcoming the problem of principal mistreatment of teachers,* Corwin Press, 2002.

Brown, Sandra, *Where there is evil,* Macmillan, 1998.

Cleckley, Hervey, *The Mask of Sanity,* CV Mosby Publishers, 1976.

Cava, Roberta, *Dealing with Domestic Violence and Child Abuse: Australia's Judicial Disgrace!* Cava Consulting, 2005 and *Dealing with School Bullying – Australia's Educational Disgrace!* Cava Consulting, 2005.

Clout-Habel, Catherine, *Work Abuse – How to recognise and survive it.*

Coloroso, Barbara, *The Bully; The bullied and the Bystander,* Harper Resource, 2004.

Crum, Thomas, *The Magic of Conflict;* Simon & Schuster, 1987.

Drew, Naomi, *Learning Skills of Peacemaking,* Jalmar Press, California, 1987.

Dyer, Wayne, *You'll see it when you believe it,* Quill, 2001 and *Your Eroneous Zones,* Torch, 1993 and *The Sky's the Limit,* Pocket Books, 1981.

Ernshaw & Cooper, *Stress and Employer Liability,* IPD, 1996.

Field, Evelyn, *Bully Busting,* Finch, 1999.

Field, Tim, *Bully in Sight – How to predict, resist, challenge and combat workplace bullying. Overcome the silence and denial,* Success Unlimited, U.K. 2001.

Graves, David, *Fighting Back; Overcoming bullies in the workplace,* McGraw Hill, 2002.

Hare, Chauncey, *Work Abuse; How to recognize and survive it,* Schenkman Books, 1997.

Hare, Robert D., *Without Conscience; The disturbing world of psychopaths among us,* The Guilford Press, 1999.

Hawke, Margaret, *Conflict Resolution,* Macmillan Education Australia, 1992.

Kinchin, David, *Post Traumatic stress Disorder – The Invisible Injury,* Success Unlimited, U.K. 2001.

Lomax, Eric, *The Railway Man,* Vintage, 1996.

Marr, Neil & Field, Tim, *Bullyside – Death at playtime – an expose of child suicide caused by bullying,* Success Unlimited, U.K., 2001.

Napier, M. & Wheat, K, *Recovering damages for psychiatric injury,* Blackstone Press, 2002.

Nelson, Jane, *Positive Discipline,* Ballantine Books, 1987.

Orion, Dr. Doreen, *I know you really love me,* Dell, 1998.

Pease, Alan, *Body Language – How to read others' thoughts by their gestures,* Carmel Publications, 1981.

Richards, Helene and Freeman, Sheila, *Bullying in the workplace – an Occupational hazard,* Harper Collins, 2002.

Rigby, Ken, *New Perspectives on Bullying,* Jessica Kingsley, 2002.

Romain, Trevor, *Bullies are a pain in the brain,* Free Spirit Publishing, 1997.

Sapolsky, Robert M., *Why zebras don't get ulcers – an updated guide to stress, stress-related diseases and coping,* Freeman, 1998.

Schaum, Melita & Parrish, Karen, *Stalked; Breaking the Silence on the Bullying in America,* Simon & Schuster, 1995.

Stanton, E. Saminow, Stanton, E.,*Straight Talk About Criminals*

Stones, Rosemary, *Don't Pick on Me,* Piccadilly Press, 1993.

Sullivan, Keith, *The Anti-Bullying Handbook,* Oxford University Press, 2000.

Southerland, V. & Cooper C., *Understanding Stress,* Chapman & Hall.

Tedeschi, R. & Calhoun, L., *Trauma & Transformation; Growing in the aftermath of suffering,* Sage, 1996.

Tehrani, Noreen, *Building a Culture of Respect: Managing Bullying at Work,* Rutledge, 2001.

Vaknin, Sam, *Malignant Self-Love – Narcissism Revisited,* Narcissus Pub., 2003.

Wilkie, Dr. William, *Understanding Stress Breakdown,* Millennium Books, 1995.

WEB CONNECTIONS

Tim Field (Success Unlimited - public speaking) Bully OnLine (web page) The Field Foundation
www.successunlimited.co.uk
www.bullyonline.org
www.thefieldfoundation.org
UK The Andrea Adams trust www.andreaadamstrust.org
Mental Health Network www.mhnet.org/guide/trauma.htm
The Healing Centre Online www.healing-arts.org
Prolonged Adaption Stress Syndrome
    www.benzinger.org/pass.html
Canadian Traumatic Stress Network
    www.Play.psych.mun.ca/~dhart/trauma_net/index.html
Australian Trauma Web www.psy.uq.edu.au/PTSD
PTSD sites www.ptsd.com
Sam Vaknin, (narcississm)
    www.geocities.com/vaksam/index/htm
Anthony M. Benis (narcissism) www.Narcissm.homestead.com
Joanna Ashmun (narcissism) www.halcyon.com/jmashmun/npd
Lifeline www.lifelinemacarthur.org.au
Together we do better www.togetherwedobetter.vic.gov.au
Buddy Bear – The Alanah and Madeline Foundation
    www.buddybear.com.au jepcaa@internex.net.au
SOFWeb eduweb.vic.gov.au/bullying/index.htm
Bullying Everybody's Business
    www.kidshelp.com.au/info7/contents.htm
Reach Out! www.reachout.com.au
Mind Matters online.curriculum.edu.au mindmatters/index.htm
Judith Paphazy, Resilience Promotion jepcaa@internex.net.au
Peer Support Foundation Victoria psupport@peersupport.com.au
Stop Bullying! bevans@alphalink.com.au
West Education Centre: ***Beat Bullying*** wested@ozemail.com.au
Eliminating violence -Managing Anger www.ses.org.nz
No Bullying Starts Today luckyduck@dial.pipex.com
Police/Telecom "Stop Bullying" www.nobully.org.nz
Bullying Online (UK) www.bulying.co.uk
Scottish anti-bullying Network, Edinburgh abn@mhie.ac.uk
Anti-bully www.antibully.org.uk
UK Dept for Ed & Employment DfEE
    www.dfee.gov.uk/bullying/pages/home.html

The Wounded Child Project www.thewoundedchild.org
Selwyn College Anti-Harassment Team (New Zealand)
    www.aht-selwyn.school.nz
Dutch school bullying www.pesten.net
QIEU Bullying Policies www.qieu.asn.au
Bullying in USA www.bullypolice.org
Communities Against Violence Network www.cavnet.org
National Criminal Justice Reference Service www.ncjrs.org
Stalking Resource Center (SRC) www.ncvc.org/src/index.html
Anti-stalking web site www.antistalking.com
The Stalking Assistance Site www.stalkingassistance.com
Survivors of Stalking (SOS) www.soshelp.org
The Stalking Victims Sanctuary www.stalkingvictims.com
Victim Advocacy Program of the Capital District VACCD@aol.com
Victim-Assistance Online www.vaonline.org
Stalking FAQ www.state.ia.us/government/ag/stalker.htm
National Victim Centre
    www.ojp.usdoj.gov/ovc/help/stalk/info44.htm
Cyberstalking www.cyberangels.org/stalking
The Message Relay Center www.MessageRelayCenter.msn.com
Not Victims www.smalltime.com/notvictims
Harassment law UK www.harassment-law.co.uk
Beyond Bullying ww.cwpp.slp.pld.gov.au/bba/default.html
Beyond Bullying www.bulliesincorporated.co.nz
The Mobbing Encyclopaedia
    www.leymann.se/English/frame.html
National Union of Teachers www.teachers.org.uk
Northern Territory Work Health (2001) www.nt.gov.au/dib/wha
WorkCover Authority of New South Wales (2001)
    www.workcover.nsw.gov.au
WorkCover Corporation, South Australia (2001)
    www.workcover.com
Workplace Standards Tasmania (2001) www.safetyline.wa.gov.au
New Perspectives on Bullying - Astam Books, Australia
    info@astambooks.com.au
UK National Work Stress Network www.workstress.net
Befrienders International (Suicide) wwwlbefrienders.org
Helene Richards and Sheila Freeman
    www.sheilafreemanconsulting.biz/bullying.htm
Canada safety Council
    www.safety-council.org/info/OSH/bullies.html

Australian Manufacturing Workers' Union www.amwu.asn.au
Symptoms of emotional abuse
    www.lilaclane.com/relationships/emotional-abuse
Beating bullies in New Zealand
    www.bulliesincorporated.co.nz
South Australian Employee Ombudsman Gary Collis
    www.employeeombudsman.sa.gov.au
    www.oeo.sa.gov.au
Working Women's Centre S.A. www.wwc.org.au
Women's Executive Network - Canada
    www.wxnetwork.com
Citizens Against Bulling Association (CABA) of Northern Alberta
    Canada www.stopbullyingme.ab.ca caba@stopbullyingme.ab.ca
Dr. Arnold Nerenberg - Road rage www.roadrage.com
Workplace Services SA www.eric.sa.gov.au
Equal Opportunity SA www.eoc.sa.gov.au
Industrial Court SA www.industrialcourt.sa.gov.au
Acts and regulations SA
    www.parliament.sa.gov.au/dbsearch/legsearch.htm
Spanish Website www.psicoter.es
The Canadian Safe School Network
    www.cssn.org/pages/home.htm
The Workers Health Centre ACT www.workershealth.com.au
    admin@workershealth.com.au
ACTU *Work on Life* e-bulletin www.actu.asn.au
Australian Services Union - workplace bullying
    asuclerical-nsw.asn.au/campaigns/w.html
International Labour Organisation, Geneva www.ilo.org
New Zealand Council of Trade Unions union.org.nz
UnionSafe, NSW unionsafe.labor.net.au
Fair Work Commission www.fwc.gov.au